Endorsements

"Tony Sgroi has developed an innovative approach to making marketing decisions on a Lean basis. Everything is done to create value and eliminate waste. He includes an interesting visual system for assessing and communicating the quality of any prospective marketing opportunity."

Philip Kotler
S. C. Johnson & Son Distinguished Professor of International Marketing
Kellogg School of Management, Northwestern University

"Very rarely does a book get published that can make a huge difference to a business. *The Innovative Lean Enterprise* is such a book. The information within this book is a road map to Success. Every business reaches a point where it has to innovate or perish. Tony Sgroi has given you the secret to succeed. By implementing each step Tony Sgroi has outlined in each chapter, you will create a building block for success. I really wish I had this book when I was developing my 35 companies."

Ken Varga
Author of How to Get Customers to Call, Buy & Beg for More!
and 10 Marketing Mistakes That Steal Your Cash

"Tony Sgroi has made an important contribution to the discipline of strategic planning. By adapting the visual management tools of "Lean" to both define 'the now'... AND envision new and innovative strategic futures, *The Innovative Lean Enterprise* makes it easy to discover and exploit unique competitive advantages for a brand, a division or a company!"

Bryan Mattimore
Co-Founder, The Growth Engine Company
Author, Idea Stormers: How to Lead and Inspire Creative Breakthroughs

"The topic of the book from Tony Sgroi is not only for people who are interested in starting a business, but also for any person involved in management of a business or government agency. The composition is very clear, and his step-by-step of how-to-do portrayal assists the readers' comprehension. In addition, the numerous diagrams and graphs add to or enhance the meaning and provide a clear and attractive presentation to the reader. In today's economic and global downturn, Tony's view on maximizing value while minimizing waste is essential to business and daily life."

Dr. Henry C. Lee
Distinguished Chaired Professor, Forensic Science
The Henry C. Lee Institute of Forensic Science

"The Innovative Lean Enterprise is a great resource for business and technical leaders and entrepreneurs! Tony has laid out his thoughtful insight in a manner that brings the full force of his over 20 years experience as an engineer, manager, and patent agent registered to practice before the United States Patent and Trademark Office to bear on the complex topic of developing a winning strategy. As an intellectual property attorney and instructor on business and legal topics, it is my opinion that Tony masterfully melded together these components to help ensure the alignment of the strategies that support your business."

Ned McMahon
Partner at Ohlandt, Greeley, Ruggiero & Perle, LLP.

"I found Tony Sgroi's book very educational with graphic examples of how to move projects forward. He explains how complicated decisions can be made by breaking them down into basic elements. A must read for entrepreneurs of every field."

Don Gringer
Chairman, Allway Tools

"The Innovative Lean Enterprise is a vital resource for employees at all levels of your business. It presents a unique strategy framework highlighted with engaging examples to demonstrate successful implementation and execution of your business plan."

Evan Anderson
President, Allway Tools

"The Innovative Lean Enterprise is an interesting perspective on the planning process. Its approach is both easy to apply and beneficial. A should read for anyone in any field of business."

Chris Mills
President, North America Consumer Products
BIC USA Inc.

"After reading Mr. Tony Sgroi's book *The Innovative Lean Enterprise* I was struck by the depth of information and knowledge Tony was able to deliver. The book ties together marketing strategy, innovation and Lean product development concepts very nicely. The information in the book is powerful and will be important reading for most types of business professionals including general managers, brand marketing executives, and R&D professionals.

I highly recommend reading *The Innovative Lean Enterprise* and believe it will be an important addition to any company's training effort focused on delivering customer value and innovation in the marketplace."

Steve O'Brien
Director, Global Human Resources
Unger Global Companies

The Innovative Lean Enterprise

Using the Principles of Lean to Create and Deliver Innovation to Customers

Anthony Sgroi, Jr.

CRC Press
Taylor & Francis Group
Boca Raton London New York

CRC Press is an imprint of the
Taylor & Francis Group, an **informa** business

A PRODUCTIVITY PRESS BOOK

CRC Press
Taylor & Francis Group
6000 Broken Sound Parkway NW, Suite 300
Boca Raton, FL 33487-2742

© 2014 by Taylor & Francis Group, LLC
CRC Press is an imprint of Taylor & Francis Group, an Informa business

No claim to original U.S. Government works

Printed on acid-free paper
Version Date: 20130412

International Standard Book Number-13: 978-1-4822-0390-5 (Hardback)

Library of Congress Cataloging-in-Publication Data

Sgroi, Anthony.
    The innovative lean enterprise : using the principles of lean to create and deliver innovation to customers / Anthony Sgroi, Jr.
    pages cm
    Includes bibliographical references and index.
    ISBN 978-1-4822-0390-5
    1. New products--Management. 2. Lean manufacturing. 3. Customer relations. I. Title.

HF5415.153.S487 2013
658.4'063--dc23   2013013204

Visit the Taylor & Francis Web site at
http://www.taylorandfrancis.com

and the CRC Press Web site at
http://www.crcpress.com

For my wife, Tammy,
my daughter, Erica,
and my son, Tony

Contents

Acknowledgments

I am grateful to many people who I have encountered throughout my journey. For the beginning of my journey, I owe many thanks to a select few professors in my early adult life. George Geyer was one particular individual who provided me with the confidence that I could learn physics. I don't know if I would have continued school if I never crossed his path.

I also thank the dedicated professors at the University of New Haven. The professors within the Department of Mechanical Engineering are second to none. The same holds true for the professors whom I experienced in the executive MBA program. Your teachings helped me to realize that a well-rounded executive extends past engineering.

Special thanks to James Champy, who spent the time to review my first manuscript. Your recommendations shaped this book to where it is today.

I owe many thanks to the team of CRC Press. My gratitude first extends to Kristine Mednansky. Thank you for seeing the book beyond the original title and suggesting the title change. I also thank Kate Gallo for all of her hard work in putting the pieces of this book together as well as Jay Margolis for his help during the editing of this book and Sophie Kirkwood, the typesetter.

I owe many thanks to my parents. Your constant encouragement to become an engineer while tinkering with everything around the house has created my career path. This has truly made me who I am today. Dad, sorry about the lawn mower, welding your toolbox shut, your lost tools, all of the loose chairs, and jamming up the key locks with toothpicks.

Finally, I thank my wife, Tammy, for standing by me all these years as I continued to build on my knowledge base. Any success that I have achieved or will achieve would not be possible without her continuous support.

Introduction

During the time period of preparing this manuscript, I was struggling with a proper name for this book. My first proposed title was *Iconic Strategy*. In the beginning, I believed the title was appropriate. But as I began to receive feedback on the book, I soon realized that *Iconic Strategy* did not properly describe the book. This book is more about innovation. I therefore struggled with other title ideas, such as *Reinnovating the Corporation, Business Model Reengineering,* and finally *Reinventing the Corporation.* Again, these titles did not properly describe this book. As I began to ponder additional titles, I soon realized that this book is more about creating and delivering customer value and innovation. I further realized that in this process, anything that did not contribute to creating customer value and innovation was waste. I then linked this process to the principles of Lean. With these thoughts in mind, the creation of the title became rather easy for me.

The broad theme of Lean resides in the concept of maximizing value and minimizing waste. Minimizing or eliminating waste is rather a straightforward concept and begins with the customer. During the beginning stages of product development, any activity that does not contribute to the understanding of the customer is waste. It is this crucial stage that fuels the remainder of product development activities. The last thing any business wants is to effectively develop a product that customers are not willing or motivated to purchase.

The motivation to purchase depends on understanding what is valued by the customer. When this value is discovered, created, and delivered in the form of an offering customers are willing to pay for, demand is created. This demand results in value generation for businesses. Lean thinking begins by focusing on these initial principles before large resources are deployed. Understanding demand in the beginning maximizes value for the company and minimizes the waste of developing and launching the wrong product.

Many principles of Lean product development are based on the works of Allen C. Ward.[1] Ward spent considerable time studying the product development methods of the Wright Brothers and how their approach to product development was similar to that of Toyota. Along with his observations and direct experience, Ward invented set-based concurrent engineering (test before design) and began the concept of Lean product development. Today, many companies are trying to understand Ward's works and are attempting the application of Lean product development to their organizations. Several books have been written about Lean and have been sold so others can make the attempt to understand the principles of Lean product development. Despite the amount of literature available, many organizations still struggle in the application of Lean.

Successful implementation of Lean requires cross-functional teamwork. Therefore, in order to apply Lean successfully, teams are formed for each product development project. Each team comprises one or more expert individuals who represent each of their respective disciplines, for example, a product development expert representing R&D, an expert tooling engineer representing manufacturing, an expert marketer representing marketing, an expert in supply chain representing operations, and so on. Each of these members must be willing to work together as a team with a systems design approach where the team has one simple and important goal: *aligning all activities to provide customer value while relentlessly driving out waste.* The team will report to a specific type of project manager dubbed the entrepreneurial system designer (ESD), who has intimate experience working across all disciplines. In addition, and probably most important, the ESD has full in-depth understanding of the customer.

Each team member must be an expert in his or her related field and must hold himself or herself and the team accountable for results. This mindset forms a team of responsible experts. The sure test for this is to verify that each team member has the ability to actually perform the work in the areas that he or she is responsible for. In addition, each team member must have sufficient levels of understanding for the needs of his or her cross-functional team members. For example, if a product's aesthetics is contributing to a difficult injection molding process, then R&D should have an appreciation of that difficulty and alter the design as required.

A Lean organization is an organization built on trust. Trust allows the team and its developers the power to make the appropriate decisions at

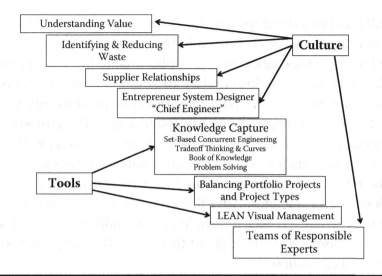

Figure 0.1 Lean tools vs. company culture. (From Anthony Sgroi Jr.)

every level necessary to move the development to a successful completion. The leaders are there for support and do not dictate orders. These individuals mentor their respective subordinates to create organizational learning, which allows for decisions to be made at all levels. A manager who merely gives orders and pushes paperwork will not be effective in a Lean organization. This concept, in addition to a skilled workforce, provides the only way organizations can develop products as quickly and efficiently as possible. Companies should strive to do whatever it takes to achieve that level of trust in their organization or Lean will never become a reality.

Lean product development has several areas of focus, each being important both on an individual basis and in combination. Understanding certain parts of Lean on an individual basis allows companies the luxury to begin to implement certain portions of Lean rather quickly. By studying the founding principles, companies can begin to understand the challenge in implementing one or more aspects of Lean. This of course will depend on the culture of the company. The reader is encouraged to study the illustration shown in Figure 0.1.

As illustrated by Figure 0.1, it is quite clear that the full implementation of Lean is heavily dependent on company culture. Roughly speaking, implementing Lean requires five-eighths cultural acceptance and three-eighths implementation of the various Lean tools. Thus, it is no accident that many companies struggle in their endeavor of Lean implementation.

This book has been developed to focus on certain aspects of Lean. In order to better target a larger audience in business, various portions of Lean will be used to drive innovation and portfolio (marketing mix) planning. This topic is certainly the optimum place to begin any new Lean endeavor, as businesses must provide an optimum product or product mix to drive sales. In addition, beginning with an understanding of the customers and what is important to them will benefit product developers as well as others in the organization. This includes marketers, strategists, senior managers, and even the officers of companies. Our journey begins with a brief discussion of various Lean principles. After these discussions, the applicable portions of Lean to drive customer innovation are identified. This will serve as the basis for the discussions throughout this book. Brief explanations of the various parts of Lean follow.[2]

Value Creation

Lean strives for the understanding and creation of customer value. Anything that contributes to a better understanding of the customer in terms of his or her needs and wants (sometimes referred to as voice of the customer [VOC]) is value. Value is also the connected activities (sometimes referred to as the value stream) that create and deliver a profitable value proposition to the customer. Value is also created if these activities fail in the procurement of a value proposition provided learning is achieved and knowledge is retained and can be reused later. This can prevent a future market miss. Markets are missed when the development team fails to understand the customer, or because the product is not innovative enough, or cost and quality problems exist. This value drives operations in the areas of manufacturing and procurement. Therefore, any activity that improves operational efficiency in the delivery of the value proposition to the customer is value.

Reduction of Waste

Lean strives to remove all forms of waste in product development. Unnecessary and time-consuming meetings, excessive reports, excessive specifications, waiting, etc. are some examples of waste. As a check, personnel should always verify that if the time being spent is not contributing to customer or company value, then this time is attributed to waste and should be eliminated or minimized. This includes overdelivery of features to the customer. If products are loaded with too many features that do not target important needs of customers, waste is present. This condition adds cost and complexity that customers may not be willing to accept and pay for. The most critical waste in product development is discarded knowledge. There is nothing worse than discarding hours of valuable knowledge that will require a future repeat of work. Knowledge must be retained and readily available.

Entrepreneurial System Designer (ESD)

Lean companies utilize a program manager who has a full understanding of the customer and all of the activities associated with delivering the value proposition. This is the one person who is responsible for the entire product development project. He or she is responsible for the engineering and aesthetic design, ease of manufacturing, quality, and market and business success of the product. He or she is also an expert in the design of the entire system. Such expertise optimizes the interactions of the subsystems of the design. For example, a robust engine for a car must be used with an equally robust drivetrain. This maintains the balance of the design. Alternate selections for drivetrains could result in unit damage or a high-cost overdesigned unit for a specific engine. ESDs understand how subsystems interact together. Think of this person as a project manager on steroids that truly understands the entire value stream of the product. Beginning with intimate knowledge of the customer and transforming the development of products that meet customer requirements, the ESD must ensure that the company can in a timely manner provide these products at the lowest possible cost, with high perceived quality, and must ensure that the organization learns and retains new leading-edge knowledge. The ESD leads a team of responsible experts in the conception and creation of products.

Teams of Responsible Experts

Lean organizations mentor their people to become experts in their respective fields. These experts also have a deep understanding of their team member's needs in their respective fields of discipline. This is necessary to drive cross-functional success. Lean product development organizations develop managers who are rewarded based on the creation and retention of knowledge that leads to profitability and customer satisfaction. These are people who are constantly learning to better themselves, their cross-functional team, and their organization. They are individuals who have working knowledge and strive to get their hands dirty, ensuring that they are achieving a full understanding of their area of discipline. These individuals know that once they stop learning, they cease to provide value. These individuals refrain from becoming bureaucrats and hold themselves responsible and accountable for results.

Set-Based Concurrent Engineering

Lean organizations are learning organizations. By testing multiple alternatives before development begins, the failure points of these alternatives can be determined prior to costly product development and testing. This allows for the rapid elimination of weak alternatives early on. The remaining, more robust alternatives can be selected if their failure points lie above the targeted range of the product requirements. Another term for set-based concurrent engineering is *rapid learning cycles* or *test before design*. Lean organizations using proper set-based methods have very little need for failure mode and effects analysis (FMEA). Another way of thinking about this is to simply perform more up-front learning, ensuring that all knowledge gaps are eliminated. This avoids expensive time-consuming modifications later, when tools are built and the product is near launch. This is especially important when learning about customer needs and wants.

Lean (Flexible) Project Management

Lean organizations reject the concept that managers plan and workers do. Rather, developers plan their own work and work through their plans under the guidance of a coach. Projects are broken down into smaller milestones or batches, and the developers plan their work to meet these milestones. This allows engineering work to be pulled instead of scheduled. Simple and visual communication networks are established so that information is made available to people requiring such information. This eliminates wasteful management structures and reports.

Visual Management Tools

Lean organizations rely heavily on visual management. With the notion that information is captured in only one place, it is not uncommon that Lean companies utilize an entire wall to hang visual project information. Lean companies also utilize effective reports that fit on a single sheet of paper. These reports are designed to fit on A3-sized paper and are thus denoted as A3 reports. They communicate a vast amount of information utilizing as many graphics, illustrations, and graphs as possible. This creates a simple, innovative, and effective communication tool. There are many forms of these reports used by companies. Some examples are project status reports, knowledge capture reports, and problem-solving reports. In this book, the concept of visual management tools will serve as the dominating framework.

Knowledge Reuse

Lean organizations strive to create and archive knowledge so that it is readily available for reuse. This allows faster and more predictable results with respect to product development, as much is learned early on. When an abundance of knowledge is available for reuse, developers can simply take what is needed from a knowledge base. This results in fewer subsystems to develop within a system. Some examples are subsystem design, research, standard parts, 3-D computer-aided design (CAD) files of widely used components and assemblies, automated spring programs, test data, etc.

Supplier Relationships

Lean organizations understand that it is essential that their suppliers share in the total available profit. By building strong relationships with key suppliers, trust is gained, resulting in higher levels of quality. It is best to have fewer key suppliers that deliver high levels of quality on a consistent basis than to shop for multiple low-cost suppliers. Strong supplier relationships can also result in shared development, ultimately lowering the cost and lead time for product launches.

Balancing Portfolio Projects and Project Types

Lean organizations understand that resources are limited. Offerings (product portfolios or the mix of product features) must be balanced with the resources of the organization. Proper planning is necessary to create a balanced offering. In some cases, innovation can occur in a single subsystem, unlocking new opportunities. In other cases, only incremental improvements are necessary for market penetration. In the extreme, new products requiring new manufacturing equipment may be necessary. These decisions are based on an understanding of the market needs in a business. This requires the vision of strong leaders. Portfolio planning is a key component that drives company success. The key is to provide a sustainable offering targeted to a market sufficient in size to profit in the long term.

Problem Solving

Lean companies systematically solve problems and transfer this knowledge throughout the organization and to new development programs. When companies learn how to solve problems at the root, problems go away and never resurface.

Go and See

Lean companies instill the notion of going to the source to fuel development and problem solving. Before new products are defined, Lean companies send the appropriate people to customer locations to better understand the customer. When a machine is malfunctioning, problem solvers automatically go to the source of the problem to verify the problems themselves. Lean organizations do not make decisions solely on the creation of reports of others. By getting close to the source of any challenge, proper decisions can be made as to the best countermeasure to be implemented.

Chosen Lean Principles

The discussions above represent some of the main topics of Lean. Although this book is not intended to teach the entire Lean system, it is rather important that the reader becomes familiar with the terms. It is the intention of this book to utilize certain portions of Lean to drive innovation and company planning using a simple and visual process. This book will accomplish this important goal as business planning must reflect a long-term strategic goal of understanding what is valuable to the customer and effectively form an offering targeting this value with little to no waste. This book will discuss customer value in the form of benefits to customers' desire. The discussions will also include driving out waste (providing unnecessary product features), leading to higher cost of offerings. By using set-based techniques, unnecessary offerings can be eliminated rather early. This will allow for fewer, more important offerings required for evaluation. The results of this planning will be communicated using visual management tools specific to this book. This will allow for simple and effective communication that will make knowledge capture easy for executives.

This book also includes a very simple step-by-step process taken from Lean principles to effectively and rapidly evaluate the current state of a company and the steps to define a totally new and unique innovative strategy. It is also equally important to format the strategy in such a way that easy and visual communication is possible. This book will form the beginning of Lean thinking for executives.

Chapter 1

Visual Strategy

What is a strategy icon? What does your strategy icon look like? The answers to these questions do not seem to coincide with the topic of competitive strategy. Before these questions can be answered, it is necessary to engage in further discussions. Surely, once understood, the answer to these questions will guide executives in better understanding the topic of strategy.

The subject of strategy has often been an interesting topic to many executives. Many books and papers have been written about strategy, each having its own unique perspective to guide executives in winning over their rivals. Many of these writings are well known and have helped many companies develop successful strategies to win in the marketplace. Despite the numerous works on this topic, there still exists confusion among executives with respect to strategy. Typically, confusion stems from a variety of reasons. Some confusion is a result of conflicting terminology (i.e., strategic planning vs. strategy). Other forms of confusion, among others, result from a lack of an intuitive framework, complexity in execution, and numerous tasks for implementation.

Despite the fact that strategy can be learned, executives still face the challenge of applying it to their business. For example, can businesses transform their current strategy to an optimum future strategy without an effective means of simple communication of their current strategic situation? The answer to this question results in additional questions, such as: What is the best method to display and communicate strategy? What are the primary parameters of strategy that businesses should understand and focus on? How can businesses optimize their strategy to win in the marketplace?

It is the opinion of this author that a main contribution to confusion is the lack of a simple and visual framework for strategy. Moreover, the sequential steps necessary to successfully transform a company's current strategy (or lack thereof) to an optimized future strategy are also lacking. It is the intention of this discussion to simplify the communication, analysis, and execution of strategy utilizing a visual framework.

To begin, one must understand the basics of strategy. For businesses, strategy is simply a choice, a choice to position oneself in the marketplace to compete that is characterized by high levels of long-term profitable opportunities. Once the position to compete is understood and chosen, companies focus on the aligned activities to create and distribute a profitable value proposition to a chosen target market. This value proposition must be unique and must define a competitive advantage over its rivals to be sustainable for some time. Thus, the key points of strategy can be summarized as:

- Create value propositions in the form of unique value-added products or services (hereafter offerings) to customers.
- Identify and optimize company cost structure necessary to deliver offerings allowing for the desired profit.
- Choose a position in the marketplace that is opportunistic in the short and long term, allowing for future market share gains.
- The strategy is sustainable and backed up by various forms of barriers to imitation.

The simplification of strategy communication is possible by defining a series of visual tools that communicate the key points of strategy. Such tools are enhanced when effectively merged together. In order to achieve this goal, the key points of strategy can be represented using a series of specific graphics. These graphics are formed by the various parameters of strategy that collectively display the entire competitive landscape for any chosen business.

First Parameter of Strategy

To define the parameters of strategy, we can first choose to focus on the value propositions that companies provide to customers. Businesses compete in the marketplace by offering value to customers. Companies' offerings must fulfill customers' needs (met or unmet) and wants in a more beneficial manner than the offerings of their competitors. Unless companies' offerings can provide better value at the same or lower cost, or provide the same or comparable value at a lower cost, customers will not have a compelling reason to purchase the offerings of companies. In many cases, beneficial offerings are those offerings that improve people's lives. For example, they can make buyers' lives more productive, more efficient, more convenient, simpler, or even more fun in the various situations they experience in their lifestyle.

Delivering value begins by first understanding what customers actually need, want, and may desire, both in the present and in the future. Value is created when companies' offerings possess exceptional utility or emotion, ultimately fulfilling their needs and wants in a *beneficial* manner. The concept of utility and emotion will be discussed in depth in Chapter 5. A brief discussion for the purposes of this chapter follows.

Utility

Utility is offering customers solutions (products or services) that perform a function. Such a function is most likely associated with problems customers are trying to solve. Utility is enhanced by offering customers solutions that perform a function faster, better, or cheaper than they are traditionally used to. Utility of a product can also come in the form of solutions that allow customers to complete tasks that normally required high skill to perform in the past.

Emotion

Many products possess certain emotional appeal and can make customers feel good when experiencing the offerings of a company. Executives must understand that the emotional component of products and services has an incredible contribution to customer purchase decisions. When customers buy products or services, companies should ask themselves what emotional triggers are associated with the purchase decision. For example, how do customers feel about the purchase of a new car? In addition to utility (getting to and from destinations), cars can trigger certain feelings as a result of specific emotional benefits, such as feeling safe due to the enhanced safety benefits of the car.

Value is then created by defining innovative solutions directed toward customers' needs and wants that are unmet. Companies satisfy customers by efficiently delivering these solutions to them without overdelivery. Overdelivery occurs when too many features are added to offerings, leading to waste. Overdelivery increases the cost of the offerings that customers may not be willing to pay. Overdelivery includes features that do not provide key customer benefits.

Thus, businesses must identify and deliver value to their target customers. Our discussion of value allows for the easy identification of the first parameter of strategy. This discussion forms the easy conclusion that value comes in the form of the benefits that offerings provide customers. Thus, our first parameter of strategy is *benefits*.

Second Parameter of Strategy

Once the benefits of offerings are understood, companies must understand that there are other areas of consideration that affect purchase decisions. Customers always balance the benefits to be gained with the cost of the purchase. This balance is compared with alternate or substitute offerings in the marketplace. Thus, companies must consider the dynamics of customer value, offering price, and their cost to deliver value. First, as discussed above, it is essential that companies discover what customers truly require in terms of their unmet needs and wants. Once this is discovered and the benefits of the product or service are determined, companies must price these offerings properly. Pricing should reflect the value being offered to customers. For example, if the offerings create a large increase in value, higher than market average prices are possible. Finally, once the optimum price is determined, profit is only possible if these products or services can be delivered at a cost allowing for the desired profit. Simply raising the offering price to produce the desired profit is unwise and may result in lower than desired sales. Therefore, companies should ensure that their "cost position" to deliver offerings to customers is low enough to profit at the price customers are willing to pay. In addition, a lower-cost position will result in greater profits to be gained. Therefore, understanding and cutting cost without affecting quality is of major importance. Thus, the second parameter of strategy is *cost position*.

Third Parameter of Strategy

Creating profitable opportunities depends on the importance of the problem to be solved compared to the level of satisfaction with the current available solutions. For example, if there is a very important problem that a group of customers is struggling with and there are very poor solutions currently available, this would indicate a high opportunity. High opportunities drive purchase decisions if such solutions are available to customers. The difference between the level of importance and the level of satisfaction is called a market gap. A large gap represents a large opportunity. On the contrary, if there is no gap, then there is little to no opportunity. Such a situation of little to no gap is a commodity situation. In most cases, finding the lowest-cost solution is the key for winning when competing in a commodity situation.

The gap can be assigned a numerical value to help identify the opportunity level. This gap can be analyzed by the business executive who understands the business he or she represents or can be integrated into a survey for potential customers to rate. The survey can be administered to a set of target customers for analyzing current and future opportunity scores. This information will help in the formulation of future strategies as new ideas are conceived. We can introduce a scale of 1 to 10 for the importance question with respect to a set of offerings (i.e., product features). A score of 0 would indicate that the product feature is unimportant. Likewise, a score of 10 would indicate that the product feature is extremely important. The same can be stated for satisfaction. A score of 0 would indicate that the product feature is not at all satisfied by current available offerings. Likewise, a score of 10 would indicate that the product feature is fully satisfied by current offerings. With these scores, opportunity is determined by subtracting the satisfaction score from the importance score. For example, if a product feature received a 10 for importance and a 3 for satisfaction, the opportunity would be a 7, indicating a high opportunity. Thus, the utilization of this method of scoring allows for companies to test their current and potential offerings for verification of the existence of high-opportunity levels. High-opportunity levels define less risk and are optimum for strategic success. Thus, the third parameter of strategy is *opportunity*.

Fourth Parameter of Strategy

To sustain a set of a company's offerings for some time, companies must ensure certain barriers to imitation. A barrier to imitation is the leverage of a company's tangible and intangible assets imposed on its competitors. Tangible assets are in the physical form and include buildings and warehouse spaces, manufacturing equipment, product inventory, inspection equipment, packaging equipment, etc. These are the items that can be seen, touched, and related to rather easily. In many cases, physical products can be reverse engineered rather easily. Intangible assets are those assets that cannot be physically touched. These assets are just as important for companies as their physical assets. Intangible assets are more difficult to imitate, as they are not as transparent as physical assets. These assets come in a variety of alternate forms and provide companies with a competitive edge when more are leveraged. Some examples of intangible assets are patents, trademarks, trade names, trade secrets, trade dress, and other various forms of goodwill.

Besides assets, there are other forms of barriers to imitation. Some of these barriers include goodwill, such as brand power. Strong brands result in a company having more market worth than the worth of their physical assets. Other barriers, some attributed to goodwill, can also include customer understanding, customer relationships, supplier relationships, product development process, great vision of management, customer lists, etc. Imagine how difficult it would be to research a company's product development process, customer lists, or the vision of its leaders. Thus, the more of these barriers a company builds, the more difficult it becomes for competitors to imitate. Some examples of barriers to imitation include:

Brand power
Firm's knowledge: Customer knowledge, product knowledge, market
 knowledge, etc.
Customer relationships
Supplier relationships
Highly efficient operations
Skill of people
Processes
Technology
Regulatory pioneering
Trade secrets
Patents
Trademarks
Copyrights
Power of patent pending

Therefore, the more barriers that can be leveraged, the longer companies can enjoy profits free of imitation. This brings us to the fourth and final parameter of strategy: *barriers to imitation.*

Strategy Icon

The identification of the four parameters of strategy will allow for the creation of a descriptive graphic. This graphic is dubbed the strategy icon and can be seen in Figure 1.1. In the figure, the icon contains four quadrants, where each quadrant communicates one of the four parameters of strategy. The upper left quadrant utilizes the symbol of a lightbulb, and this is indicative of the benefit(s) of the offering. To further enhance the icon, each quadrant can be further configured to communicate the effectiveness of each parameter. The introduction of a shading scale (colors or grayscale tones) will allow for the *levels* of each parameter to be communicated. For example, with respects to the *benefits* parameter, green on the color scale indicates high benefits, whereas yellow indicates medium benefits and red indicates low benefits. Similarly, black on the grayscale could indicate high benefits, where gray could indicate medium benefits and white could indicate low benefits. Thus, this convention (symbol plus shading) communicates the benefit levels of the offering. Similarly, the remaining quadrants are described in the table as shown in Figure 1.2.

Upon inspection of the strategy icon, managers can easily determine the position of their offerings. In addition, strategy icons can be created for

Figure 1.1 The strategy icon. (From Anthony Sgroi Jr.)

Strategy Icon (Grayscale Key)

Strategy Parameter	Symbol	Black Shade Indicator	Gray Shade Indicator	White Shade Indicator
Benefits	Lightbulb	High-benefit level	Medium-benefit level	Low-benefit level
Cost position	Money bag	Low-cost position	Medium-cost position	High-cost position
Opportunity	Partially filled circle	High opportunity	Medium opportunity	Low opportunity
Barriers to imitation	Padlock	High barriers to imitation	Medium barriers to imitation	Low barriers to imitation

Figure 1.2   Quadrant shading for the strategy icon (grayscale). (From Anthony Sgroi Jr.)

competitors' offerings for analysis and comparison. For example, consider the strategy icon in Figure 1.3. In this figure, the icon displays offerings having medium *benefits* targeting a low *opportunity*. Such a low opportunity indicates an overserved market. The *barriers to imitation* are medium, which may allow some degree of imitation. Finally, the *cost* to produce the offerings is rather high. Upon inspection, one can surmise that this offering is not desirable and more work is needed to optimize the strategy. Thus, by answering the question "What does your strategy icon look like?" managers can begin to understand their strategic view in the marketplace.

The understanding of the strategy icon is integral in drawing the entire competitive landscape. However, to be more descriptive, there are still two key graphics that require discussion. To reiterate from the discussion above, companies must create and distribute a profitable value proposition to a *chosen target market*. Of course, the chosen market must be suitable in size and must allow room for growth. This allows for the definition of the next visual graphic, dubbed the market size gage (MSG). The MSG is illustrated in Figure 1.4.

As seen in Figure 1.4, the chosen target market consists of $100,000,000 of annual sales. The gage illustrates that our company enjoys 50% share. The gage also illustrates that the top two competitors have 25% and 18% market share, respectively. The MSG allows for the instant viewing of market size and relative market shares. This aids in decisions as to either further

Figure 1.3   Strategy icon-shaded example. (From Anthony Sgroi Jr.)

| Rival 2 (18%) |
| Rival 1 (25%) |
| Our Market Share (50%) |
| Total Market Size (100,000,000 Annual Sales Dollars) |

Figure 1.4   The market size gage. (From Anthony Sgroi Jr.)

penetrate the market or grab share from rivals. This can also indicate a saturated market where divesture may be the optimum choice.

The MSG works in two ways. The first is the communication of the present state of the company (current market size and share). The second is the communication of the proposed future state defined by a transformed strategy. Depending on the proposed transformed strategy, the MSG could indicate a newly proposed target market and the share desired some time after the transformed strategy.

The final graphical tool to be introduced communicates the entire competitive landscape. This tool is referred to as the visual strategy map (VSM), and it incorporates the strategy icon, the market size gage, and the offerings of the competitive landscape. The visual strategy map can be used to analyze and communicate the current strategy (visual strategy map—current state) or the proposed future state (visual strategy map—future state). The VSM is best explained utilizing an example.

Consider a large office building employing a thousand employees. In order to minimize employees leaving the building during lunch hours, there are two restaurant locations within the office building. The first location (Eatery A) includes a restaurant that offers traditional foods, including a full salad bar, pasta bar, hot meals, grilled foods, and various desserts. The food is prepared by average chefs, as the dishes are simple. Despite the low offering prices, the first restaurant enjoys healthy profits, while the second location has remained vacant for some time.

The owner of Eatery A recently received a notification that the second location was leased. Very concerned, the owner of Eatery A began to investigate his new competitor (Eatery B) in order to assess the potential threat. Upon his investigation, the owner of Eatery A determined that Eatery B will be offering nontraditional foods in an effort to target foreign visitors of the various businesses in the office building. Upon investigation, the owner of Eatery A verified some of the menu items from a brief conversation with the owner of Eatery B. Some of these items included Peking duck, chicken tikka, water bugs, frog, turtle soup, liver, horse meat, eel, snake, and pigeon. The owner of Eatery B stated that many of these items would be available during random times as the availability of these menu ingredients was very sporadic. To better attract potential customers, Eatery B was also in the process of elaborately decorating its establishment with rare and unique artwork from various countries.

The owner of Eatery A was more at ease as he realized that Eatery B was targeting a much smaller group of people. However, to put his mind more at

Offering Comparison Based on a Scale of 0–4 (Eatery A vs. Eatery B)

Offering Description	Eatery A Value with Logic	Eatery B Value with Logic
Consistent menu	3.5: Various popular items offered with 1 varying hot meal per day	1: Menu highly dependent on availability of nontraditional food ingredients
Food variety	3.2: Good general mix of popular foods always offered	1: Very limited menu and focused on nontraditional recipes
Service speed	3.9: Fast due to an efficient operation	1: Slow, each dish is made to order
Skill requirements of chef	2.8: Simple traditional recipes that taste good	4: Chef must be familiar with several unfamiliar dishes
Elaborate environment	2: Simple wallpaper and clean environment	4: Decorated using elaborate art forms
Spoilage concerns	1: Good predictability on demand of meals	3.8: Not a good prediction on demand of meals
Price to patron	2: Can profit at a fair price	3.9: Must price higher to reflect higher fixed and variable costs

Figure 1.5   Offering comparison: Eatery A vs. Eatery B. (From Anthony Sgroi Jr.)

ease, he decided to gather additional information. During lunch sessions, the owner of Eatery A surveyed members of the various businesses. He found that a very small percentage (5%) of the building population enjoyed nontraditional foods. He also determined that the office building would receive only 20 (approximately 2% of the building population) foreign visitors on average per week. Armed with this knowledge, the owner of Eatery A no longer feared the future presence of Eatery B.

From the information discussed, we can begin to list the applicable offerings and form a comparison for the eateries. We can choose a scale that ranges from 0 to 4 and on a comparative basis, the offerings for the eateries can be assigned a value based on their comparisons in our chosen scale. The offerings and their values are shown in Figure 1.5. Figure 1.5 also includes a discussion for the logic of the chosen value within the scale. As a note, for this example, the comparison is based on the preferences of the target market, which consists of the individuals that work at the office building.

Strategy Icon Generation Grid

Strategy Parameter	Eatery A	Eatery B
Benefits	High: Good healthy food at good prices, fast service	Low: Does not appeal to the population majority
Cost position	Low: Low overhead, low-cost ingredients, high volume allows for buying power	High: Elaborate environment, skilled chefs, rare and higher-cost ingredients
Opportunity	High: Food is appealing to most of the building population	Low: Food is not so appealing to most of the population
Barriers to imitation	Medium: Efficient streamlined process can be difficult to imitate	Medium: Unfamiliar elaborate recipes, but can be copied with some effort

Figure 1.6   Icon generation grid: Eatery A and Eatery B. (From Anthony Sgroi Jr.)

Similarly, the parameters for the Strategy Icon can be assigned as illustrated in the strategy icon generation grid in Figure 1.6 for each eatery using the preferences of the target market as a baseline.

Finally, the market size gage is constructed (Figure 1.7) with reference to the target market.

Based on Figure 1.6, the respective strategy icons can be drawn for each eatery. By use of Figure 1.7, the market size gage can also be constructed. Figure 1.8 illustrates the strategy icon for Eatery A, Figure 1.9 illustrates the strategy icon for Eatery B, and Figure 1.10 illustrates the market size gage.

Market Size Gage

Restaurant	Market Size Potential and Logic Based on 1,000 Employees
Eatery A	68% (680 people daily)
	25% eat out, bring lunch, or are not interested
Eatery B	7% (70 people daily)
	5% interested + 2% visitors

Figure 1.7   Estimated market size for Eatery A and Eatery B. (From Anthony Sgroi Jr.)

Figure 1.8 Eatery A strategy icon. (From Anthony Sgroi Jr.)

The visual strategy map (VSM) can now be constructed based on the discussions above. By reference to Figure 1.11, the VSM is illustrated and the reader can immediately depict the entire competitive landscape on a visual perspective. Along the horizontal axis are the seven offering attributes. The first solid curve depicts the offering and their levels for Eatery A. The dashed line depicts the offering and their levels for Eatery B. Each eatery has a corresponding strategy icon providing the key strategic information discussed above. Finally, the market size gage is also included. Upon immediate inspection, it is clear that Eatery A commands a better strategy than Eatery B. From the VSM, the two curves follow alternate paths indicating a unique strategy for each eatery. Based on the strategy icon, one can immediately gather that Eatery A offers higher benefits at a lower-cost structure, allowing for higher profit margins. This lower-cost structure allows Eatery A to price

Figure 1.9 Eatery A strategy icon. (From Anthony Sgroi Jr.)

Eatery B (7%)		
Eatery A (68%)		
Total Market Size (1000 Daily Patrons)		

Figure 1.10 Market size gage (Eatery A vs. Eatery B). (From Anthony Sgroi Jr.)

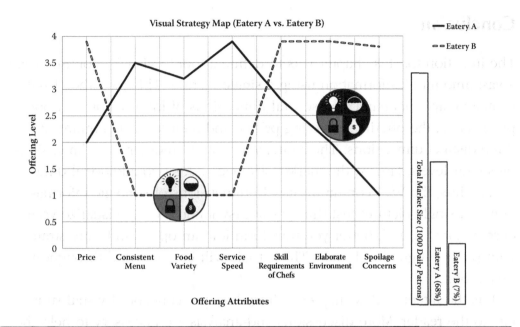

Figure 1.11 Visual strategy map (Eatery A vs. Eatery B). (From Anthony Sgroi Jr.)

its offerings less than those of Eatery B. The offering attributes of Eatery A also define a greater opportunity to a larger target market. Eatery A has a consistent menu filled with variety coupled with fast service. In the event that Eatery A loses a chef or two, it can easily fill the position, as the skill requirements to work at Eatery A are of average levels compared to those of Eatery B. Eatery B has a high fixed cost (elaborate environment) and also has higher variable costs (higher-cost ingredients and spoilage).

Upon inspection, a simple one-sentence description can be stated for each business. For Eatery A, we can state, "A fast, affordable eating experience that appeals to everyone." This statement is positive and descriptive. However, the same is not true for Eatery B. Perhaps the statement for Eatery B would be, "An expensive and unique dining experience for the chosen few." Common sense dictates that the strategy of Eatery B could not be sustained indefinitely. If maintained, the rate of cash burn would exceed operating income, forcing Eatery B to close its doors.

On the other hand, Eatery B could modify its strategy to form an offering that better appeals to a larger population of the people in the office building. Eatery B can also study surrounding office buildings for verification of a larger market that would potentially pose an interest in their offering. Such modifications are possible by use of the principles of this book and will be detailed in later discussions.

Conclusion

The intention for this chapter was to define a tool to visually communicate a vast amount of information using a single picture. This tool, the visual strategy map, communicated several dimensions of information. On one perspective, the offerings, offering prices, and their levels communicate three distinct dimensions. The strategy icon adds another four dimensions plus their levels. Finally, the market size gage adds two additional dimensions. Thus, the VSM communicates 10 dimensions of strategic information in a single picture! Just think how easy it could be to visualize your current strategy and, better yet, transform it to an optimum future strategy with powerful graphical tools. These tools will be illustrated throughout this book.

It is the intent of this chapter to introduce the concept of visual strategy to the reader. More discussions and analysis are necessary to help the reader apply the various concepts introduced in this chapter. The subsequent chapters of this book will refine the discussions above for a better understanding of the subject matter. It is also the intention of this book to present the subject matter utilizing several examples. These examples will help deliver the content more effectively. Such delivery can allow executives to apply the principles of this book to their business. Whether managers wish to evaluate a product or service concept, a product portfolio, or an entire business model, these concepts will allow the readers of this book to better understand their business so that improvements can be made. This chapter closes with a high-level overview of the remaining chapters.

Chapter Overviews

Chapter 2: Understanding the Current State

Strategy transformation begins with the understanding of the current state of the business in relation to the competitive landscape. Not until the current state is understood can a company begin to explore an optimized strategy. This chapter will discuss how to depict the current state of strategy on a graphical perspective utilizing one or more examples.

Chapter 3: Opportunity Identification

Once the current state is understood, the steps of identifying the opportunity levels of offerings are explained in detail. This chapter will describe how to identify such opportunity levels on a quantitative basis for current and proposed offerings. This chapter will also introduce another tool, referred to as the product fulfillment map, to evaluate the effectiveness of offerings.

Chapter 4: Idea Generation

Once the market opportunities are understood, this chapter will run through several techniques for idea generation. From both an internal industry perspective and an external industry perspective, this chapter will provide several methods of idea generation that can unlock new offerings for growth and differentiation. By including several methods of idea generation, the creation of new themes, new product or service features, new markets, new customers, etc., can be possible. The reader will verify that finding new opportunities can be as simple as identifying a new market gap or can result in the blending of offerings from a different industry altogether.

Chapter 5: Delivering Profitable Innovation to Targeted Customers

In this chapter, the concept of customer value will be discussed in detail. This topic will describe the value that companies' offerings provide customers in terms of the benefits they deliver. This chapter will also cover cost considerations for the offerings. With the understanding of fixed and variable costs, an innovative profit model is introduced and is discussed in detail in this chapter. This chapter also presents discussions for defining the largest target market as possible to achieve maximum revenue potentials. Finally, the topic of pricing power is also discussed.

Chapter 6: Barriers to Imitation

In this chapter, various forms of barriers to imitation that companies can utilize to protect their offerings are discussed in detail. This chapter will cover certain assets that can be leveraged against the competition to prolong or even prevent imitation. From high levels of brand power to intellectual property, companies should have a good understanding of this subject matter, as high levels of barriers to imitation can allow for premium pricing for longer periods of time. A section on patents is also discussed, unlike traditional business books.

Chapter 7: Applications of Graphical Strategy Tools

This chapter expands on the visual tools introduced earlier in this book. In the discussions that follow, the reader will learn how to customize the visual strategy map according to the principles of this book. Later, alterations of the visual tools will be illustrated so that the reader can apply the principles of this book in use with his or her favorite business framework, including strengths, weaknesses, opportunities, and threats (SWOT) analysis, balanced score card approach, and the disruptive innovation model.

Chapter 8: Ranking Offerings

In this chapter, techniques for ranking product or service offering ideas will be discussed. The ranking system will allow readers of this book to customize the parameters of the rank, thereby allowing for more weight on user-specific parameters (unequal weights), if desired. This chapter also teaches the reader how to prefilter offerings for early elimination of weak ideas, allowing for more rapid strategy transformation.

Chapter 9: Strategy Transformation Process

In this chapter, the steps discussed above are brought together to teach the reader how to create the visual strategy map (both current state and future state). Such a simple and effective tool will also allow for companies to test for the uniqueness of their proposed strategy. The framework presented in this book will allow managers to assess and test their current strategy, form and test a new strategy, and reformulate the strategy as needed. This will be presented in a simple and easy to follow step-by-step process.

Chapter 10: Strategy Transformation Example

This chapter will run through the entire strategy transformation process using a detailed example. The example will begin with the defining of the current state using a visual strategy map (current state). The example will then run through the entire transformation process to ultimately deliver a visual strategy map (future state), followed by an analysis of the future state using the visual strategy map.

Chapter 11: Alignment and Position Statements

Since there are many possible themes that can develop during the strategy transformation process, this chapter introduces the concept of position statements. Position statements can help companies focus on a theme for their new strategy that is more aligned with companies' capabilities.

Chapter 2

Understanding
the Current State

In Chapter 1 we introduced the Lean concept of visual strategy by merging a series of graphics together. This allowed for the communication of a vast amount of information in the display of the entire competitive landscape. We talked about benefit levels of offerings and how a company's offerings should provide customers with better solutions compared to their competitors'. This was communicated using the strategy icon displayed on the visual strategy map (VSM). Included on the strategy icon were the cost position, opportunity levels, and levels of the barriers to imitation. Finally, the market size and the respective market shares were also displayed on the VSM using the market size gage. Included on the VSM along the bottom horizontal portion were the general offerings of the competitive landscape.

In this chapter, we will explore in more detail the graphical display of the various competitive offerings and how they can be displayed. This will allow executives to paint a picture of the current state for their company's competitive landscape. This picture will provide the means for any company to begin to map its current strategy (or lack of strategy) compared to its competitors and general industry perceptions. Such industry perceptions are sometimes referred to as industry factors. The graphical display of the competitive offerings forms the initial comparison for companies and their competitors. The graphical depiction of the offerings may begin to provide companies with confidence that their current strategy is acceptable. However, companies may discover that their current strategy in not acceptable. This marks the occasion for improvement.

Before any company begins to alter its strategy, it is necessary that it clearly understands its current strategy. By understanding their current strategy compared to competitors' and the general industry factors, companies can begin to make the appropriate changes for improvement.

2-D Perceptual Map

There are several methods of visually displaying a strategy. One simplistic approach is to utilize a 2-D perceptual map. This map is a simple approach of graphically depicting two distinct offerings and allows for comparison of the offerings of multiple companies on the same map. Consider the example of the visual representation of three cars. We can list a few of the cars' attributes where we can visually compare them using the 2-D perceptual map. From a quick search on Edmunds.com we can compare the new Chevy Sonic, Audi A8, and Toyota Camry XLE V6. All three cars are unique. The Chevy Sonic is an economical car with an MSRP starting at $13,865. The Sonic gets 40 MPG on the highway due to its smaller size and has lower horsepower than the Camry or the A8. Due to the low cost, this car does not have loaded levels of luxury. The Toyota Camry XLE V6 is a midlevel car having adequate horsepower and more features than the Sonic. The MSRP begins at $29,845 and it gets about 30 MPG on the highway. The Audi A8 has an incredible 500 horsepower and gets 21 MPG on the highway. The MSRP is about $78,050 and it is loaded with more features than the Camry or the Sonic. The features of the three cars can be charted as shown in Figure 2.1.

With the information contained in Figure 2.1, the cars can be graphically compared using the 2-D perceptual map. As will be apparent, the 2-D

Car	Price	Fuel Consumption (MPG)	Luxury Level (1 = Low, 2 = Medium, 3 = High)
Chevy Sonic	$13,865	40	1
Toyota Camry XLE V6	$29,845	30	2
Audi A8	$78,050	21	3

Figure 2.1 Various car features. (Adapted from www.edmunds.com.)

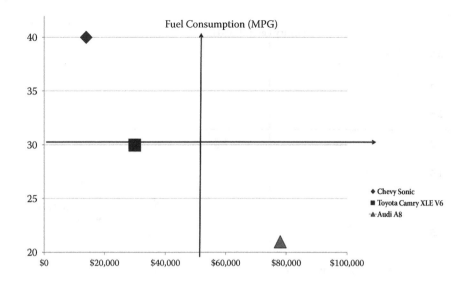

Figure 2.2 Two-dimensional perceptual map (fuel consumption vs. price). (From Anthony Sgroi Jr.)

perceptual map compares two distinct parameters, and therefore only two attributes can be chosen for a single map. In the first example, price vs. fuel consumption is chosen for comparison. Figure 2.2 illustrates the perceptual map of price vs. fuel consumption for the three models.

As verified in Figure 2.2, each car has its own unique position in the defined space on the 2-D perceptual map. By visualizing the 2-D perceptual map, managers can begin to verify if their products reside in the same space or are truly unique. As one can see, the display of only two attributes can be problematic. The limited display of only two attributes makes it difficult to depict an entire strategy if similar attributes are present. For example, if we were to compare the Audi A8 to the Mercedes S Class, it most likely would occupy the same space for many chosen offering attributes. Thus, in many cases, utilizing a single 2-D perceptual map may not provide enough information to make intelligent decisions. To mitigate this problem, one can create multiple 2-D perceptual maps to gain additional information. For example, perhaps we want to compare luxury level vs. miles per gallon (MPG). This can be analyzed utilizing another 2-D perceptual map, as shown in Figure 2.3. Again, it is clear that each car occupies a distinct space as in the first map. We can also verify that having two 2-D perceptual maps does not provide the necessary information to properly compare product attributes. In addition, utilizing multiple 2-D perceptual maps for mapping a strategy can be tedious for executives to analyze. Thus, using this type of

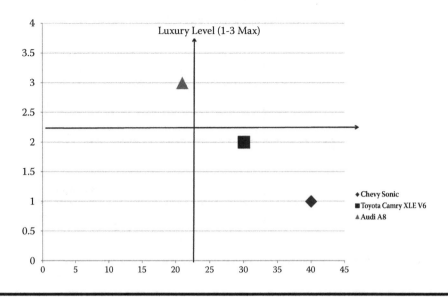

Figure 2.3 Two-dimensional perceptual map (luxury level vs. MPG). (From Anthony Sgroi Jr.)

map may be acceptable if a product has two major characteristics, but for more than two, we can see the shortfalls of this approach.

2-D Map

To better visualize the multiple characteristics of the three cars, an alternate approach is desired. Such an approach is the use of a 2-D map,[1] which is illustrated in Figure 2.4. As seen in Figure 2.4, the characteristics (price, fuel consumption, and luxury level) can be placed along the bottom of the 2-D map. On the vertical direction, a series of levels can be defined based on their *relative comparison* of the three cars. For example, instead of mapping MSRP price and fuel consumption, which have different units of measure ($ in thousands compared to tens in MPG) along the vertical direction, the compared levels of each can be mapped. Thus, for the Audi A8, price, fuel consumption, and luxury are all higher levels compared to the Camry and the Sonic. Therefore, for all of the features, each characteristic can be included on a single 2-D map as shown in Figure 2.4.

The structure of the 2-D map in Figure 2.4 allows for the three characteristics that each car offers to be visually and instantly compared despite the different units of measure. The description of the structure of the 2-D map begins with the bottom portion of the map. This portion along the lower

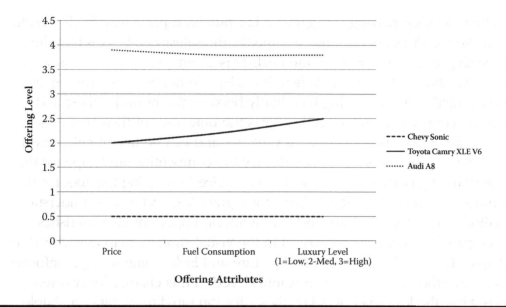

Figure 2.4 Two-dimensional map. (Adapted from the strategy canvas in W. Chan Kim and Renee Mauborgne, *Blue Ocean Strategy*, Harvard Business School Press, 2005.)

horizontal section of the 2-D map captures the offering attributes and factors that the industry competes on. The first item along the horizontal direction is typically price, followed by the offerings and any applicable factor related to the industry. This allows for direct comparison of price vs. offerings. In some cases, the 2-D map allows one to determine what its competitors are investing in based on the levels of their offerings. The left vertical portion captures the levels for each offering, industry factor, and price in relation to the company and its competitors.

The factors, sometimes referred to as industry factors, require further discussion. This phrase refers to the general perceptions of the industry. It usually excludes the main attributes of price and the offerings, but can affect any business. For example, when comparing car dealerships, a factor that one cannot ignore is "game playing" on the part of the dealership. How many times do dealers offer people a fair price from the start? In most cases the answer is never. The buying experience typically begins with a salesman dictating that the initial price quoted for a particular car is the lowest price one can ever be offered. The buyer then counters where the salesman has to whisper in the general manager's ear to only come back with a piece of paper folded in half. They continue with the game playing by proceeding to explain that the price written on the paper is the best they can do and they are now breaking even. This process goes on and on, and if one chooses to continue to keep playing this game, a fair purchase price may finally result. To make the situation even more comedic, the salesman dictates that the dealership is losing money on the deal. This example applies to most people that have shopped for a car. Although dealers do not advertise their game-playing tactics, game playing has simply become the norm for most and must be considered, as it directly affects the outcomes of their businesses.

The 2-D map has many clear advantages and can be taught rather easily. This allows executives to visually display the competitive landscape for the understanding of their current state. The choice in utilizing this tool for the definition of the current state allows for a graphical and easy-to-understand method to develop, analyze, and communicate important characteristics of a company's strategy. As compared to the visual strategy map introduced in Chapter 1, the 2-D map is a partial picture and lacks some strategic information. Nevertheless, the 2-D map is introduced in this chapter for two reasons. First, the low level of detail allows for the rapid teaching of a simple graphical method of depicting offerings and industry factors of strategy. Second, after some practice using this tool, it will serve as a background for later chapters when the visual strategy map (current and future states) is explained in greater detail.

In conclusion, the 2-D map is a two-dimensional graphical tool that:

■ Captures the current and proposed states of offerings
■ Maps companies' offerings compared to the competitors' offerings and the general factors of the industry
■ Allows companies to understand the offering levels of their strategy in relation to what the competition is offering
■ Allows executives to visually compare the relative prices paid for those offerings in relation to one another

This chapter will derive a second set of 2-D maps utilizing a more detailed example. The first map will graphically depict the current state of a particular industry. From that current state, the offerings will be analyzed so that a new and unique product can be defined. Once defined, the offerings of this product can be compared with its competitors on a second 2-D map.

Before deriving the first 2-D map, a few details of the chosen industry are discussed. This discussion will allow the reader to verify how price, offerings, and their levels are extrapolated and placed on the 2-D map. Our example targets the utility knife industry. This example is chosen to illustrate the increasing innovation that has taken place in this industry. After some time, innovation slowed until the development of a new product dubbed the switchback, which was created by the Allway Company.

Utility Knife Industry

Utility knives come in many styles and forms. Their main purpose is to allow the use of disposable blades for cutting. This prevents the user from the chore of sharpening the blade as the blade becomes dull. In the event that the blade becomes dull, the user simply removes the worn blade and inserts a new blade. Such a concept allows for efficient use of these knives. Through the years, these blades have become standardized so that multiple manufacturers can produce utility knives and blades where interchange is possible. The standardization also allowed for blades to be produced at low costs, allowing for the disposable blade concept to be accepted by users. Standard blades are trapezoidal in shape, allowing for the use of two cutting edges. Thus, when the first side is worn, the user can reverse the blade for use of the second side. This allows for two uses of the blade before replacement is necessary.

The first styles of utility knives were simple. They allowed the user to assemble a blade to a handle with the use of a fastener such as a screw. When the blade required to be changed, the user had to utilize a screwdriver to complete this task. This design placed the blade in a constant exposed position. Such a concept proved to be unsafe during use and storage. For example, during use, these knives maintained the blade in an exposed condition that put the user at risk during grasping. It also prevented the placement of these knives in the user's pocket in between tasks. These drawbacks began the development of several innovations with respect to these knives. Each innovation led to the next as users demanded better solutions to various problems of the industry.

First Innovation: The Retractable Utility Knife

The problem of utility knives having blades in a constant exposed position led to the development of retractable utility knives. These knives allowed for the blade to be contained in the handle for safe handling and storage. The blade was attached to a sliding blade holder that contained a button. This button extended from the blade holder and was exposed on the outer portion of the utility knife. When use of the blade was required, the user actuated the button of the utility knife. This button unlocked the blade holder for sliding the blade in the exposed position. After the cut was completed, the blade could be retracted for placement in a pocket of the user or for long-term storage. These types of knives consisted of a two-piece housing secured by a screw. When the blade required reversal or replacement, the user was required to separate the housing with a screwdriver. These housings were long enough to allow for the storage of spare blades. Despite this improvement, in time it became inconvenient to utilize a screwdriver for blade change-out.

Second Innovation: Quick Blade Change

To eliminate the requirement of removing and reinserting a screw for blade reversal and replacement, new retractable utility knives were developed. With the blade in the extended position, the user is required to simply push a button to remove the blade with a simple grasp. The blade can then be placed in a storage compartment with the sharp side facing toward the front of the knife. This designed allowed for automatic engagement of subsequent blades. By placing the sharp side toward the front, the user was assured that when that particular blade was engaged, the sharp end would be in use. Although these knives were convenient, they were bulky and more costly. The need to cost-reduce these knives led to similar variations that were more labor-intensive for blade reversal, removal, and insertion. For example, the automatic reload feature was eliminated and required the user to remove, reverse, and reinstall a new blade from a separate storage compartment. This eliminated the need for the more complicated automatic loading mechanism.

Third Innovation: Folding Utility Knives

The next innovation in this industry was the introduction of folding utility knives having a locking feature when in the open position. This knife also featured a relatively quick blade removal mechanism. This next contribution sparked sales to new levels. No longer were utility knives purchased to be stored in a toolbox or tool belt. People were purchasing these knives for a variety of reasons. Some like the compact style, which easily fits in their pockets. Others like the locking feature of the knives when in the open position. Others prefer folding knives that never needed sharpening. When the blade becomes dull, it can be reversed or replaced. However, the main reason for high sales was the "coolness factor." Folding utility knives delivered high levels of emotion to people. People would make special trips for the sole purchase of these items. Such demand sparked new designs increasing the coolness factor of these knives. Some of these designs included rapid blade-opening features. Others were the gravity opening release. Still others were a combination folding and retractable function. Finally, others included blade storage. After some time, innovation in the area of folding knives slowed. Despite the new colors and styles, these knives did not show intensified innovations with respect to the coolness factor—not until the development of the switchback knife.

Switchback Knife

The need to boost emotion, particularly the coolness factor, led to the development of the switchback. The switchback utility knife is unlike all other folding knives. With a simple push of a button, a spring-loaded blade flies open as if it were a switchblade! How cool is that? Please don't worry, there are no legal issues in owning a switchback. The switchback is actually safer than all other folding utility knives on the market. When the blade flies open, it first locks in the open position with the blade guarded. The blade edge and the front point of the blade are covered when the knife automatically flies open. This prevents accidental cutting or stabbing as the blade guard is also locked in the guarded position. Once the knife is locked open, the user can use the same hand and easily retract the blade guard. This is accomplished by sliding the blade guard against spring pressure toward the rear of the knife until it locks in the unguarded position. The knife is now ready for use. When the knife is to be closed, the user pushes the same button that opened the knife. This action produces two events. First, the blade guard automatically locks in the guarded position. This occurs as the blade guard is spring loaded in the guarded position. Second, the knife is unlocked so that the user can fold the knife and lock it back in the closed position. For the first time, the blade is completely covered before closing begins. This prevents accidental cutting every time the knife is closed. The switchback also includes features for rapid removal and insertion of the blade.

From the above discussion, a 2-D map can be created for a visual representation of the utility knife industry. To begin, the features of the switchback and the main competitive knives will be studied so that the offerings and industry factors can be identified. This will allow for a visual comparison of the knives on the 2-D map. The offerings and industry factors will populate the horizontal axis of the 2-D map. Upon study of the competitive knives, their price and features are analyzed and discussed below. This discussion will serve for the creation of the first 2-D map. The first 2-D map will display the competitive landscape prior to the invention of the switchback knife. This illustration will aid in the identification of several gaps that the switchback will ultimately fill, resulting in a boost in customer fulfillment. As a note, this discussion will not identify the competitive knives by brand, but will identify them by their main attributes.

Product Features: Lock-Back-Style Folding Utility Knives

The lock-back-style folding utility knife was the first folding utility knife, and it set the standard for many versions to follow. It is equipped with a machined steel body and blade holder. The blade holder holds the blade in a constant exposed position. This knife has a locking feature having a latch along the rear top portion of the knife. This locking feature is spring loaded, similar to classic lock-back knives. To maintain the knife in the locked position, the locking feature has a pin that fits into a slot on the blade holder. This slot is positioned to align to the pin when the knife is opened and keeps the knife in the open position. Prior to closing, the user simply pushes on the latch against the spring pressure to unlock the blade holder. Opposite the slot of the blade holder is a flat surface. This surface maintains the knife in the closed position as the pin pushes on the flat surface to prevent accidental opening of the knife. When the knife is opened, the blade holder is pulled and the flat surface rotates and forces the spring pressure of the locking pin away. This force continues until the flat surface is rotated out of contact with the pin. If the user releases the blade prior to this point, the spring pressure will force the blade holder closed. This is a major safety concern since the blade is exposed. This same condition is present during closing of the knife. As the knife is closed, the spring-loaded pin will engage the flat surface. This point of contact will begin to accelerate the blade in the closed position. If the user is not expecting this, the acceleration of the blade can cause injury.

These style knives suffered some drawbacks. First was the safety concern, as discussed above. Next, the user is required to open these knives using two hands. The high spring force to maintain the blade in the closed position required one hand to grasp the knife and the other to open the knife. The next drawback is the weight of the knife. Although compact, the steel body and blade holder resulted in a rather heavy unit. Finally, although the blade is easy to change, its design has inherent variations in the force required to unlock the blade-retaining feature. In some cases, the force to unlock the blade-retaining feature is rather high. In other cases, the force is low, allowing for unintentional opening. The coolness factor has also diminished over time as new innovations flooded the market. This also caused prices to drop over time.

Despite safety concerns, these knives set the standard for new versions to follow. These new versions reduced some of the drawbacks of these knives and boosted utility. In addition, new innovations introduced attempted to boost the coolness factor for this category. Our analysis continues with two additional offerings.

Product Features: Folding Retractable Utility Knife with Blade Storage

The next style knife is the folding retractable utility knife. This knife features a folding blade carrier that opens in a blade-retracted position. Once opened and locked, the knife allows for the blade to extend out of the blade carrier for cutting. It features a dual-material handle for gripping. To further enhance utility, this knife features a storage compartment to store extra blades. The features of this knife require the knife to have a larger body, thus increasing bulk and weight. As compared to most folding utility knives, this knife is priced on the high end of the range due to the abundance of features. Although this knife is designed to open using a one-handed operation, it lacks some of the coolness factor that others offer. Finally, since this knife can be closed with the blade extended, there is a risk of cutting injuries upon this step.

Product Features: Fast-Open Gravity Utility Knife

The next knife is the gravity opening folding utility knife. This knife features a folding blade carrier loosely connected to the handle. With use of a single locking button, this knife can be locked in the open and closed positions. When in the closed position, the user unlocks the knife and performs a rapid acceleration of the wrist to open the knife. The same operation can be repeated for closing of this knife. Upon some practice, this knife can be operated using a one-handed operation. Thus, there is a high level of coolness factor with respect to this knife. This style knife is priced higher than the folding knives discussed above. They are also compact and light. In terms of safety, there can be a safety risk, as the exposed blade is moving at relatively high speed during the opening and closing operations.

Based on the study of these knives, the offerings and industry factors that are relevant in this industry can be extracted and listed for placement along the horizontal portion of the 2-D map. These offerings define the important attributes of the knives and are comparable to one another. In addition, the offerings chosen are those features that can drive purchase decisions. The industry factors are noted in parentheses and will be discussed further. These offerings and factors, beginning with price, are:

Price
Actuation using one-handed operation
Compact storage
Ease of blade change
Knife safety
(Bulkiness/weight)
(Coolness factor)

The industry factors are those that are present as a result of the offerings. In other words, during development, certain features and benefits are targeted. Depending on the choice of these combined features and benefits, certain factors can develop. In this case, certain features of the folding knives can create a level of coolness never anticipated. From the discussion above, another possible factor to be considered is bulkiness/weight. For example, during the development of the first folding lock-back-style knife, the developers selected machined steel, resulting in a compact but heavy product. This created a resultant high-weight factor for this particular knife and has led to lighter materials to be chosen for some of the newer versions.

The offerings and industry factors can now be compared using assigned levels based on a user-defined scale. The assigned level will be plotted along the vertical axis of the 2-D map for each offering and industry factor. The user-defined scale can be any desired scale. For the examples of this book, a scale of 0 to 4 is used. One can choose a scale of 0–5 or 0–10. It is up to the reader of this book to choose any scale and, once chosen, to always maintain consistency as the scale maps relative information of a chosen strategy. For example, you can use a scale to compare similar offerings (low-cost autos to high-cost autos) on a first 2-D map. On a second 2-D map, you can use the same scale to map low-cost pens to high-cost pens. However, one may never typically compare autos to pens on the same 2-D

Offering Description	Lock-Back Folding Utility Knife	Folding Retractable Utility Knife	Fast-Open Gravity Utility Knife
Price	2	3	4
One-handed actuation	1	3	4
Compact storage	4	4	4
Ease of changing the blade	3	3	3
Knife safety	1	2	2
Bulkiness/weight	1	3	2.5
Coolness factor	3	2	4

Figure 2.5 Offering levels for various utility knives. (From Anthony Sgroi Jr.)

map, as these are dissimilar offerings and do not define a single strategy or a common theme.

A scale is analogous to comparing the length of a bar. If measuring systems did not exist (i.e., inches, millimeters, etc.), then one could compare one bar to another. For example, bar 2 is twice the length of bar 1. This method is used to assign levels for offerings and the industry factors. This task will become easier as more examples of offerings and their respected levels are mapped. The offerings and their factors are shown in Figure 2.5 with the appropriate assigned levels.

From Figure 2.5, the choice of the assigned levels is explained using the "one-handed actuation" offering description. On a comparative basis, the lock-back folding utility knife is very difficult to open using one hand. If it were totally impossible to open using one hand, the assigned value would have been a zero. Since the knife can be opened using one hand, a somewhat difficult task, the assigned value of 1 is appropriate. Next, on a comparative basis, the folding retractable utility knife is very easy to open. Using one hand, the knife can be "flicked open" upon some practice. However, once open, the user must reposition the hand to extend the blade out of the retractable holder. Although this is not a difficult task, the dual handling of the blade prevents an assigned value of 4, as the fast-open gravity knife is easier to open using a one-handed operation. The fast-open gravity knife simply requires a push of a button and a flick of the wrist for opening. Thus,

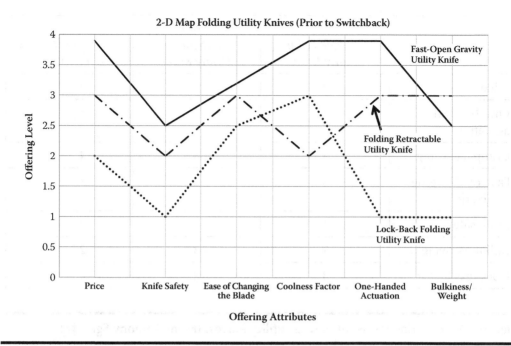

Figure 2.6 Two-dimensional map for folding utility knives (prior to the switchback). (From Anthony Sgroi Jr.)

for this example, the fast-open gravity knife is the easiest of the three and receives an assigned value at the top of the 0–4 range. The same logic is used for the remaining assigned values in Figure 2.5. As a note, this example illustrates a purely subjective exercise. If desired, the assigned values can be derived using consumer testing, focus groups, in-depth research, etc., to arrive at more factual numbers. It is up to the reader of this book to choose a convention that best fits his or her situation.

From Figure 2.5, we can draw a 2-D map to form an understanding of the competitive landscape with respect to the folding utility knife industry prior to the introduction of the switchback. The 2-D map is shown in Figure 2.6. The reader should note that the offerings/factors have been presented in a different order than in Figure 2.5. This allows for the smoothest possible display of the curves (i.e., minimum peaks and valleys).

From the 2-D map, we can begin to get a quick understanding of the industry. First, the folding retractable utility knife is positioned in the middle of the 2-D map. It has an abundance of features and is more utilitarian than the other two. Thus, we can determine that this model is targeting those focused on getting certain jobs done, for example, a carpenter or other tradesman that requires the retractable function with blade storage. Despite the utilitarian function, there is some level of coolness associated with this product.

Next, the lock-back folding utility knife can be analyzed. Although initially this knife was very successful in terms of driving sales to a larger target audience, in time other models have emerged and this model lost some of its relative coolness factor. This knife also posed a danger during use, especially during the closing of the knife. Thus in time, other models having more innovative features began to overtake this model. This led to the development of the more innovative fast-open gravity knife. During the time period of preparing this book, this knife is better targeted to those seeking a cool knife.

From the analysis of the 2-D map in Figure 2.6, the information necessary to determine the benefits of the switchback was determined. To win, a knife having a higher degree of coolness factor was required compared to the fast-open gravity knife. In addition, safety on these folding knives needed improvement. Therefore, the creators of the switchback created such a knife. With its automatic opening function, the coolness factor has been boosted to a new high. Safety has also been enhanced as per the features previously discussed. Finally, the geometry and material selections have minimized cost and bulkiness/weight that have been ignored for some time. Thus the switchback can now be compared to its competitors on another 2-D map. As a note, the switchback has been created to target the same buyer group as the fast-open gravity knife and the lock-back folding utility knife compared to the buyers of the folding retractable utility knife. Since the folding retractable utility knife is more utilitarian in function, it will not be reflected on the next 2-D map.

The offerings and levels of the switchback are compared to two competitive models and are shown in Figure 2.7. Similar to Figure 2.5, the assigned values are based on a relative comparison of the three models that are being compared. Again, these values are subjective in nature and can be modified using external information such as customer feedback data, customer surveys, etc.

We can now create a 2-D map to graphically compare the three knives. From the assigned values depicted in Figure 2.7, the switchback can now be visually compared to its two competitors. This 2-D map is illustrated in Figure 2.8, and the offerings have been reordered to depict smoother curves. From the 2-D map shown in Figure 2.8, we can immediately verify that the switchback has superior offering attributes compared to its competitors. Comparing the offerings from left to right on the 2-D map, beginning from

Offering Description	Switchback Knife	Lock-Back Folding Utility Knife	Fast-Open Gravity Utility Knife
Price	3	1	4
One-handed actuation	4	0.5	3.5
Compact storage	4	4	4
Ease of changing the blade	3	2	3
Knife safety	4	1	2
Bulkiness/weight	1	3	2.5
Coolness factor	4	0.5	2

Figure 2.7 Offering levels for various utility knives (including the switchback). (From Anthony Sgroi Jr.)

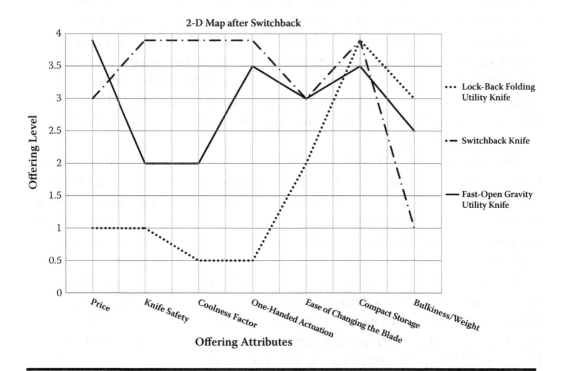

Figure 2.8 Two-dimensional map for folding utility knives (after the switchback). (From Anthony Sgroi Jr.)

one-handed actuation, we see the switchback meets or exceeds the levels of its competitors. However, the main purchase decision driver is the result of a very high relative coolness factor. The enhanced safety also helps to deliver the value proposition. Finally, the switchback will be offered at a lower price than the fast-open gravity version. From the 2-D map and the discussion that follows, we can derive a simple one-sentence statement for the switchback that tells its story. Such a statement could be "more coolness and safety for a lower price."

At the time of writing, the switchback is near completion of the tooling phase. Once the molds and assembly process is completed, the switchback will soon be offered in the marketplace. The elements of this product as dictated by the 2-D map in Figure 2.8 should define a successful strategy. We shall see how the market perceives this offering in due time.

Since assigning relative values on a chosen scale can be difficult to grasp initially, our discussion of the 2-D map concludes with another discussion of this topic. Let us reference another chosen offering for the discussion of the logic used to assign relative values. In this case, the knife safety offering is chosen for discussion. On a comparative basis, we begin with the switchback knife. This particular model is loaded with safety features. The blade and blade point are always in the covered position during opening of the knife. Upon closing, the blade is automatically placed in the safe position. No other folding utility knife possesses these attributes. Therefore, this feature deserves the maximum possible level on our scale, and in this case a level 4. Next, we compare the version lacking the abundance of safety features, the lock-back folding knife. Since the blade can be stored in a nonexposed position when folded, there exist some levels of safety. However, as previously discussed, during closing of this knife, the blade can accelerate and cause injury. This knife can also promote a hazard when trying to open using a one-handed operation. Therefore, it seems appropriate to assign a level of 1, as this knife has relatively low levels of safety. Finally, the fast-open gravity knife is compared to the prior offering features. In this case, this model is safer than the lock-back but is not as safe as the switchback. Therefore, an assigned level of 2 is a logical choice for this feature after study.

When two or more curves are displayed on a single 2-D map, the strategies of the offerings and price are clearly illustrated for the products being considered. If the curve looks choppy and unsmooth, you may need to switch offerings in different locations in order to obtain a smooth curve for comparing offerings. Once the desired curve is obtained, you can analyze the strategy where verification of the levels can be further analyzed. If you do in fact modify the levels, you may be required to shuffle around the offerings to obtain a smoother curve.

A smooth curve may illustrate more of a clear and focused strategy. A focused strategy may not necessarily represent a successful strategy, as the 2-D map does not provide a complete analysis. In Chapter 10, we will draw additional visual strategy maps, including strategy icons and market size gages, which will provide additional information allowing for a more thorough picture.

From the depiction shown in Figure 2.8, we can see multiple curves varying in shape. The curves, being different, are said to diverge from each other. A divergent curve depicts a totally different strategy and is usually desired since it invokes uniqueness. From our previous discussion, the offerings of a company must fulfill unmet consumer needs/wants within a defined market. If this is the case and the strategy diverges from the competition, then the strategy has a chance for success.

In the example above, Allway created a unique position by defining a series of unmatched and consumer-preferred offerings. It blended certain attractive elements of multiple product types. By bridging elements of the locking folding knife, the utility knife, and the switchblade knife, Allway created something truly unique. One may ask, is there a method of selection for bridging ideas from one product to another? How about one industry to another? The answer is yes. In subsequent chapters in this book, these techniques will be revealed and discussed to allow for anyone to blend ideas from alternate sources for the purpose of creating new opportunities.

As a final note, the above example was used to analyze a single product offering. It should be noted that the above technique can also be used to compare service features or even an entire business model. For example, when comparing two or more business models, the main attributes of the business models are labeled along the horizontal axis, and the levels of these attributes are indicated along the vertical axis, allowing for the creation of multiple curves. These attributes are analyzed in the same manner as the example above and can be shifted around if required so the curves have focus. Similarly, if a company is made up of one or more business units that are strategically unique, the process can be used for each business unit. For example, General Electric could compare GE aircraft engines to Pratt and Whitney aircraft engines and Rolls Royce aircraft engines. These similar business units are directly comparable to each other, and a clear graphical comparison is possible. However, General Electric would not use a single 2-D map for its entire business model. It wouldn't make sense to compare jet engines to appliances to power plants on the same 2-D map.

Conclusion

This concludes the topic with respect to the current state. If you are unclear in defining levels for offerings, refer back to the earlier portion of this chapter. It is rather important to understand the concept of defining the offering levels, as this will serve as a basis in defining a future state strategy.

Chapter 3

Opportunity Identification

In Chapter 2 we learned how to create a visual representation of a current strategy for a company using the visual management tools of Lean. This was reflected in the 2-D map. We also learned how a company can define a totally new strategy that is unique and offers a new and improved customer experience. We saw by example that this new experience can come at a lower cost by simply choosing alternate materials or lower-cost manufacturing methods. In many cases, eliminating or reducing those offerings that do not contribute to customer benefits (value) can reduce complexity and provide lower costs. Our example illustrated how ideas from different products can be combined to create a new and unique product offering. Finally, we analyzed the new business model by using the 2-D map to study the new strategy in comparison with the strategy of the current industry.

In this chapter, the topic of identifying new opportunities will be discussed in detail. These discussions will work in combination with subsequent chapters regarding the topics of finding new opportunities and filtering the optimal or more value-added opportunities. Such a process will minimize waste. By targeting large customer opportunities, companies add value to their customers and to themselves. Thus, the topic of opportunity identification is strongly linked to the principles of Lean.

Opportunity identification begins with the understanding of customer value. Providing customers with value-added products or services results in customer satisfaction. High levels of customer satisfaction lead to high levels of customer loyalty. High levels of customer loyalty in turn lead to steady streams of cash flow and lower transaction costs since the cost of attracting customers is lower. Companies have learned that it costs more to acquire a new customer than to keep an existing one. Customer satisfaction reduces price elasticity, since satisfied customers are willing to pay more for higher-quality products and services. Customers with high loyalty and low price sensitivity are easy targets for acquiring additional sales (i.e., cross-selling). These customers will also be easier to convince to trade up to more premium products or services. Finally, loyal customers are more likely to engage in free word-of-mouth advertising for your business.

Growth opportunities in any market can be gained through a better understanding of the customer's lifetime value. For example, in the ski industry, the average customer spends approximately $700 per purchase. Typically, these customers buy a new pair of skis every three years. That is about 15 to 20 pairs in a lifetime, leading to $10,500 to $14,000 of sales. This is why it is beneficial to any company to strive to keep its customers satisfied.

Studies have also shown that customer loyalty differs substantially depending on whether customers are *very satisfied* or just *satisfied*. These studies have shown that on a scale of 1 to 5, where 5 is "very satisfied" and 4 is "satisfied," customers are six times more likely to repurchase a product when "very satisfied" than those who are just "satisfied." Knowing that moderate satisfaction does not have a high impact on customer loyalty, companies need to *exceed* customers' expectations and delight them on a continual basis. Very satisfied customers lead to repeat sales, word-of-mouth advertising, and the gain of new quality customers willing to pay more for a company's products or services.

Companies that possess high levels of customer satisfaction tend to have increased market share compared to companies with lower levels of customer satisfaction. Therefore, the question is how do companies achieve high levels of customer satisfaction? Besides the methods of doing business and other important operational details when dealing with customers, the key to customer satisfaction is in the offerings companies provide customers. This needs to be amplified. As stated in Chapter 1, companies must provide customers those offerings that improve people's lives. This can be accomplished by making buyers' lives more productive, more efficient, more convenient, simpler, or even more fun in the various situations they experience in their lifestyle. In addition, providing better or cheaper solutions to current needs and wants is also beneficial to customers. This also includes the jobs buyers need to perform and solving problems they typically encounter. If the customer is a business-to-business customer, then these offerings must provide the buyer and its direct customer solutions to their unmet needs or wants, compared to the competition.

There are three types of offering requirements that need to be discussed in detail that will be used throughout this book. These requirements are vital for the understanding of customer satisfaction. After the discussion, you will understand how to create customers who are very satisfied. The three requirements are must-be requirements, one-dimensional requirements, and attractive requirements.[1]

Must-Be Requirements

These are the basic must-have features of the offerings of products or services. If these features are not present and not fulfilled, customers will be extremely dissatisfied. In some cases, customers may not explicitly demand these requirements and may even take these requirements for granted. Therefore, companies may not realize that certain requirements are unfulfilled, resulting in the total loss of interest in various products or services. Moreover, the fulfillment of these requirements will not lead to increased customer satisfaction. Consider this topic in terms of on-time departures at airports. As a flyer, I was always satisfied when flights were on time. In addition, if my flight was boarding early, I was never very satisfied. Earlier boarding did not contribute to an increase in customer satisfaction. However, when my flight was delayed, I became very dissatisfied, as did all passengers waiting to board. This example of on-time flights is a must-be requirement, as this requirement is already expected and does not lead to higher levels of customer satisfaction when achieved.

One-Dimensional Requirements

These requirements result in levels of customer satisfaction proportional to the level of fulfillment. In other words, the higher the fulfillment, the higher the customer satisfaction. One-dimensional requirements are usually explicitly demanded by the customer. For example, the more miles per gallon a car can achieve, the more satisfied the customer will be. Therefore, as customers want more or less of something where no limit exists, companies should strive to deliver as much value as they can. Of course, there may be barriers for this delivery (i.e., cost barriers, technology barriers, etc.). For instance, in order to achieve higher miles per gallon, there may be a new engine technology that is beyond the reach of what customers are willing to pay. Would you pay $250,000 for a car that can get 100 miles per gallon? The average consumer would not.

Attractive Requirements

These requirements have the greatest influence on how satisfied a customer will be in terms of an offering. These requirements are neither explicitly expressed nor expected by the customer. Fulfilling these requirements leads to more than proportional levels of satisfaction. If they are not met, there will be no feeling of dissatisfaction since they are not expected. Satisfying these requirements enhances customers' perceived value and their satisfaction. These are the most important requirements to fulfill in order to obtain very satisfied customers.

An explanation of the three customer requirements can be better understood by the use of an example. Consider the purchase of a car. A 23-year-old adult male performs a study of a few cars within his predetermined budget. He requires a car that can get at least 30 miles per gallon at a minimum due to his daily commute requirement. However, if he found a car that can get better mileage (one-dimensional requirement), he will be even more satisfied. He began to filter out some of the selections based on style. He was sure that certain styles would look too feminine and would result in a mockery from his peers. He narrows his selection to three models for test-drives. The first car drives very well and gets 38 miles per gallon. He determines that the car meets his level of expectation and the improved mileage provides a small added bonus in his purchase decision. He then test-drives the second car. This car is available in a shade of red unlike others that appeals to him. In addition, the second car can take corners better than any other car that he has driven. The feature that took him by surprise was the voice interaction device. He could talk to the car for the performance of specific car functions. The downside to the second car was the mileage. The second car only achieved 29 miles per gallon, slightly less than his original requirement but still workable for his commute. He then test-drove the third car, which had good style but was a little plain in the interior and in the wheels. However, this car was designed to get 40 miles per gallon.

After the three test drives, it was easy to make the purchase decision. Each car was very close to his original mileage requirements, and some exceeded his requirements. However, as we learned above, it was the attractive requirements that ultimately led to the purchase decision of the second car. The second car had a unique and appealing shade of red paint, hugged corners like he never experienced, and had that really cool voice interaction system. Despite the slightly lower mileage (one-dimensional requirement), this would not lead to low levels of customer satisfaction. Thus, with all other requirements being slightly different, the three attractive features prevailed in the end.

Next, we can further discuss the significance of the must-be requirements continuing with this example. The best way to discuss the must-be requirements is to note that the car purchased (second car) must be free of any significant and unexpected issues that may lead to total dissatisfaction. If this is the case, then the must-be requirements are fulfilled. On the other hand, consider this example where the buyer learns that the must-be requirement is *not* fulfilled. The buyer is enjoying his purchase for a couple of weeks. He then pulls into a parking lot and drives over a speed bump and hears this very odd and unpleasant sound of crushing metal. As he pulls away from the speed bump, he notices that his car is running rough. He takes the car to the dealer and learns that due to the robust suspension design, the exhaust system was positioned lower than normal. The lower position does not permit the car to be driven over speed bumps. He also learns that this type of damage is not covered under warranty. Upset and in need of the repair, he agrees to pay for it. Upon receipt of his car from the repair, his view regarding the car is no longer the same. He is constantly worried that he cannot drive over a speed bump. But he knows that at any time, a speed bump can show up. What can he do? How can he avoid them? This begins to stress him out to the point that he no longer enjoys his new car. Thus, the car did not fulfill this must-be requirement. You may ask yourself the question of why the buyer didn't ask the dealer if this car could be driven over a speed bump. In reality, who would ask this? This is typically always expected.

With the understanding of the three customer requirements, companies can begin to become sensitized as to what drives customers to purchase or not purchase certain products. In a later chapter, a tool to analyze and determine these requirement types will be discussed and illustrated in detail.

Now that you have an understanding of the types of requirements that lead to customer satisfaction, it is time to discuss various tools to identify opportunities in the marketplace. This will be attacked utilizing a variety of methods from both an internal and an external perspective. You can choose one tool or a plurality of tools, depending on your preference. Two or more forms of validation are always better than one. To begin, we will introduce a tool that can be used to analyze an already existing set of offerings. This tool has been

Product Fulfillment Map

	Product Life Cycle Touch Points				
	Acquisition (purchase/ destination/ setup)	*Product Use*	*Barriers to Use (skills or supplements)*	*Product Reliability (service/ maintenance)*	*End of Life (trade-in/ residual value/ disposal)*
Product Fulfillment					
Utility (job completion)					
Risk (safety, technical, etc.)					
Simplicity or Convenience					
Emotion or Social Well-Being					
Supports Green Movement					
Financial					

Figure 3.1 The product fulfillment map. (Adapted from "The Buyer Utility Map," in W. Chan Kim and Renee Mauborgne, *Blue Ocean Strategy*, Harvard Business School Press, 2005.)

worked through and enhanced to allow for quick and valued results when analyzing current or future strategies. As we are interested in the continual creation and delivery of customer value, this tool can be used to both verify if a business is delivering customer value and provide guidance in idea generation for producing customer value. This tool will also be used to test future ideas from techniques introduced later in this book. This tool is denoted as the product fulfillment map[2] and is illustrated in Figure 3.1.

The map in Figure 3.1 will allow for the analysis of offerings from a variety of forms, such as product or service features. By running the features of the offerings through this map, new opportunities can be discovered by analyzing unfulfilled portions of the map. In addition, new ideas can be generated via the use of the product fulfillment map. Before illustrating how this is used, a brief discussion of the map is necessary for clarification.

Top Portion of Product Fulfillment Map

The top horizontal portion of the map represents the touch points of the product life cycle. These are the basic touch points that customers experience during the purchase, use, and up to the disposal of products. It is equally important that customers obtain an exceptional experience during all touch points in order to be completely satisfied. Below is a brief description of each touch point within the product life cycle.

Acquisition

This is the purchase phase of the product. You want to ensure that customers can easily purchase your products and bring them to their desired location with an easy setup. If two companies offer the same product and one is extremely difficult to purchase and install, that company may never experience a repeat sale. Let us recall our dealership example. Buying a car is so difficult when dealing with dealers and their sales staff. Some people would rather get a root canal than deal with a dealership. Just think how many more cars a dealer would sell if the experience was improved. Ask yourself if your products are easy for customers to acquire. If they are not, then do something about it. This also includes effective packaging so that buyers can immediately understand the value proposition of products. The location of products is also important. A product developed to remove haze from a car's headlight should be merchandised near the car wax section of the store and not be merchandised in the cleaning aisle. Most people would not think of visiting the cleaning aisle for this type of product. Always make it easy for buyers to find and purchase products.

Product Use

Does your product perform as intended? Is your product easy to use and intuitive so the customer can get the job done? Do you provide directions that are clear and easy to follow? Do your competition's products do a better job than yours? Always face the truth about your products or services.

If they do not work too well, improve them as soon as you can so they are easy and effective to use soon after purchase.

Barriers to Use

Does your product require a high skill level to operate? Does your product require excessive fine-tuning to operate properly? If so, can the product be configured to allow for the average user to operate without extensive training or practice? Is your product offered such that the average (not too intelligent) customer can make it work out of the box with ease? If the answer is no, then do you provide clear and visual instructions? These are some of the necessary questions to ask customers, as those who purchase products have an expectation that the products will work for them. You should always configure products to be used that allow customers to tap into their value immediately. If a customer has to spend a long time to learn how to use the product, you may have missed the opportunity.

Does your product require supplements to use? If you must rely on supplements, ensure that this is clearly communicated and simple so the customer can understand this at the point of purchase. Make sure that you are not asking customers to rely too heavily on supplements. For example, if your competitor's product does not require supplements but your products require them and you exclude them to save on shipping cost, you may be losing sales to your competitor. Make sure the use of supplements is agreeable and easily implemented by the customer. Perhaps a new and innovative product that overcomes a required high skill or experience level can be created. This would allow an average person to complete a task that originally required specialized know-how or an experienced individual.

Product Robustness

Does your product break down rather easily and require service on a continual basis? Can your product be configured so that it is reliable and does not require frequent service? If this is the general nature of your industry, do you offer your customers a worry-free and convenient process so they are not affected by the delay of repairs? Do you offer warranties on your products to remove their financial risk of repair? Is your product easy to service so that customers can repair the products themselves? Does your product require specialized equipment to repair, or can it be configured otherwise so the customer can maintain the product?

These questions are important to consider, as people these days do not have the time to be inconvenienced. Do what it takes to increase the robustness of your products.

End of Life

Is your product costly to dispose? Is your product safe for the environment when disposing? Does your product contain residual value at it moves toward the end of its useful life? Can your product be traded in for a newer version? During trade-in, does the customer receive fair market value for the trade-in? These are the necessary questions to ask so that programs can be in place to remove as much inconvenience for the customer as possible when the product is at the end of its life. This can also provide companies with opportunities for their customers to purchase new products from them via trade-in.

Left-Side Portion of Product Fulfillment Map

The left side of the map represents the product fulfillment target categories of the map. These targets represent the actual reasons why customers purchase products. These targets are the needs or wants that drive customer satisfaction. They are the functional and emotional components that drive purchase decisions. All companies should understand and fulfill the appropriate number and levels of these targets regarding their products or services. The product fulfillment targets are briefly described below.

Utility: Product Function Category

This target is focused on the ability of the product to get a specific task completed. When a functional product is sought out by a customer, he or she is looking for this product to get a specific job or task completed in the most efficient manner. For example, when purchasing a tool, the tool is expected to perform a specific function as the buyer perceives based on the product's claims and general perceptions of that particular type of product. If one were to purchase a cordless drill, this product is expected to have the ability to drill holes and drive screws into drywall. When a user purchases the drill, it must allow the customer to be productive in installing drywall. Depending on the features of the drill (i.e., motor, battery, drill chuck, etc.), the drill may be more or less productive than others. An inferior and less productive drill may stall during screw installation, may have a short battery life, or some chucks may not grip well, causing slippage of the screws and ultimately providing low forms of customer productivity. Always ask yourself, for a particular purchase price, do your products offer customers improved productivity (speed, efficiency) compared to the alternatives available?

Risk: Category in Which Customers Seek Risk Avoidance

Are you afraid of heights? Do you dislike climbing a ladder? If the answer is yes, do you seek products that achieve a specific task without the requirement of climbing a ladder? Perhaps you are painting a two-story foyer and you purchase a long tele-pole, thereby allowing the task to be completed without the use of a ladder. This is an example of a customer eliminating a safety risk or simply the risk of falling. Another good example is the purchase of life insurance. Do you fear that your family will be in a financial crisis if your life suddenly ended? The purchase of life insurance eliminates the worry of financial risk to your family. There are other types of risk, but know that customers are constantly trying to reduce or eliminate risk in all aspects of their lives. Perhaps your product or service can be altered to provide increased risk avoidance for customers.

What about company risk? Companies must understand certain risks associated with investments, more specifically technologies. Certain technologies can spark large financial and people resources. Therefore, it is important that companies determine that chosen technologies are better adapted to solve customer problems in a more desirable fashion and can be sustained for some time, allowing for profitability of the technology.

Simplicity or Convenience

Are your offerings simple or convenient to use? Are your offerings simple and convenient to purchase? If they require a high skill to use or inconvenience to purchase, customers will get frustrated. This may alter the customers' purchase decision and prevent repeat sales. Customers want and need simplicity and convenience. Ensure they get it.

Emotional Well-Being or Social Well-Being

For the most part, all products can touch buyers on an emotional per-spective. There are some products that are purely functional and offer little to no emotion, such as computer paper or raw materials (e.g., wood, Styrofoam, etc.). On the other hand, there are products that have mostly emotion and offer little to no function, such as jewelry or cosmetics. Finally, there are products that offer both function and emotion, such as electronics, apparel, and even some appliances. In many cases, emotion can be added to functional products. For example, a car is functional. Its basic job is to provide transportation. However, these days, most auto purchase decisions are based on pure emotion. Most people want to buy a car that is just cool to drive. This provides pleasure to the buyer made possible by the large emotional component offered in some autos. This is an example of emotional well-being, where the customer feels good about the product he or she owns. In addition to the coolness of the automobile, people also purchase a car for social well-being. Social well-being deals with the way people are perceived in society. For example, some people like to be perceived as successful in society based on the type of car that they drive. Driving a Mercedes Benz would allow one to feel success-ful. This is an example of social well-being. In some instances, functional characteristics can be added to pure emotional type of products to unlock hidden value. Adding new features to a designer handbag can unlock new sales potential, as those seeking functional needs can now be satisfied with a designer look. Always ask yourself if your products exhibit ade-quate levels of emotion. Try adding emotion to functional products, and you may also consider adding function to emotional products.

Supports the Green Movement

This has been an increasingly growing topic. Our planet is in jeopardy of pollution and the depletion of natural resources. The time is now to start saving the planet, and many customers are willing to pay more to do so. However, be careful. One must truly find how much more the customer is willing to pay. Never assume that your products will sell just because they support the green movement. In addition, companies must ensure that their products, although green, perform as good as their nongreen counterparts.

Financial

Since consumers are always concerned with their finances, it is appropriate to include this in the product fulfillment map. The financial component is existent along the entire product life cycle. Ensure that you keep the views of your customers in mind financially, as cost is most often a decision driver.

Product Fulfillment Map Example

With the elements of the product fulfillment map defined, we can begin to work through an example. I chose a topic that most people can relate to on a daily basis. Consider a tire manufacturing company that has a long-time existence in the marketplace. It wants to offer customers a tire that performs as good as a high-cost tire but at an average cost. This particular company surpasses most in the areas of product development, material science, and testing. It truly feels that it can enter the market of supplying high-performance tires at average prices that every consumer can afford. In order to achieve this objective, the designers verified that a unique tread design will achieve this goal. The designers also verified that only a slight formulation modification to their already existing material configuration will be needed for product success. This will allow for a low-cost product offering. The design team has already performed preliminary testing in various situations and has confirmed that the new tread grips the road in snow and rain almost as good as premium, more costly tires. The designers have communicated that this unique tread design is not a symmetrical design and will require one set of tires for the driver's side and another set of tires for the passenger side.

To begin using the product fulfillment map, the company decides to work through each product fulfillment target individually, scanning through each corresponding product life cycle touch point. For example, beginning with utility, fulfillment (or unfulfillment) is investigated for acquisition, followed by product use, barriers to use, product reliability, and finally, end of life. Once this is completed, the same is done for risk, simplicity or convenience, emotional or social well-being, and finally, financial. Each cell is labeled using the following label convention:

- F-number: *F* denotes fulfillment and *number* indicates the level of fulfillment, where 1 is very low fulfillment and 10 is completely fulfilled. An example is F-10, where 10 indicates completely fulfilled. Another example is F-5, where the 5 indicates 50% fulfillment (based on a scale of 1 to 10). The scale is relative and can be compared to current levels of fulfillment with respect to the particular industry.
- U: U indicates unfulfilled.
- N/A: N/A indicates not applicable for this cell. Also, for N/A, the cell can simply be left blank.
- An integer can be placed in front of the label for purposes of cell identification, allowing for an action plan description (e.g., 1F-5 or 2U, etc.).

The team on an internal perspective begins to populate the product fulfillment map using the convention above. The output is illustrated in Figure 3.2.

The convention from above allows for the instant identification of opportunities. The cells illustrating an F with a number substantially less than 10 and a U represent an opportunity for improvement. In our example, the team identified six cells for discussion:

- 1F-8 illustrates that the newly proposed tread works almost as good as a very expensive premium tire. This indicates that the tire tread will be very productive when the tire is in use. At this stage, the team decides that a score of 8 is almost three times better than tires of average price. Thus, the team decides that the proposed tire represents a good opportunity.
- 2U indicates that there can be a risk during routine maintenance. In many cases, customers are used to rotating their tires by switching them around. If the "do it yourself" person places a specific tire on the wrong side, the car will become unsafe. The team must revisit this issue and work through a solution.
- 3F-9 indicates that purchase will be simple and convenient, as the company will sell in its large and already existing distribution channels.
- 4F-10 indicates that the owner of these tires will feel safe during the use of them, as they grip the road very well.
- 5F-10 indicates that the cost of acquisition is highly fulfilled, as the consumer is getting a high-end tire for the cost of an average version.
- 6U indicates that the user will not have the same options available for rotating tires to minimize wear. This will result in more tire purchases than average. Although this seems to be the optimum situation for the company, consumers may not go for this over the long term.

Product Fulfillment Map

	Product Life Cycle Touch Points				
	Acquisition (purchase/ destination/ setup)	*Product Use*	*Barriers to Use (skills or supplements)*	*Product Reliability (service/ maintenance)*	*End of Life (trade-in/ residual value/ disposal)*
Product Fulfillment					
Utility (job completion)		1F-8			
Risk (safety, technical, etc.)				2U	
Simplicity or Convenience	3F-9				
Emotion or Social Well-Being		4F-10			
Supports Green Movement					
Financial	5F-10			6U	

Figure 3.2 Product fulfillment map tire example, first pass. (From Anthony Sgroi Jr.)

The analysis revealed some important opportunities to target. The company determined that the nonsymmetrical design was not a good position to be in. The company could not risk automobile crashes if any tire were to be installed on the wrong side of the car. Another decision maker was the fact that consumers may not be too pleased if they were unable to rotate tires to minimize wear over time.

The design and materials science team then decided to develop a symmetrical tire tread design. This would allow for the tire to be installed on any wheel location. After many tests and material iterations, the team determined that a symmetrical design was possible with the following changes, compared to the first version:

■ A new symmetrical tread was developed to meet the design targets.

Product Fulfillment Map

	Product Life Cycle Touch Points				
	Acquisition (purchase/ destination/ setup)	*Product Use*	*Barriers to Use (skills or supplements)*	*Product Reliability (service/ maintenance)*	*End of Life (trade-in/ residual value/ disposal)*
Product Fulfillment					
Utility (job completion)		1F-7			
Risk (safety, technical, etc.)					
Simplicity or Convenience	2F-9				
Emotion or Social Well-Being		3F-10			
Supports Green Movement					
Financial	4F-8				

Figure 3.3   Product fulfillment map tire example, second pass. (From Anthony Sgroi Jr.)

- New material costs necessary for optimum results grew by 12%.
- Performance was reduced by 8% in terms of gripping the road compared to the nonsymmetrical tread.

The team then decided to run a second analysis through the product fulfillment map for final verification before talking to lead customers. The results are shown in Figure 3.3.

From the results in Figure 3.3, the product reliability issues have been resolved. As feared, the team has confirmed that performance has diminished slightly as well as there being an incremental cost increase. However, the team was optimistic that the much improved tread/material characteristics at a slightly higher cost were a far better offering than the current available average tire. The team also verified that customers were willing to pay more for the new performance levels using a series of customer focus groups and surveys administered to customers and distributors. The company also learned at the end of the study that the new formulation allows for virtually any color tire, which created a new level of uniqueness never realized.

The product fulfillment map is a good tool for immediately analyzing and finding opportunities in the marketplace. It can be used for a current set of offerings as well as proposed offerings. This tool can be expanded to compare your offerings to those of your competitors if desired. In later chapters, additional examples of the product fulfillment map will be illustrated.

As previously stated, opportunities exist when customers purchase products to fulfill some sort of need or want, typically in the form of a problem to be solved. If customers do not think they have a particular problem, they will not purchase unless they can be enlightened that they do in fact have a problem. These are called unarticulated needs, and they usually show themselves when customers see a solution, for example, the microwave oven. Before the microwave oven was invented, people never explicitly asked for such a device. There was no knowledge in the public that the creation of the microwave oven would be in demand. However, once the technology was discovered, the application of employing microwaves to cook food presented a solution that made sense to consumers. Once customers learned that a product was created that allowed them to quickly prepare food with minimal cleanup, they sought microwave ovens. The solution to a large unarticulated need opened a very large opportunity of considerable market size. Therefore, if companies can define problems in terms of the desired outcome[3] (minimize the time to prepare food and clean up), new offerings can be discovered. Running through the product fulfillment map can surely help companies discover new opportunities within the confines of their business model.

Opportunity Scores

Creating opportunities and gaining high revenues depend on the importance of the problem to be solved and the level of satisfaction with the current solutions. For example, if there is a very important problem that a group of customers is struggling with and there are very poor solutions currently available, these customers would pay for these solutions if available. Consider the chore of washing clothes. One has to take the clothes to the washer and separate. The next step is to place them in the washer and load the soap. Then after the cycle is complete, the clothes must be taken out of the washer and fed into the dryer. Finally, these clothes must be taken from the dryer and folded before wrinkling occurs. Finally, pressing of the clothes is done for those who desire wrinkle-free clothes. Now, let us assume that a device can be invented that performs all of the above tasks in a single step. The only thing to do is to simply load the clothes into the device and the output is washed, dried, pressed, and folded clothes. This is an example of creating an opportunity by satisfying an important task for buyers. Such a device would most likely drive people to pay a vast amount of money if it were offered.

With respect to market offerings, the difference between the level of importance and the level of satisfaction is called a market gap. A large gap represents a large opportunity. On the contrary, if there is no gap, then there is little to no opportunity. Such a situation of little to no gap is a commodity situation, and your best bet to find opportunities is to find a lower-cost solution to unlock new opportunities.

The gap can be assigned a numerical value to help identify the opportunity level. This gap can be analyzed by the business executive who understands the business he or she represents, or can be integrated into a survey for potential customers to implement. The survey can be administered to a set of target customers for analyzing current or future opportunity levels. This information will help in the formulation of future strategies as new ideas are conceived. We can introduce a scale of 1 to 10 for the importance question with respect to a set of offerings (e.g., product features). A score of 0 would indicate that the product feature is unimportant (waste). Likewise, a score of 10 would indicate that the product feature is extremely important (value). The same can be stated for satisfaction. A score of 0 would indicate that the product feature is not at all satisfied by current available offerings. Likewise, a score of 10 would indicate that the product feature is fully satisfied by current offerings. With the scores, opportunity is determined by subtracting the satisfaction score from the importance score.[4] For example, if a product feature received an 8 for importance and a 3 for satisfaction, the opportunity would be a 5. As a note, for negative opportunity scores, the negative value is preserved, as this can allow for the ranking of opportunity scores if desired. For the purposes of ranking, I prefer to rank beginning from the highest opportunity to the lowest opportunity. I then use a second ranking for those offerings having the same opportunity. Thus, two or more offerings of the same opportunity can be subranked by arranging from highest importance to lowest importance. This is illustrated below.

To explain further, let us state another example. Let us assume that an importance score was 9 and a satisfaction score was 2; the opportunity is: opportunity = importance − satisfaction, or 9 − 2 = 7. Therefore, we can surmise that a perfect opportunity score would be 10 (importance = 10, satisfaction = 0), and the worst possible opportunity score would be 0. Therefore, we have defined an opportunity score range of 0 to 10 if we exclude the possible negative values of opportunity.

We can formulate a scale for the opportunity scores and define market conditions. An opportunity score of 0 to about 3 can represent an overserved market, where an overserved market is not worth too much time and effort to pursue unless a truly innovative feature can be added to boost productivity, emotion, or substantially lower the cost of the feature. An opportunity score of 4 to about 6 can represent an adequately served market and allows for more opportunity in terms of innovation and lower cost. An opportunity score of 7 to 10 can represent a large opportunity or an underserved market where the simple delivery of that product feature can unlock new revenue growth. Of course, an innovative and low-cost method to hit a large opportunity only builds more confidence in the introduction of the offering. Note, the ranges as defined for the opportunity scores are introduced by example only. The reader of this book is free to employ any chosen convention for defining the ranges that best align to a particular market condition.

We can brainstorm and obtain some potential ideas for opportunity evaluations by obtaining importance and satisfaction scores. We can also obtain ideas from utilizing the product fulfillment map. The product fulfillment map is one way to generate new potential product or service ideas. From any method of idea generation, a list of potential ideas can be evaluated for performing opportunity calculations. We can tabulate the features and also include satisfaction columns of current competitor products in order to paint a picture of what is currently being offered. From these satisfaction scores, we can determine their opportunities for evaluating new product ideas. Such a table is illustrated in Figure 3.4. In it, we are exploring four features for a cordless drill. This table will allow us to verify if there is an opportunity for development of one or more new features by an internal analysis or obtaining importance and satisfaction scores from customers. We will also learn if our three main competitors are doing a good job with respect to their features.

Product Features (abbreviated form)	Impor-tance	Competitor Satisfaction Scores			Maximum Satisfaction	Oppor-tunity
		Competitor 1	Competitor 2	Competitor 3		
Maximizing the time the battery delivers full power	8	4	5	3	5	3
Minimizing the time to charge the battery	9	4	6	8	8	1
Sufficient torque to drive large deck screws	9	2	2	2	2	7
Zero-slip keyless chuck at high torque	6	3	4	5	5	1

Figure 3.4 Opportunity calculation scores (importance minus satisfaction). (Adapted from Anthony Ulwick, *What Customers Want: Using Outcome-Driven Innovation to Create Breakthrough Products and Services*, McGraw-Hill, 2005.)

From the results shown in Figure 3.4, we can immediately see that there is a large potential opportunity to create a cordless drill that can drive large deck screws.

If you have generated a rather large list of opportunity scores, it is best to rank them from highest to lowest. By beginning with opportunity, you can first list all of the features by the opportunity they represent, and study the opportunity scores. If two or more features have the same opportunity, a second ranking can be made using the highest importance. Thus, you will be left with a prioritized list, and the features at the top of your list would have the highest probability of success. Figure 3.5 illustrates the ranked opportunity scores for the features shown in Figure 3.4.

Product Features (abbreviated form)	Impor- tance	Competitor Satisfaction Scores			Maximum Satisfaction	Oppor- tunity
		Competitor 1	Competitor 2	Competitor 3		
Sufficient torque to drive large deck screws	9	2	2	2	2	7
Maximizing the time the battery delivers full power	8	4	5	3	5	3
Minimizing the time to charge the battery	9	4	6	8	8	1
Zero-slip keyless chuck at high torque	6	3	4	5	5	1

Figure 3.5   Ranked opportunity scores. (Adapted from Anthony Ulwick, *What Customers Want: Using Outcome-Driven Innovation to Create Breakthrough Products and Services,* McGraw-Hill, 2005.)

If a customer survey is desired, the questions should be asked in a more complete form rather than in an abbreviated form like that shown in Figures 3.4 and 3.5. For the importance question, the question should begin with the phrase: "How important is it that you are able to ...?" Similarly, for the satisfaction question, the question should always begin with the phrase: "How satisfied are you with your ability to ...?" This format allows for the reader to adjust his or her answer according to the scale that you provide. If your scale is 0–10, the question for importance regarding a kitchen stove top may state, "On a scale from 0 to 10, how important is it that you are able to boil a large pot (4 gallons) of water in under 5 minutes?" where 0 indicates not important and 10 indicates very important. Similarly, for the satisfaction question, you can state, "On a scale from 0 to 10, how satisfied are you with your stove's ability to timely boil a large pot (4 gallons) of water?" where 0 indicates not satisfied and 10 indicates fully satisfied.

Conclusion

The tools provided in this chapter represent two methods to discover opportunities. These discussions allow the reader to better understand opportunities associated with current products and new ideas. This chapter is placed before the idea generation chapter for a few reasons. The first is that you can directly apply these tools to your present set of offerings for evaluating your current strategy. Second, having an understanding of the best opportunities allows you to focus on these opportunities during the idea generation process. This can provide maximum value to the new ideas. Since practice makes perfect, and since you are familiar with your current products or services, you will have better insight running through the exercises of these tools. After some practice, you can verify the level of fulfillment of your current offerings and understand if you are overserving, adequately serving, or underserving your customers. Don't spend too much time trying to verify if your offerings are must-have, one-dimensional, or attractive. In later chapters, we will run through a complete process in determining these aspects for current and future product and service features using the Kano model.

Chapter 4

Idea Generation

In Chapter 3 we learned about finding and quantifying new opportunities and the understanding of various customer requirements. We learned that customer satisfaction depended on certain must-have requirements, one-dimensional requirements, and attractive requirements. We also learned how each of these requirements contributes to customer satisfaction. In Chapter 3, we introduced a new tool called the product fulfillment map, which utilizes all of the customer touch points with the various categories of product fulfillment targets. We learned how this tool can be used to test current and proposed strategies and, in some cases, can unlock new opportunities by the application of the tool.

We also learned about a method to quantify market opportunities. We defined a scale for importance and satisfaction with respect to offerings and how to calculate the opportunity based on the scores of importance and satisfaction. Finally, we defined a method to categorize the opportunities based on their calculation and defined three potential markets. The first was the overserved market, the second was the adequately served market, and the third was the underserved market.

In this chapter, the topic of idea generation will take any company from where it is to where it could be. Two perspectives will be discussed regarding idea generation. The first is the internal industry perspective. This will take an approach that is in tune with your industry. The internal perspective of idea generation will help you to create new ideas that will fill gaps according to those problems and solutions familiar with your current industry. The second alternative will take the form of an external industry perspective. This perspective will unlock new offerings based on gathering new ideas from external frames of reference, such as a different industry.

Internal Perspective Techniques

We begin by looking at some of the most common ways to generate new ideas, beginning with the internal perspective approach. This approach deals with the industry's current customers and the current problems these customers are solving. There are many techniques to gather feedback from customers, lost customers, and competitor customers that ultimately lead to new ideas. These new ideas fuel product changes, new product concepts, and new services. We begin by discussing various voice of the customer (VOC) techniques.

The understanding of a target market allows one to choose certain VOC methods that will provide customer insight. Target customers can be a set of people who represent some sort of common need or want. Another example of target customers is a group of people or customer group that shares a common problem, for example, men in the age range of 45 to 60 looking for products to solve the problem of gray hair. It is desirable to choose a set of target customers of adequate size, allowing for high levels of sales. In later chapters, we will discuss various forms of target customers so that the largest possible group can be defined and targeted.

VOC techniques will allow the acquisition of quantitative data, qualitative data, or a combination of both. Some techniques are more costly and time-consuming than others. Special consideration should be taken as to which method is best for you.

The use of qualitative data will be subjective. For example, you may ask an individual to rate a product's performance. The individual may provide you with feedback that the product's performance is inferior. How does one interpret such a response? Do you deem the product as inadequate, or do you look for more clarifying feedback? In any case, you must always get to the root cause of the feedback. For example, you may realize that the participant was not using the product properly, and that resulted in an unfair rating of the product. Qualitative data mining requires that participants properly understand the question in view of the facilitator. If the product is available, errors can be reduced by having the participant demonstrate the use of the product. This technique can ensure that data received will be relatively accurate.

Quantitative data and analysis allow aspects of the product to be ranked using a numerical scale. As defined in Chapter 3, obtaining a numerical value can provide a measurable method of evaluation. This can substantially aid in measurable decisions. As in qualitative analysis, quantitative analysis must also

be understandable to the participants. When participants can easily understand the questions that are being asked to them, they can provide more accurate answers, which will reduce the number of possible errors that may occur.

We now turn our attention to some of the common methods[1] regarding
the internal industry perspective approach.

Surveys

The most common form of obtaining the voice of the customer is through
the use of surveys. Surveys typically involve the use of a questionnaire and
basically come in four forms. The first form is typically a person-to-person
survey where the survey questionnaire is explained to the participant in
person and then administered. The second form is a telephone survey
where the participant is called and asked a variety of questions over the
phone. The third method is a mail survey where a vast amount of people
are mailed a questionnaire and are encouraged to participate in the survey. The final form is administered online using a survey type of website
such as surveymonkey.com. In all cases, some sort of incentive is needed
in order to obtain enough people to participate in the survey. For example,
the participant can be told that he or she will receive a free product for his
or her participation. In other instances, the participant can receive a coupon
or even cash. When administering surveys, the questions must be clear and
understandable to reduce possible errors when evaluating the results.

Focus Groups

Focus groups are an interactive discussion of 5 to 15 people administered
by a moderator that can last for about two hours. The discussions typically begin by focusing on the current levels of satisfaction with products
and the problems these products are intended to solve. The moderator can
then begin to find the root cause issues to customer dissatisfaction, thereby
exposing ideas for new opportunities. Visual aids and products can be made
available to give more validation to the information being exchanged.

Focus groups can be costly, as travel may be necessary to reach the lead
users of certain products. Also, focus groups typically require the use of
a facility equipped with a two-way mirror so that product developers and
business executives can anonymously listen to the discussions to unlock
new ideas. Recruiting can also be time-consuming, as first you must find
qualified people to invite, and then you must entice them to attend.

One-on-One Interview

One-on-one interviews provide qualitative and detailed information that cannot be gathered from a large population, such as the utilization of focus groups. These types of interviews are performed when there is not enough information available to form a survey questionnaire.

One-on-one interviews can be particularly useful for people with limited availability when it is impossible to get these people together in a room for a focus group. This is typical when dealing with high-level executives or high-profile people. These types of interviews can be planned more easily around a busy individual's schedule, as the interviewer can travel to the interviewee's location.

The cost of a one-on-one interview is usually low unless a large compensation request is made from the individual.

Intercepts

Intercepts consist of approaching an individual in a public location. The most common place for intercepts is typically at shopping malls. In many cases, the interviewer will approach people associated with the target market. For example, if a sporting equipment provider wanted to gain new insights regarding baseball gloves, an interview can be conducted to those shoppers entering and leaving a sporting goods store within the mall. In many cases, these individuals are provided an incentive to participate.

Product User Testing

This form of testing requires asking individuals to use a product, often while they are being observed. If they are not being observed, the individuals may be asked to fill out a survey during or after the product trial. This type of testing can help designers understand how to make their products more intuitive and easier to use. Often, a set of instructions is supplied with the product for further evaluation. To gain a thorough understanding, product testing may require more than one to two weeks to complete. Based on the types of questions to be asked, this type of testing can be both qualitative and quantitative.

Customer Feedback and Complaints

Customer complaints can provide useful information regarding products. However, companies must find the root cause of these complaints, as there are many people out there that make it a habit to constantly complain. Some of these people may want free products as a result of the complaint, or they may simply have nothing better to do with their time. Don't feel compelled to modify your products right away. Investigate the complaint and make sure there is a true issue with your product before making investments. In addition, other forms of feedback can highlight possible product issues. Such forms include warranty claims and product return data. In addition, feedback from the sales force may surface issues and unlock new potential opportunities.

Ethnographic Research

Ethnographic research is a qualitative method of researching customer needs based on studying the anthropology or culture of the user. This method involves spending time in the field observing customers and their environment to better understand their lifestyle or culture as a basis for understanding their needs for a product. A deep understanding of your customer can lead to fundamental insights that impact product design, feature sets, product positioning, marketing communications, advertising execution, etc.

Idea Generation

We can now get into some details with respect to idea generation on an internal perspective using a technique referred to as the problem solution statement. I find that problems to be solved within an industry can lead to solutions when the *problem* is properly defined. Therefore, by writing multiple phrases or problem statements, one can properly identify the problem. Another way of thinking about this is to find the root cause of the problem. Consider this example: If your faucets at your house continue to feed dirty water, what is the problem? Is the problem dirty faucets? Is there a problem with the plumbing (i.e., corrosion of the pipes)? Is the water entering the residence dirty? These types of questions must be understood before a solution can be implemented. For this example, let us assume that we have investigated the root cause of the problem. At the end of the investigation, it was determined that the root problem was the water that was entering the house was in fact dirty. The problem solution statement[2] can be used to find the solution as well as formulate possible solutions.

Problem Solution Statement

The problem solution statement has the form: The problem of _____ is best solved by _____.

Once we understand the root cause of the problem, we can then turn to the problem solution statement for possible solutions. For example, consider the following possible solutions:

1. The problem of faucets discharging dirty water is best solved by placing a water filter on each faucet in the house.
2. The problem of faucets discharging dirty water is best solved by placing a water filter on the entrance pipe of the house.
3. The problem of faucets discharging dirty water is best solved by forcing the city to ensure clean water is delivered to the home.
4. The problem of faucets discharging dirty water is best solved by placing the house on the market and moving to a different area with cleaner water.

From the four problem solution statements, it is clear that solution 2 makes the most sense. Therefore, to apply this concept to practice, companies should first identify the root cause(s) of the problem and write a series of problem solution statements. Once the statements are complete, the optimum solution can be chosen for implementation.

Job Mapping

Another useful technique for brainstorming is job mapping.[3] Job mapping focuses on a specific task or job and breaks down the steps necessary to complete the task or job perfectly. This is essential because if you do not seek perfection, an opportunity for innovation can be lost. From each step, new innovations may be possible to significantly simplify one or more of the steps defining a new product. For example, with respect to washing clothes, let's revisit our previous example and list the steps in list form, as shown in Figure 4.1.

Now from the listing of the steps, it seems that there are a variety of new possible innovations. We can simply develop the best and most innovative laundry basket that has separable compartments for separating clothes during

Task or Job: Cleaning Clothes

Steps	Perfection Recommendation
Transport clothes to wash room	Laundry baskets with wheels
Separate clothes	Laundry baskets with insertable compartments
Load washer	Configured laundry basket that hooks up to washer for easy loading
Load soap and fabric softener	Washer to automatically draw from containers
Turn on water valve	Automatic water valve (turns on during wash cycle and shuts off after wash cycle)
Turn on washer	Voice commands
Load washed wet clothes into dryer	Combination washer-dryer that can automatically load the washed clothes into the dryer; this will eliminate waiting and handling
Remove clothes from dryer and load into basket	Configured laundry basket that hooks to dryer for easy unloading
Fold clothes	Sorry, this still has to be done manually.
Transport clothes to destination	Laundry baskets with wheels

Figure 4.1   Steps to clean clothes. (From Anthony Sgroi Jr.)

loading. Also, we can include wheels for easy transport of the clothes. Finally, we may choose to add a self-lifting device to the laundry basket that allows for quick loading into the washing machine and quick unloading from the dryer. We could go even further and develop washing and drying machines that attach together, automatically load washed clothes into the dryer, and automatically draw soap and fabric softener. On the other hand, we can develop a new and innovative water valve that automatically turns on for use by the washing machine and automatically shuts down the water when the washing machine is not in use. This would allow for the sense of security that if the water hose were to fail when the machine was not in use, floods would never occur. The key to job mapping is that it is not essential to solve the entire problem. We can generate incredible innovations and unlock great new ideas by solving only one problem associated with the entire job.

Internal Ideation Methods

In addition to the ideations techniques above, it is also desirable to engage the organization for new ideas to creative challenges. This is made possible by running various internal ideation sessions. In his book *Idea Stormers*, Bryan Mattimore teaches several of these sessions.[4] In most cases, these sessions should be facilitated to keep the participants on track. Some techniques require a group setting and others do not. Below are a few techniques that can be incorporated into any company's idea generation process. As a note, ideation sessions typically involve the use of several techniques. This improves the chance of inspiration occurring, as some techniques may not work with certain groups. In the event one technique does not produce the desired results, others may allow for a productive day.

Brain Writing

This technique is an anonymous type of ideation technique. In it, the facilitator presents a creative challenge such as a problem that certain customers are struggling with. Each of the participants is given a blank sheet of paper and writes down an initial idea for meeting the challenge for this first step. At this point, each participant passes the paper to his or her nearest neighbor. Each person builds on the initial idea and passes it to the next neighbor for further building of the idea. This process continues until each participant gets the opportunity to build on each initial idea. At this point, the first step of the session can end where the idea is passed back to the originator. However, if desired, the paper can be passed to each individual multiple times prior to completion of this first step. When the paper is given back to the originator, the second step begins. For the second step, the originator of the idea studies the paper and circles the two best ideas for group discussion. During group discussion, the best ideas from each paper are optimized. The ideas left can be later prioritized for possible selection.

Brain Walking

Similar to brain writing, this technique utilizes a large flip chart called ideation stations in place of passing around a sheet of paper for the first step. Each participant has an assigned ideation session and writes his or her first idea directed to a creative challenge. In this technique, participants shift to the nearest ideation station and build on previous ideas. Shifting is continued until completion of the first step as mandated by the facilitator. Each participant returns to his or her respective station for step 2. In step 2, the best two ideas are selected for group optimization. Since brain walking is public, this exercise creates synergy among the group, allowing for a shared purpose.

Worst Idea

The worst idea technique can surely generate a ton of fun. In it, a creative challenge is proposed. The participants respond by creating a list of really bad ideas. Not just bad, but really off-the-wall ideas that can be gross, stupid, and even illegal, if desired. Once the list is complete, the exercise continues with efforts of turning the bad ideas into good ideas by using two methods. The first is to simply think in terms of the opposite of the bad ideas for sparking a good idea. If this doesn't produce the desired results, then new ideas can occur by finding something of interest or value in the bad idea to inspire a good idea. If this technique does not produce the desired results, it is sure to spark energy and humor into the session.

Patent Prompts

Prior to this session, the U.S. Patent database is searched based on keywords that are related to the creative challenge. The abstracts of several patents are printed and given to the participants. This session is a two-step technique and begins with the individuals working alone. Each individual is given three to five patent abstracts and is instructed to select one or two abstracts that he or she believes can help the group with its creative challenge. Once the abstracts are selected, teams are formed and the chosen abstracts are used to inspire a new idea to the creative challenge. This technique uses existing inventions to inspire a new invention.

Picture Prompts

Picture prompts is a very similar technique to patent prompts. The difference with this technique is that pictures, illustrations, and even videos are used instead of patent abstracts. This technique can use either random or targeted pictures for inspiration. In the random technique, an abundance of pictures from various sources are handed out to the participants for sparking ideas to a creative challenge. Pictures can come from magazines, posters, etc. In this technique, the participants try to find aspects of the pictures to solve the creative challenge. In the targeted approach, pictures are selected that are related to the creative challenge. Performing Internet searches for pictures and videos can spark ideas to creative challenges. Targeting is achieved using keywords taken from the creative challenge. In this example, pictures can be given to the group for inspiration, or the technique can begin on an individual basis, as discussed with patent prompts.

White Board Technique

This technique is a type of visual suggestion box. By mounting a large white board in a neutral or common location, employees from the company can post ideas in a more private, nonthreatening format. The technique begins by posting a creative challenge on the white board. In many cases, the one writing the creative challenge (facilitator) may choose to post an idea or two to invite others to build upon. A timeline is also posted on the white board to provide a sense of urgency. Each day, employees from all over the company can post new ideas or build upon previous ideas. The facilitator also adjusts the timeline to indicate the days remaining on a daily basis. During this process the facilitator should encourage the addition of ideas. Once the timeline has ended, the facilitator summarizes the ideas for prioritization and selection. In order to ensure that employees take this technique seriously, it is essential that some type of action is taken upon completion. For example, lunch can be provided to all those who have contributed, and a cash prize can be given to the individual who posted the best idea.

External Perspective Techniques

We now turn our attention to some of the methods regarding the external perspective approach.[5] Instead of looking within the confines of a company's business, companies can look beyond them to create a totally new business. In addition to alternate industries, companies can also look to alternate strategic groups, at the different buyer groups, and at complementary product and service offerings; add or remove functional or emotional characteristics of their industry; and finally, adapt to current trends or even identify and create new trends.

Looking to Alternative Industries

Companies not only compete with other firms in their own industry, but also with companies offering alternative products and services. These products or services can have the same form and provide the same function (e.g., snap-on wrench vs. an SK wrench regarding the hand tool market). Companies also compete with firms that provide substitute products. These are products or services that have a different form but provide the same type of function (e.g., owning a motorcycle vs. a car; both provide the same transportation function, but in a different manner). Finally, companies compete with firms offering alternatives. These are products or services that have different forms and different functions but achieve the same objective. For example, take the objective of traveling to a certain destination. You can take a taxi or go to the extreme of getting a ride in a helicopter. In this example, the helicopter is in a different form with a different function but does provide the same objective. When companies study the purchase decisions of customers, these objectives may not be so easy to detect since when making purchase decisions, buyers weigh these alternatives, often unconsciously. Should we go to dinner, have a drink, go to the city, rent a DVD, or get dessert? Alternative choices like these are sometimes difficult to relate to. For example, a restaurant owner would typically focus on the competitive activities of other restaurants and would not suspect that a promotion from a movie theater could potentially take away sales. Rarely do sellers think about how their customers make trade-offs across alternative industries. A price reduction or a new product launch can cause a fearful response from rivals within an industry, but the same actions in an alternative industry do not draw attention to many companies. This is a result of sellers abandoning the normal thought process of buyers where buyers automatically and subconsciously make these trade-offs.

Consider the example of a leading medical device company[6] that was the first to pioneer a wireless electrocardiogram data communication system for use in the hospital. The leader created a system that allows caregivers to easily convert existing bedside monitors to wireless technology. With this solution, caregivers and their patients can get total freedom from lead wires, enabling focus on patient care, not on wire management and false alarms. In addition, patients can move about more freely without the need to unplug these bedside monitors. In this example, the pioneering company looked beyond the traditional industry of hospital monitoring equipment and utilized Bluetooth technology. The company realized that this alternate

Benefit–Disadvantage Chart

Alternative	Main Disadvantage	Main Benefit
Your industry		
Enter name		
Alternative industry		
Enter name		

Figure 4.2 Benefit–disadvantage chart. (From Anthony Sgroi Jr.)

industry and other innovative design features could provide a new offering for patient care.

Since there are a vast number of industries to choose from, where can a company start to generate ideas from different industries? A good way to start is to figure out the most painful part about your industry and list that as a disadvantage. This disadvantage may be in the form of customer complaints, high-cost areas, items well known within the company, etc. You may choose to include more than one pain point if applicable. Once the pain point(s) is identified, you can begin to search for those industries that mitigate or eliminate the pain point. A simple chart can help accomplish this. Figure 4.2 illustrates such a chart, referred to as the benefit–disadvantage chart.

Utilization of this chart will help a company pinpoint some of the main disadvantages of its products or services to allow the search into other industries that may have a better handle on the particular disadvantage. Let us utilize the chart on the patient monitoring example to see how it can help. We begin by entering the company name and list its main disadvantage. From that, we begin to search alternate industries by looking at various technologies, products, etc., that eliminate the disadvantage. We can then fill in the rest of the table to add more description to the analysis. The completed table is shown in Figure 4.3.

From Figure 4.3, the exercise begins with the identification of the patient monitoring industry and its main disadvantage of having too many wires to plug in and working around. We then list the main advantage of our industry to form a more complete picture. The next step is to explore different technologies or products that solve this main disadvantage. In our example, we know that the hands-free devices for cell phones use Bluetooth technology. This certainly can be a viable option to explore. For Bluetooth technology, we insert the advantages for verification and any potential

Benefit–Disadvantage Chart for Chemical Cleaning

	Alternative ⟶	Main Disadvantage	Main Benefit
Your industry	Patient monitoring	Too many cumbersome wires to move and plug into	Life-saving patient monitoring in the room and at the nurses' station
Alternative industry targeting the main disadvantage of your industry	Bluetooth ear device	Battery life; may require the design of an integrated connector	No wires needed
Industry 3, etc.	Enter another if applicable	Enter another if applicable	Enter another if applicable

Figure 4.3   Benefit–disadvantage chart example. (From Anthony Sgroi Jr.)

disadvantages that may require investigation. If the benefit–disadvantage chart does not spark any new and useful ideas, another chart has been created to help companies identify alternate industries. This chart is called the substitute-alternative chart and is shown in Figure 4.4.

The substitute-alternative chart identifies those substitutes and alternatives that may be part of a customer's purchase decisions. With the identification of certain substitutes or alternatives, new ideas can be blended with your current industry. I have included a description in the input fields of the substitute-alternative chart. To bring life to this chart, I find it useful to include an example. Consider a leading padlock provider.[7] This particular

Substitute–Alternative Chart

Industry	Basic Objective	Substitute Offering Different form same function	Alternative Offerings Different form, different function, same objective
Enter your industry	State the basic objective	Enter an industry that has the same function in an alternate form	Enter an industry having the same objective but different form and function
Notes	Notes	Notes	Notes

Figure 4.4   Substitute–alternative chart. (From Anthony Sgroi Jr.)

Substitute–Alternative Chart

Industry	Basic Objective	Substitute Offering Different form same function	Alternative Offerings Different form, different function, same objective
Padlock	Security	Bank vault	Safety deposit box
Goal is to refresh the old padlock creating a new icon identifiable to the company.	We are selling security solutions; the lock mechanism is to be enhanced for added security. The lock should be used in more locations; thus, we need to develop the lock so it will not scratch adjacent surfaces.	Bank vaults have added security by utilizing a more secure mechanism. We will explore this for the new padlock.	Safety deposit boxes are at locations easy to recognize. Perhaps, our locks can be designed for quicker recognition from a distance.

Figure 4.5   Substitute–alternative chart example. (From Anthony Sgroi Jr.)

company's commonly known padlock had not been significantly redesigned for more than 50 years. Like many leaders, this company had been the lock icon for some time and was subjected to heavy imitators. It realized that it was time for a redesign to refresh its product line. The results of its strategy are represented in Figure 4.5.

This leading company created a new lock having an enhanced lock mechanism. Its new designs allowed for scratch-free use and are visible from a distance. By running through the chart using the example, one can verify how the substitute-alternative chart can bring about new ideas from alternate industries. By focusing on how the substitute and alternative industries target a basic objective, ideas can be endless, as multiple substitutes can be tested.

Looking to Alternate Strategic Groups

Our next method to explore new ideas is to look across the various strategic groups within the same industry. The search for ideas using this concept is simpler than looking at alternate industries, as your company should have a basic understanding of the various strategic groups within your industry. A strategic group refers to a group of companies within an industry that pursue a similar strategy but differentiate price from performance. In any industry, customers make trade-offs based on price and performance. For example, when purchasing a car, many would enjoy the very expensive luxury import. The import would be filled with many performance features and other various luxury-loaded features. Of course, this would come at an expensive price. Some will choose to purchase a Mercedes Benz; however, others will choose the lower-prestige, lower-performance features, and lower luxury at a lower price. In this example, some buyers may trade up to the Mercedes Benz at the higher price, and other buyers may trade down to lower performance at the lower price. Each added feature or performance enhancement usually brings a higher-value proposition and an associated jump in price. Likewise, when features are removed, this brings a lower-value proposition and lower price of ownership. These choices of product position represent different buyers who have different needs or wants, and thus define the various strategic groups within an industry.

Most companies focus on improving their competitive position within their strategic group. For example, Mercedes, Lexus, and BMW focus on their luxury strategic group and do not focus extreme energy on what the economic car strategic group is doing. Mercedes and Hyundai do not intensely compete with each other since they are not subject to the same consumer demand. Just like looking at alternate industries, new ideas can be created by looking across alternate strategic groups. The key in discovering new ideas is to understand which factors determine customers' decisions to trade up or trade down with respect to various products. The process begins with use of another chart. I call this chart the strategic group blending chart. It is illustrated in Figure 4.6 and includes a description regarding the cell inputs.

Consider the example of a leading computer-aided design (CAD) provider. Before any type of CAD system was invented, engineering drawings were drawn to scale by hand in two dimensions. Engineering drawings represented the "cookbook" of information for the fabrication of parts and assemblies. They were similar to the drawings for the plans of a house. Later, two-dimensional (2-D) computer programs were developed to facilitate the creation of 2-D drawings. Although this was able to speed things up, there still existed errors in the interpretation of the 2-D drawings when parts and assemblies were constructed. Later, the invention of 3-D CAD programs made life simpler. These sophisticated programs began to allow

Strategic Group Blending Chart

Strategic Group	Disadvantages	Benefits
Enter name of first strategic group (target for comparison)	List the disadvantages of the first strategic group	List the benefits of the first strategic group
Enter name of second strategic group	List the disadvantages of the second strategic group	List the benefits of the second strategic group that attack the disadvantages of the first strategic group
Enter description of the proposed strategic group	In this field, provide a brief description of the new business model (proposed changes to the first strategic group)	

Figure 4.6   Strategic group blending chart. (From Anthony Sgroi Jr.)

designers to create complex 3-D solid-shaped geometry where a 2-D program could never dream of performing. These software programs required the use of expensive workstations. Over time, they began to get loaded with a vast amount of bells and whistles to justify the $30,000 price tag per user. Advanced surfacing capability, advanced assembly, and advanced feature generation, to name a few, were incorporated in the software, and if other modules were desired, the price was adjusted accordingly. Thus, a company would invest heavily for each CAD user.

This leading provider recognized that it could be successful if it could combine 3-D solid modeling with the use of a desktop computer. In 1993, this leading CAD provider developed the first 3-D CAD technology that ran on the Windows platform. For the first time, 3-D CAD modeling didn't require expensive hardware to operate. The strategy of this leading CAD provider is compared to those of the alternative CAD systems using the strategic group blending chart shown in Figure 4.7.

Today, this leading CAD provider has more than two million users in 80 countries around the world and is growing.

Looking at Different Buyer Groups

Our third area to explore new ideas is to understand the influence with respect to the purchase decision. In most industries, companies focus their

Strategic Group Blending Chart: Leading CAD Provider

Strategic Group	Disadvantages	Benefits
High-cost 3-D CAD system	Very expensive; loaded with options not widely used; difficult learning curve; requires expensive equipment to run	Robust in geometry creation
Low-cost 2-D CAD system	Cannot create any forms of 3-D solid geometry	Low cost and easy to learn
A new software that combines 3-D solid modeling with the ease of use of the desktop	Develop the first 3-D CAD technology that can run on the Windows platform and doesn't require expensive hardware and software to operate	

Figure 4.7 Substitute–alternative chart for leading CAD provider. (From Anthony Sgroi Jr.)

efforts toward a specific target group. In reality, there exists a chain of potential buyers who can contribute to the purchase decision within the specific group. The first set of buyers is the actual purchasers, those who pay for the product or service. The second set is the users, those who use the product or service. The final set is the influencers, those who can influence a purchase decision. In many cases, the purchasers may differ from the users or the influencers. Take the pharmaceutical industry, for example. In years past, pharmaceutical representatives would travel to doctor's offices with the latest samples of various products. They would also include a vast amount of promotional materials, such as branded pens, paper pads, magnets, etc. These promotional materials would highly advertise the brand and the drug with the efforts of keeping that particular drug on the forefront of the physician's mind. In many cases, the pharmaceutical representatives would also take the doctors and their staff out to dinner. This effort was targeted to the influencer. If the doctor believed in the drug, he or she would recommend it to the patient, and in most cases the patient was influenced. As years passed, pharmaceutical companies began targeting the general population with heavy commercials and advertising. They understood those people who actually paid for the product should be more aware and demand these drugs during a doctor's visit. In this case, the pharmaceutical companies targeted the users.

Buyer Chain Grid

	Purchasers	*Users*	*Influencers*
Which group are your offerings focused on?			
Who makes the purchase decision?			

Figure 4.8 Buyer chain grid. (From Anthony Sgroi Jr.)

With respect to cleaning buildings, a user of cleaning equipment may choose equipment designed to clean the quickest (*user influenced*). On the other hand, a building maintenance manager may purchase cleaning equipment that is less likely to cause injury instead of the rapid cleaning version (*purchaser influenced*). Finally, the CEO may choose a piece of equipment that does the most thorough and complete job (*influencer influenced*).

In many cases, industries usually focus on a single buyer group. Challenging an industry's focus regarding the target buyer group can unlock new opportunities. Companies should dedicate focus on the group that has the most influence on the purchase decision. This can be studied by reference to the buyer chain grid, illustrated in Figure 4.8.

Utilization of this table will allow companies to better align their efforts to those most influential to the purchase decision. Vertical alignment of this grid is the key to achieve proper focus. When vertically aligned, this can indicate that a company's efforts are focused on the people making the purchase decision. For example, if the users make the purchase decision, then it is better to focus your marketing efforts on the users. Similarly, if there is a heavy influencer with respect to a product purchase, then the company's efforts should target this influencer, highlighting the benefits of the product.

The buyer chain grid is explained by use of an example. For this example, let us return back to the pharmaceutical industry and assume a time where pharmaceutical companies were targeting the doctors. After a study, the pharmaceutical companies realized that one doctor could see a patient every half hour on average. That would be approximately 14 patients per day. If a doctor worked 5 days per week, then on average a doctor could treat 70 patients per week. That would be 3,360 patients per year, assuming the doctor was off for approximately 4 weeks per year for vacations and

Buyer Chain Grid: Doctor Focus

	Purchasers	*Users*	*Influencers*
Which group are your offerings focused on?		Prescription drugs are targeted for the users, those people suffering from an illness	
Who makes the purchase decision?		↓	In this case, doctors are making the recommendation as to which drugs are being prescribed. A large factor is due to the pharmaceutical companies focusing on doctors only
		These 2 columns (Users & Influencers) are not aligned vertically	

Figure 4.9   Example buyer chain grid unaligned. (From Anthony Sgroi Jr.)

conferences. Now multiply 3,360 by the total number of doctors and you will get the number of patients seen in one year. The pharmaceutical companies realized that the U.S. population is over 300 million. That is a much larger number of people that the pharmaceutical companies could reach compared to targeting doctors. The pharmaceutical companies realized that with national advertising, a good portion of the population could be influenced with hopes that patients would request certain drugs. In addition, the pharmaceutical companies realized that if a particular drug targeted their medical condition, patients may go out of their way to go see a doctor to request the drug. Therefore, with heavy national advertising, the pharmaceutical companies could boost sales by focusing on the user. Figure 4.9 illustrates the buyer chain grid when the focus was specific to the doctors. From that, we create another buyer chain grid where the focus is better aligned

Buyer Chain Grid: User Focus

	Purchasers	Users	Influencers
Which group are your offerings focused on?		Prescription drugs are targeted for the users, those people suffering from an illness	
Who makes the purchase decision?		Pharmaceutical companies are now targeting their advertisements to the general public. The general public is those who actually need the drugs and, in most cases, influence the doctors to prescribe the wanted drug	.
		Vertical alignment is now achieved (alignment in the Users column)	

Figure 4.10 Example buyer chain grid aligned. (From Anthony Sgroi Jr.)

to a larger quantity of individuals that can influence the purchase decision (Figure 4.10).

As seen in Figure 4.9, vertical alignment is not present. The two columns are not positioned in a vertical format. Thus, the user is not making the purchase decision in most cases.

Let us now prepare a buyer chain grid where the general public is targeted. As shown in Figure 4.10, by the pharmaceutical companies targeting their heavy advertisements to the general public, they have achieved vertical alignment. This vertical alignment focuses on the largest group of influencers and unlocks a larger opportunity.

Always remember when developing products or services that the purchasers who pay for the product may differ from the actual users. You must ask yourself the question, what is the chain of buyers in your industry? Which buyer group does your industry typically focus on? If you shift the buyer group, can new value be unlocked? Use the buyer chain grid to help you find the best buyer group so you can unlock new opportunities.

Looking to Complementary Product and Service Offerings

Our fourth concept in the exploration of new ideas is to look for and create the total solution. By finding those complementary products and services that may deter or prevent the use of your product, or by modifying a product, companies can unlock new opportunities. In most cases, products and services are affected by various situations that are never considered. Many times, companies focus only on those offerings in which they typically specialize. For example, going out to dinner can be affected by the ease and cost of parking the car at the restaurant. How many times have you heard of a great restaurant and been forced to park several blocks away? This certainly can deter one from going out to dinner to a particular restaurant. Few managers worry about how difficult or costly it is for people to be fulfilled by their offerings. This condition can affect the perceived value of a company's offerings. This should *not* be ignored since it affects the demand of its business. New value is often hidden in complementary products and services. The key to unlocking new potential opportunities is to define a total solution buyers seek when they choose a product or service. Think about what happens before, during, and after your product is used. You can also verify what happens before, during, and after your product is used by running your offering through the product fulfillment map described in Chapter 3.

Consider the example of hybrid cars. Hybrid cars utilize an external battery that is charged during certain situations from the operation of the car. These batteries power specific functions of the car so that the car is not fully reliant on fuel consumption. These situations are defined by those energy absorption events so that actual fuel consumption is not required to charge the battery. As dictated by the conservation of energy (energy cannot be created or destroyed, but only change in form), the charging of the car battery can be accomplished by using the energy absorbed by braking, coasting down hills, and even a solar panel for the sunroof door. In these examples, the power to charge the car is not dependent upon engine power, which of course consumes fuel. Hybrid cars soon began to gain popularity. People enjoyed the lower fuel consumption (one-dimensional requirement).

However, as the battery approached its end of life, it could no longer hold a charge. The result was the requirement of a new battery. Surprisingly, people soon realized the high cost of battery replacement. In many cases, the cost of a new battery was in the thousands. As word began to spread regarding the cost of the battery, people realized that any money saved with respect to fuel consumption was largely offset by the cost to replace the battery. Demand for hybrids began to drop as people became more educated on the high cost of battery replacement. Hyundai recognized this simple concern by those desiring hybrid cars and offered a free lifetime replacement of batteries for its cars. This was being communicated in television advertisements during the writing of this book.

In this example, Hyundai provided a complementary product and service. Hyundai now guarantees the installment of a new battery when the battery reaches its end of life. These insights can be determined by use of a tool. Figure 4.11 illustrates this tool, called the complementary offering grid.

On the grid, locate the pain points of one or more of your offerings. Think about any pain points that may happen before, during, or after use of the product or service. Next, under the appropriate box, indicate a method to eliminate the pain point.

We will illustrate an example using this tool. Consider going to the grocery store. Does it upset you that customers buying eight items or less are rewarded with fast checkouts and you are waiting 20 minutes with an "overloaded" cart? How many times do you go to the grocery store and load up your cart? You then go to the checkout lines and there are always three people working the registers and 10 registers closed. As you wait in a long, endless line that just keeps building, you think to yourself that you just want to leave the full cart where it is and exit the supermarket. But the practical side of you kicks in and you realize that you do in fact need these items. Therefore, you are forced to wait. During your wait, you see three or four

Complementary Offering Grid

	Before	*During*	*After*
Pain point			
Pain point elimination method			

Figure 4.11 Complementary offering grid. (From Anthony Sgroi Jr.)

registers open for those purchasing eight items or less, and these people just fly through the lines. They are being rewarded for small purchases! How can this be? Nevertheless, you finally get to the register, and you now have to unload your cart. In some instances, you may be required to bag your items and then load them back in your cart. Finally, you have to bring the cart to your vehicle and load it with the groceries. When you get home, you again have to handle the groceries by unloading them from your car and finally put them away. Isn't there a huge opportunity to remove all of these tasks? Let us make use of the complementary offering grid to see if we can remove some of these pain points. The result of this exercise is shown in Figure 4.12.

Now just think how busy this supermarket would be if the plan of Figure 4.12 was implemented. Think about what happens before, during, and after your product is used

Can you identify the pain points? How can you eliminate these pain points through a complementary product or service offering? Use the complementary offering grid to unlock these pain points.

Adding or Removing Functional or Emotional Characteristics

Our fifth concept in the exploration of new ideas is to look at the emotional component of products and services. Competition not only depends on the functional aspects of your products and services, but also can depend on the emotional aspect. Over time, functionally oriented industries can become more focused on utility (i.e., function or the mechanics of the product features). Similarly, emotionally oriented industries can over time focus more on the emotional aspects of their offerings, with zero levels of utility.

Functionally oriented companies compete largely on utility, whereas emotionally oriented companies compete largely on feeling. Two common patterns occur: Emotionally oriented industries offer many extras that add price without enhancing functionality. If these companies began to strip away those extra emotional aspects of their offerings, this can result in a simpler and lower-cost business model that would welcome new customers. Similarly, functionally oriented industries can bring ordinary products to life by adding new levels of emotion that can stimulate new demand. When companies challenge the functional or emotional orientation of their industry, new opportunities can be gained.

Complementary Offering Grid: Supermarket Shopping Experience

	Before	*During*	*After*
Pain point	Have to find a parking space. In many instances, parking can be distant from the store. Have to find a shopping cart as there are times where they are scattered in the parking lot and none are available in the store.		Long lines! People have to wait a long time to pay. People have to handle their groceries multiple times. People then have to load their vehicle with the groceries. These are four touch points before the consumer gets home.
Pain point elimination method	When it comes time to receiving money from customers, this step should be as painless as possible. We must ensure that our customers can pay their hard-earned money as fast as possible, and we also want to ensure them that they do not have to handle the groceries multiple times. We will greet customers with a cart and place their parking lot location on the cart. As soon as they are done, we will bring them to a snack area or where they can sit down and relax while we process the order. Once processed, the groceries will be ready for transport to the vehicle. The store will transport the groceries and load the vehicle after the customer approves the transaction, making sure that the expectations of the purchase are correct (i.e., verification for on-sale items). After approval of the transaction, the store will load the groceries into the vehicle and drive the car to the front near the snack area, like valet parking experience. The customer can then simply drive home. As this system becomes more efficient, we may offer full valet parking so the customer can simply drive to the front of the store.		

Figure 4.12 Complementary offering grid example. (From Anthony Sgroi Jr.)

I have created a tool that can help companies compare their main competitor(s) to their company. In many cases, the functional or emotional aspects of business models are relatively consistent within an industry. If this is the case, then it becomes easier to differentiate one's company, as you can simply add utility to an emotional-offering company or add emotion to a

Functional Emotional Grid

	Functional Appeal	*Emotional Appeal*
Your company (Company 1)		
Main competitor(s)		
Action plan regarding adding emotion to a mostly functional type of business or adding function to a mostly emotional type of business		

Figure 4.13   Functional emotional grid. (From Anthony Sgroi Jr.)

functionally oriented company. The tool is called the functional emotional grid and is illustrated in Figure 4.13. Differentiation can occur if you can add function or emotion to your offerings compared to those of your main competitor(s).

We can illustrate the use of the functional emotional grid by reference to an example. We will use the classic example of Starbucks. Drinking coffee is popular throughout the world. Many consumers drink coffee as part of a daily routine. In the late 1980s, General Foods, Nestle, and Procter & Gamble dominated the U.S. coffee market. At this time, coffee was considered a commodity, marked by heavy price cutting and an ongoing battle for market share. Customers shopped for coffee based on price and attractive coupons. The industry, through its price cutting and discount coupons, taught customers to shop based on price only. The result was low profit margins and low growth. The visionaries of Starbucks saw that this market was free of all emotion, and instead of viewing coffee as a functional product, Starbucks set out to make coffee an emotional experience. Instead of preparing coffee from a can, Starbucks sold its coffee in a relaxing and unique environment. The environment became a gathering place offering relaxation, conversation, creative coffee drinks, and free Internet. It allowed for the premium price per cup of coffee. With very little advertising, Starbucks became a national brand with margins roughly five times the industry average. The comparison of Starbucks to its main competitors is illustrated in Figure 4.14. Figure 4.14 illustrates how the functional emotional grid would look utilizing the Starbucks example.

We can utilize another example where emotion can be added to a pure functional product. Consider the high-end watch industry.[8] Many people cannot afford these watches. In reality, a watch has a simple function, telling basic time, and in many cases also displaying the date. Sure, some watches

Functional Emotional Grid

	Functional Appeal	Emotional Appeal
Starbucks		Creative coffee having multiple flavors, relaxing environment with free Internet, highly unique
Main competitor(s) Donut shops, fast food restaurants, etc.	Quick ordering, good-tasting coffee, normal sit-down environment that does not act as a gathering place	
Starbucks sold its coffee in a relaxing unique environment that became a gathering place offering relaxation, conversation, and creative coffee drinks. This environment offers free Internet, which invites our customers to stay. If modeled as a gathering place, we can see repeat sales in the same day. Students can study here as well, with their friends providing even more sales potential.		

Figure 4.14 Functional emotional grid example 1. (From Anthony Sgroi Jr.)

have more bells and whistles, such as a calculator, altimeter, etc. However, these are more functional characteristics. Many high-end watchmakers created a desirable watch by adding a large emotional (i.e., status) component to the simple task of telling time.

The most popular high-end watch brands are the most recognized watches in the world and are known for their elegance and perfection with respect to their category. Rolex was the first to invent the waterproof watch case, the first to invent a date feature on the dial, the first to invent a dual-time zone (GMT) timepiece, and the first to achieve the Contrôle Officiel Suisse des Chronomètres (COSC) chronometer certification.

This brand offers a multitude of exquisite lines. Its Oyster Perpetual automatic chronograph chronometer mechanisms highlight their market position of offering both enhanced functionality and elegance of design. Available in a variety of men's and ladies' styles, as well as exotic materials such as gold, diamonds, and Tahitian mother of pearl, these watches are a symbol of status and excellence.

Let us input this example into the functional emotional grid. The result is shown in Figure 4.15. As a note, this example looks back in time when this high-end company pioneered these high-status types of watches.

Functional Emotional Grid: High-End Watch

	Functional Appeal	*Emotional Appeal*
High-end watch		Desirable materials Design and workmanship Exotic materials
Main competitor(s) All functional brands	Basic time keeping	
We will add high-end and desirable materials to our watches. Our workmanship and design will be so great, that those who purchase our watches will easily display their high status.		

Figure 4.15 Functional emotional grid example 2. (From Anthony Sgroi Jr.)

Identifying New Trends

Our sixth concept in exploring new ideas is to look for trends and align our business toward them to create new opportunities. All industries are subject to external trends that affect their businesses over time. Technologies such as advances in the use of the Internet are driving many new business models. Looking at, adapting to, and creating new trends with the right perspective can create new market opportunities. By looking at these new movements and themes of popularity, companies can actively take advantage of these trends and create new opportunities by aligning to these trends. By observing changes within the competitive environment, such as new technologies, new initiatives, regulatory changes, etc., companies can align to these changes and create new opportunities. For example, let us assume that new regulatory changes will directly affect butane cigarette lighters in terms of withstanding high temperatures. A responsive company competing in this market can either fight this change or simply be the first to adhere to it. By being the first, the company can educate the public and the retailers, boasting the new elevated levels of safety in terms of resisting high temperatures. By educating consumers and retailers, companies can boast new benefits of safety, ensuring that if the lighter is left in a car on a hot summer day, there would be no safety concerns associated with the product.

In order to minimize risk, there are three considerations that must be adhered to. The first deals with the predictability of the trend. One must ensure that it is predictable, or at least somewhat predictable, meaning that the trend makes sense and takes hold. For example, if we align our business to the technology of the Internet, it is somewhat predictable that this technology is proper to align to, as the general population utilizes the Internet. However, if a new technology is to emerge and we do not know too much about it, proper investigation would be necessary, as the new technology may not be adapted by many, making it less predictable. The second consideration deals with the trend's staying power. Is the trend irreversible? Will the trend last? Just think about the green movement. I would not suspect that after 20 years of positioning the planet for the green movement, we would begin a large pollution movement. The third consideration deals with the influence factor of the trend. Will this trend be adapted by more people over time either by choice or not by choice? When we say not by choice, this can mean some sort of enforced regulation.

We can introduce a new tool for this, as we have done for the previous five concepts for exploring new external opportunities. The new tool is named the time trend matrix and is shown in Figure 4.16.

By answering the questions in the time trend matrix, companies can study the responses and determine if a new trend can be defined. They can also use the tool to verify if their current trend is clear, will last for some time, and is influential. We can illustrate an example regarding the creation of iTunes from Apple. Apple observed the vast amount of illegal music file sharing that began in the late 1990s. Music file sharing programs such as Napster and LimeWire had created a network of illegally sharing music across the globe. By 2003 more than two billion illegal music files were being traded every

Time Trend Matrix

Trends Applicable to Your Business	Predictability Can you visualize the future activities based on this trend?	Staying Power Will this trend last?	Influence Factor Will many people be influenced by this trend?
Enter trend for analysis or discussion	Answer the above questions from the perspective of your business	Answer the above questions from the perspective of your business	Answer the above questions from the perspective of your business
Business Assessment	Briefly discuss the actions required to implement the answers to the above questions		

Figure 4.16   Time trend matrix. (From Anthony Sgroi Jr.)

month. The recording industry tried to stop these acts of copyright infringement but was unsuccessful. The availability of Internet technology made it too easy for the general public to share songs. Before iTunes, paying the price for songs (i.e., CD) was a far extreme compared to the free downloads.

The trend of music downloads also fueled the demand for MP3 players so that the forms of music could be made portable. Such devices included Apple's iPod and the Microsoft Zune, among others.

Apple studied these actions by the general public and determined that if a set of offerings were to be defined that was much more appealing than the free downloads, people would begin to purchase songs. Apple did just that; it launched the iTunes online music store in 2003. Apple offered legal, easy-to-use, and flexible à la carte song download solutions. Apple was successful in creating an experience that was more appealing than music sharing. What Apple did to entice buyers with iTunes was:

- Allowed buyers to freely browse among hundreds of thousands of songs with a free 30-second preview.
- Leapt past free downloading services by providing the highest sound quality possible, compared to the low-quality illegal songs.
- Offered an individual song for only 99 cents or an entire album for only $9.99. The ability to purchase a single song broke a key customer annoyance factor of the need to purchase an entire CD when he or she wanted only one or two songs on it.
- Provided intuitive navigating and browsing functions that allowed easy searching. The easy searching was unlike the illegal downloads, where it was difficult to find an entire album in one location.
- Created various searching categories, such as best hair bands or best love songs, staff favorites, celebrity play lists, and Billboard charts.
- Allowed users, through the iTunes music store, to burn songs onto CDs up to seven times, enough to easily satisfy music lovers, but far too few times to make professional piracy an issue.

Apple began iTunes with agreements with five major music companies. Customers have been flocking to iTunes, and recording companies and artists are also benefiting, as more than 70% of music downloads are now legal. Apple's search and browsing functions are considered the best in the business.

The results of the implementation of the time trend matrix with respect to iTunes are illustrated in Figure 4.17.

Time Trend Matrix: Apple iTunes

Trends Applicable to Your Business	Predictability Can you visualize the future activities based on this trend?	Staying Power Will this trend last?	Influence Factor Will many people be influenced by this trend?
Music download	This trend presently indicates music downloads will continue to grow; new songs/artists will provide additional activity.	As the Internet gains popularity, it is clear that this trend will last.	Most people have Internet access, and most people love music. This indicates that many people will be influenced by this trend.
Business Assessment	We will create iTunes, which will have the easiest searching capabilities, second to none. We will have the highest sound quality and offer individual songs for a very low price. This product will complement our iPod, and we will allow seven burns to a CD, so our customers can take their music with them. This high-value offering will deter illegal, low-quality music downloads.		

Figure 4.17 Time trend matrix example. (From Anthony Sgroi Jr.)

Apple iTunes is a classic example of a new trend having incredible staying power. As previously discussed, a new trend can be defined by a new technology, a new regulation, and also a new event. Refer to Appendix 1, where we explore another example using the time trend matrix.

Conclusion

No matter the method you use for idea generation, it is always important to create a rather large and applicable list. You can always rank and eliminate the weak ideas later. In later chapters, I will illustrate methods to rank and prioritize ideas. I will provide some tools that will allow for a quick analysis, so the very weak ideas can be removed rather quickly. Later, I will provide tools that allow for the assignment of different weights for ranking. This will allow executives to apply more criteria of importance to certain aspects of ideas. For example, if customer benefits are twice as important as barriers to imitation, we can adjust the ranking to reflect this.

Chapter 5

Delivering Profitable Innovation to Targeted Customers

In previous chapters we learned how to define and display the current state of a business using Lean visual tools. We learned how to identify opportunities in the marketplace by using the product fulfillment map and also by calculating opportunity scores from importance and satisfaction ratings. Finally, we learned how to generate new ideas based on internal and external industry perspectives.

In this chapter we will explore the value portion of Lean in depth in terms of delivering innovation to target customers. Before these discussions, the term *innovation* deserves a proper definition. As defined, innovation is the process of translating an idea or invention into a good or service that creates value for which customers will pay.[1] In order for an invention to be referred to as an innovation, the idea must be deliverable at an economical cost and must satisfy a specific need. As previously stated, satisfying needs begins with understanding the concept of value.

Businesses compete in the marketplace by offering value to customers. Companies' offerings, typically in the form of a product or service, must fulfill customers' needs (met or unmet) and wants in a more beneficial manner than the offerings of their competitors. Unless companies' offerings can provide better value at the same or lower cost, or provide the same or comparable value at a lower cost, customers will not have a compelling reason to purchase the offerings of companies. In many cases, beneficial offerings are those that improve people's lives. For example, they can make buyers' lives more productive, more efficient, more convenient, simpler, or even more fun in the various situations they experience in their lifestyle.

Once these offerings are identified, profitable opportunities are possible when companies create solutions to these unmet needs and wants. Unmet needs and wants are made apparent by use of the importance and satisfaction scores, in addition to working with the product fulfillment map, as described in Chapter 3. For example, high importance scores indicate high benefits, and low satisfaction scores lead to opportunities. If companies can exceed customer expectations by timely delivering unmatched value, this will result in enhanced profitability, repeat business, and free word-of-mouth advertisement.

Finally, companies must timely deliver these solutions to customers in an efficient and cost-effective manner, allowing for maximum profit. Companies generate value for themselves if they can profit from delivery of customer value. For companies, delivery of solutions has value only if it enables its operations to deliver better, more reliable, and/or cheaper products to the customer faster than competitors. Products are unsuccessful for one or more of the following reasons:

■ Companies fail to understand the customer's needs or wants.
■ The products or services do not offer a large enough increase in value.
■ The products offer too many features.
■ Quality problems exist.
■ Products are too costly compared to the alternatives on the market.
■ There is not enough emotion to spark interest.

Delivering value begins by first understanding the specific customer benefits that are important and currently unmet. Unmet offerings are those that that do not satisfy customers in their present form. These offerings do not target what customers actually need, want, and may desire in the present or future. In addition, value consists of a balance between utility and emotion. When companies learn how to incorporate both exceptional utility and emotion into their offerings, they provide important *beneficial* offerings to customers. In many cases, it is best to offer both utility and emotion, or at least communicate an emotional outcome. The concepts of utility and emotion can be difficult to grasp; therefore, the two will be discussed on an individual basis.

Utility

Utility is offering customers solutions (products or services) that perform a function. Such a function is most likely associated with problems customers are trying to solve. Utility is enhanced by offering customers solutions that perform a function faster, better, and cheaper than customers are traditionally used to. Basically, this can be performing a task in half the time to allow for more recreational time. This can also be in the form of creating a product that does the job better than any other option in the marketplace. Finally, this can be a product that completes the job with the same results, but is much cheaper. In many cases, the utility of a product or service completes a specific task or job customers deem important. In other cases, the utility of a product completes a task that typically required high skill or cost to perform in the past. If companies can make an expensive or difficult task easy and cheaper to perform by using an innovative new product, innovative service, or a combination of both, customers will seek out these solutions to their desired outcomes.

Emotion

Many products possess certain emotional appeal and can make customers feel good when experiencing the offerings of a company. Executives must understand that the emotional components of products and services have an incredible contribution to customer purchase decisions. When customers buy products or services, companies should ask themselves what emotional triggers are associated with the purchase decision. For example, how do customers feel about the purchase of a new car? In addition to utility (getting to and from destinations), cars can trigger certain feelings as a result of specific emotional benefits, such as:

- Feeling safe due to the enhanced safety benefits of the car
- Feeling important and successful due to the status the car delivers
- Feeling in control due to the performance suspension
- Feeling attractive when driving the car

Thus, with any product, there is typically some sort of emotional trigger that can be identified. This point can be highlighted by considering a pure utilitarian product such as a roof rake. A roof rake is a compact rake on a long pole that allows one to remove snow from a roof. How emotional does that seem to be? Consider this message: "We don't sell roof rakes, we sell safety. Our message has always been about offering the safest solutions to all of your house maintenance needs, and we always ensure that you can perform any task in your home without the use of a ladder. You will always be safely positioned on the ground when using our products, as your safety is important to us. Please allow us to keep your family safe." As one can verify, this message is not just about selling roof rakes, but is more focused on emotion.

Value is the appropriate mix of certain offering features. These features form various customer requirements and target important customer benefits. These requirements can be in the form of pure utilitarian features or can be more emotional focused. In most cases, beneficial offerings contain a combination of both. Value can also be defined as the appropriate mix of certain customer requirements without overshooting (waste) or undershooting (not enough value) the benefits customers seek. Therefore, from our previous discussion of customer requirements, by blending the appropriate levels of one-dimensional and attractive requirements, and by ensuring the must-have requirements are present, value is created.

Once the concept of value is understood, pricing considerations can be discussed in detail. There is an optimum sequence with respect to value, price, and cost structures that businesses must consider. First, it is essential that companies discover what customers truly value in terms of their unmet needs and wants. Once this is discovered, and the features of the product or service are determined, companies must price these offerings properly. Pricing should reflect the value being offered to customers. For example, if the offerings create a large increase in value, higher than market average prices are possible, as will be elaborated later in this chapter. Finally, once the optimum price is determined, company profit is only possible if the products or services can be delivered at a cost allowing for the desired profit. As will be highlighted later, raising the offering price to produce the desired profit is unwise and may result in lower than desired sales. To begin our discussion of the optimum sequence of value, price, and cost, we must first begin to understand the cost structure companies face.

Businesses exist to create and distribute wealth to their shareholders. Businesses generate revenue by selling products or services to customers. Businesses also consume money to keep their operations running. Money is typically spent on items containing fixed costs and variable costs. Fixed costs are usually consistent over time and have minimal variation unless management imposes a change that affects the fixed costs. Some examples of fixed costs are salaries, building and office space, equipment, utilities, insurance, and other forms of overhead. Money is also spent on variable costs. Variable costs change with respect to one or more dependent items and are typically associated with the product or service being offered. For example, variable costs with respect to a product are the cost of raw materials and the labor necessary to assemble the product. If a company produces more of a product, it will be subjected to higher variable costs of raw materials and labor. Consider the variable costs to manufacture a car. One particular plant utilizes $3,500 in materials for a particular car model and also requires $1,500 in direct labor. Therefore, it will cost this carmaker $5,000 to manufacturer a single car. Thus, the variable cost to manufacture a single car is $5,000. To manufacture 10 cars, the plant would bear the cost of $50,000 (10 × $5,000) in variable costs, and similarly, to manufacture 100 cars, the variable costs would be $500,000 (100 × $5,000).

The above car example can also be used to describe fixed costs. Let us assume that the above car manufacturer dedicates a manufacturing plant for the production of the car. The plant has a total annual fixed cost of $150,000,000, in which this includes the annual cost of the building, utilities, insurance, salaries, manufacturing and inspection equipment, depreciation expenses, building upkeep, and other miscellaneous items. These fixed costs must be absorbed by the revenue generated, as fixed costs typically remain constant over time. Thus, when performing profit analysis and pricing scenarios, we can spread the total fixed costs across the quantity of cars sold. Therefore, if 10,000 cars are sold annually, the fixed cost per car is $150,000,000/10,000 or $15,000. Adding the 15,000 fixed cost to the $5,000 variable cost yields a $20,000 total cost to produce the car. This seems costly to produce a single vehicle and should be analyzed from a different perspective. If the volume were to increase to 100,000 cars, what would this annual cost become? First, we calculate the fixed cost per vehicle of $150,000,000/100,000 to yield $1,500. Next we add the variable cost of $5,000 per car. Therefore, to produce 100,000 cars annually, the total cost is $1,500 + $5,000, yielding $6,500 per car. Therefore, the more cars that can be sold results, the lower the fixed cost per car produced.

Companies can lower their cost of delivering products by taking certain cost-cutting measures. When dealing with fixed costs, some options are moving to a smaller and less expensive location, improving operating efficiencies by removing all forms of waste in operations, allowing for reductions in salaries, installing timers on lights, outsourcing certain activities, etc.

Depending on the type of business, lowering fixed cost can be a continual process. With respect to variable costs, the best place to start is to remove costs and labor from the offerings your company delivers. For example, variable costs can be removed from products by switching to lower-cost materials, removing components by consolidating features of multiple components to a single part, using lower-cost manufacturing methods, reducing the number of touch points, i.e., removing assembly steps, etc. Again, depending on the type of business, companies have numerous options in lowering the overall cost of delivering customer value. Thus, companies must understand their *cost structure* so they can produce products and services at the lowest possible cost.

This is being emphasized for two main reasons. The first is obvious: when companies run at the lowest cost possible, they are maximizing their profits. The second reason deals with the fact that if companies do not have pricing power, they are at the mercy of market forces. This dictates that customers typically will not pay any more for an item unless the item offers them a large increase in customer value compared to competitive offerings. The consumer of today is well educated and wants a good bang for his or her buck. If the products that your company offers are similar to the current available features and benefits of products already on the market, then you will have to charge similar prices for your products. If you cannot profit at these prices, there may be a few options to consider. The first is to lower your cost structure so you can achieve profitability. This can be targeted to the product cost itself or to the cost structure of your company. The second is to create a large increase of unmatched value in your products by enhancing the benefits that your products provide that are not offered by your competitors. Sounds simple, but companies fail to differentiate themselves in terms of creating products that have unmatched value in the form of large consumer benefits.

Once companies understand the value their products provide compared to the alternatives within the marketplace, they can begin to price accordingly. Pricing has nothing to do with a company's cost structure. In many cases, companies take the cost of their product and apply a formula to that cost to arrive at their offering price. This is called cost-plus pricing. The fact is customers do not care what it cost companies to deliver products. Customers only know that there is a set price in their head as to what they are willing to pay for the value to be received. In most cases, when several alternatives are available for the same product, premium pricing is only possible for those companies that have brand power. Brand power creates an automatic higher perceived value in the mind of some customers. Why do customers pay so much for a Cadillac Escalade when it is substantially similar to a Chevy Tahoe with various upgrades and alternate branding? The answer to that question is the power of the brand. A new soda company can formulate a new cola that may taste better than Coke or Pepsi but cannot demand higher prices initially. Perhaps over time, as this new company builds brand equity and consumers begin to demand the product, premium pricing may become possible.

Brand power is associated with those companies that have high degrees of brand equity. To understand brand equity, we must first understand the marketing equation:[2]

$$\text{Brand value} = \text{Equity/Price}$$

Brand value is what your product or service is worth, as perceived by customers. Price is simply what the product or service costs. The difference between the two is equity. The real purpose of marketing (though few people, even in business, fully understand this) is to build brand equity. This is achieved by the constant support, strengthening, and increases in the perceived equity in the brands you serve.

Think of equity as the worthiness of the brand in the eyes of the customer. Of course, worthiness or value means different things to different people. Some may choose utility components, and some may choose emotional components. Some may require a combination of both. Whatever the source, worthiness is always measured by the premium that customers are willing to pay for the brand compared to its lowest-cost competitor.

Here is another way to think about brand equity. Imagine a large company purchases all of the assets of the Coca-Cola Company, all of its buildings, equipment, factories, delivery trucks, and even its famous "secret formula" for Classic Coke—every asset except for its brand name. This company can use all of the assets to begin producing, marketing, and selling its own cola drink. It would be identical to today's Coca-Cola, except for its brand name. To begin, this company creates a new name for its company. Let us assume that it chooses Cory's Cola Company. The question to ask is, would the new Cory's Cola Company be worth as much as the original Coca-Cola Company? Also, would the new Cory's Cola Company produce the same sales as the original Coca-Cola Company? The obvious answers to these questions are no. Nobody has ever heard of Cory's Cola Company. Its name stands for nothing, does not give rise to positive images, captures no memories, and stimulates no taste buds despite being identical to the original Coca-Cola Company except for the brand name. Despite owning all of the assets, the value as a business is much less. What makes the difference is brand equity. Thus, the greater the perceived equity in the product or service, the greater the brand value and the more one can demand from the associated product or service. By contrast, when marketing fails at building high levels of brand equity, there is little perceived value and customers demand lower prices.

Premium pricing is also possible if the offering benefits are protected by other forms of barriers to imitation. Such barriers are in the form of legal protection, for example, utility patents, design patents, etc. Another form of barriers to imitation is the difficulty of the technology employed. If a company's product line is extremely difficult to copy, this can provide a large barrier to imitation. When companies also have brand power, this enhances the barriers to imitation.

We can map brand power and barriers to imitation for comparison of pricing alternatives. Figure 5.1 illustrates the pricing power compared to brand power and barrier to imitation. Thus, it is clear that for maximum pricing power, companies should always concentrate on enhancing their brand reputation (brand equity) in addition to building barriers to imitation. Barriers to imitation can be created rather quickly, as we will explore in Chapter 6. However, building brand equity takes considerable time and effort. Brand equity or brand power can be intensified through position, awareness, consistency, and reminder. For example, consider the line of Audi cars. Audi has been successful in positioning its cars as a premium brand. Through the consistency in the performance and style of its cars, coupled with its messaging through advertisements, Audi has increased awareness in its brand. Audi also capitalizes on simple themes, as it was

Pricing Power

Brand Power	Barrier to Imitation	Pricing Power
High	High	High
High	Low	Med
Low	High	Med
Low	Low	Low

Figure 5.1   Pricing power. (From Anthony Sgroi Jr.)

the first to pioneer the multi-LED lights, and even portrayed these lights as the ultimate Christmas decoration in one of its advertisements. Its continual product enhancements and communications serve as a reminder that Audi cars are here to stay.

With the discussions of fixed and variable costs, pricing, and number of units sold, we can begin to discuss pricing models. This requires understanding price elasticity. Price elasticity deals with the concept of quantity of items sold with respect to offering prices. For example, if a carmaker can sell a maximum of 100,000 cars at $25,000 per car annually, then it is feasible to make the statement that if the price is lowered to $15,000, it is very likely that the carmaker will sell more than 100,000 cars. Likewise, if the price is increased to $35,000, it is very likely that the car manufacturer will sell less than 100,000 cars. Thus, for the type of business a particular company competes in, executives must understand the price elasticity relationships for their offerings. This information can be extrapolated from purchased data that can be obtained from various market research firms. In some cases, companies may have this information already on hand. Price elasticity begins by understanding the demand curve. A demand curve is a two-dimensional graph of price vs. quantity. A typical demand curve for our car example is illustrated in Figure 5.2. Along the horizontal axis is the quantity of cars sold. Along the vertical axis is the offering price for the

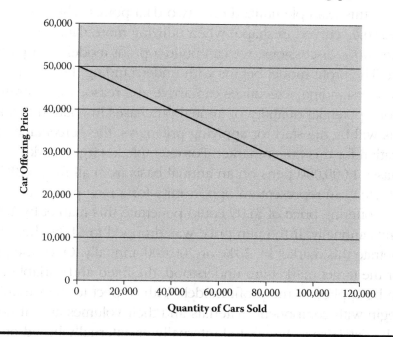

Figure 5.2   Linear price elasticity curve. (From Anthony Sgroi Jr.)

particular model of car. To begin, the firm determines the offering price that would result in zero sales. Note, this number should be the minimum offering price to reach zero sales. For example, it is easy to assign the value of $1,000,000. This would not prove useful, as the value of $900,000 would still produce zero sales. The key is to obtain that value so as the price drops by a small increment, a low volume of annual sales will be possible. In our example, the firm believes that a $50,000 offering price will result in zero sales for the chosen model. It also believes that at $45,000, it should expect some annual sales. Next, the firm determines the number of units that can be sold when the price is lowered at a targeted value. This can be based on the understanding of the consumer representing the target market. For example, a newly proposed minivan would target young families with young children in the combined salary range of $50,000 to $75,000 annually. From this statistic, the firm can obtain, through a census report, how many families fit this category. It can then purchase research data as to the amount this target market is willing to spend on a new vehicle. With that information, the firm can begin to assign price vs. quantity models. Returning to our example, the firm decides that an offering price of $25,000 would produce annual sales of approximately 100,000 cars. These data points can be graphed as shown in Figure 5.2.

From inspection of Figure 5.2, the line is linear (i.e., straight line). It should be noted that this example utilized only two data points. The line could also be nonlinear (i.e., curved in shape) when utilizing more data points.[3]

With the above discussions, we can build a profit model for a particular product. The profit model begins with understanding the target market. With this understanding, executives can arrive at a reasonable representation as to the total potential quantity of annual purchases in relation to various prices. This will be the start for applying pricing vs. the percentage of market penetration for this target market. For example, a target market (students) that purchases 1,000,000 pens on an annual basis from all firms (BIC, Paper Mate, Pilot, etc.) can represent an opportunity for a new pen. This new pen with an offering price of $1.99 could penetrate this market by 10%, or 100,000 units annually. If the pen price was dropped to $1.25, then the pen could penetrate this market by 20%, or 200,000 annually. Once the pricing models for the target market are understood, the fixed and variable costs are studied, to be applied to the profit model. With respect to the variable costs, we can begin with component materials and their volumes and, if needed, send out the database to be quoted internally or externally based on annual quantity. It is also necessary to obtain the costs of assembly, rejects, shipping, etc., in order to arrive at the most accurate variable cost per unit. Next, the fixed costs are to be determined. If you are not dedicating a complete operation to the product, then you will have to do some homework as to how much of the operation will be required to manufacture the product. You can then take a proportion of the operation to properly allocate the annual fixed cost for the product. As explained previously, the fixed cost will be spread across the number of units.

The profit model is built and tested, which allows firms to understand the profit to be gained with respect to the costs and various prices. Before we build the profit model, it is essential that we discuss various terms. The first is *revenue*. The revenue is the money received from sales and is obtained by multiplying price and quantity sold and is denoted as $Q \times P$.[4] The next term is *unit profit*, sometimes referred to as margin per unit, and this is obtained by subtracting the fixed cost per unit and the variable cost per unit from the price (unit profit = price − fixed cost per unit − variable cost per unit). *Total profit* is the product of unit profit and quantity sold (total profit = unit profit × quantity). Finally, we can define the *percentage of total profit* (total margin %) as total profit (total margin) divided by revenue multiplied by 100 (% total profit = (unit profit) divided by $(Q \times P)$ multiplied by 100). Note: The % total profit is also called the total margin %.

We can then begin to approximate various penetration percentages with respect to various offering prices to arrive at our profit model. Let us begin with another car example. This example is different than the previous auto example and represents a proposed low-cost auto. We begin by defining the target market associated with this proposed auto to arrive at the potential annual market size for this product:

Approximate number of people over 25 (strong tendency to purchase):
185 million
Total approximate number of applicable households in the United
States: 10,000,000
Average approximate purchase cycle: 10 years
Approximate annual auto purchases: 1,000,000

Next, we insert the fixed cost per car and the variable cost per car as per our analysis:

Approximate fixed cost (to be shared over all units): $300,000,000
Approximate variable cost (cost per unit): $5,000

Finally, as a team, the firm begins to determine the percentage penetration for this auto for various pricing options. We know, of course, that if the car were to be offered at a price of zero (0), the entire market (and more) would grab the car. A pure fictional situation, but the number (185,000,000) is to be captured. From the firm's analysis, it believes it could capture 30% market penetration at a $6,000 offering price for the value being offered and its brand reputation in the marketplace. The firm then runs through the various pricing scenarios. As a note, the offering price must of course be greater than the sum of the variable costs and the fixed costs to profit. These scenarios can be tabulated with the corresponding revenue and profit calculations as described previously. The results are tabulated in Figure 5.3.

Figure 5.3 can be made flexible (i.e., allow for variable user input). By the utilization of a spreadsheet tool, the gray cells are shaded to indicate items to be input by an individual. The remainder of the table is driven by calculations. This allows the firm to test a variety of situations. With the values obtained from Figure 5.3, we can also graph the various items of importance to help the company visualize the analysis more clearly. Figure 5.4 illustrates the nonlinear elasticity relationships of price with respect to quantity sold.

Likewise, we can graph total % profit (margin) with respect to price per unit. This is depicted in Figure 5.5. From the graph, the profit is at a maximum at around a $14,000 offering price and represents 10% market penetration. This certainly seems feasible, and this information is proper for the purposes of decision making. With the information obtained from Figure 5.5, managers can also utilize these data points if they must price differently for various reasons. For example, the firm realizes that its manufacturing plant cannot fabricate 100,000 units on an annual basis. Therefore, it decides to increase the price a bit to reduce demand more aligned to its production capacity of 70,000 annually. It determines that the offering price would then be increased to $16,000. Thus, from Figure 5.5, the total % profit drops very minimally and still represents a viable decision. In addition to the % profit vs. price, we can also graph total profit vs. price if one prefers working with absolute numbers instead of percentages. This is illustrated in Figure 5.6.

Finally, we can bring all of this together for the purposes of decision making. Remember, we are looking for the optimum price that we can offer to drive sales and also maximize profits. With the results of the analysis, we first must obtain the market alternatives that will compete with our car. Once we obtain these, we require understanding of the offering prices with respect to the value provided. If our car offers a large increase in customer value, then premium pricing is possible. If our brand name is

% Penetration	Price (P $)	Quantity	Q × P ($m)	Fixed Cost	Variable Cost	Unit Profit	Total Profit ($)	Total Margin %
	$0	185,000,000	$0	$2	$5,000	-$5,002	-$925,300,000,000	
30.0%	$6,000	300,000	$1,800,000,000	$1,000	$5,000	$0	$0	0.0%
20.0%	$8,000	200,000	$1,600,000,000	$1,500	$5,000	$1,500	$300,000,000	18.8%
15.0%	$10,000	150,000	$1,500,000,000	$2,000	$5,000	$3,000	$450,000,000	30.0%
13.0%	$12,000	130,000	$1,560,000,000	$2,308	$5,000	$4,692	$610,000,000	39.1%
10.0%	$14,000	100,000	$1,400,000,000	$3,000	$5,000	$6,000	$600,000,000	42.9%
7.0%	$16,000	70,000	$1,120,000,000	$4,286	$5,000	$6,714	$470,000,000	42.0%
5.0%	$18,000	50,000	$900,000,000	$6,000	$5,000	$7,000	$350,000,000	38.9%
4.0%	$20,000	40,000	$800,000,000	$7,500	$5,000	$7,500	$300,000,000	37.5%
2.0%	$22,000	20,000	$440,000,000	$15,000	$5,000	$2,000	$40,000,000	9.1%
1.0%	$24,000	10,000	$240,000,000	$30,000	$5,000	-$11,000	-$110,000,000	-45.8%

Figure 5.3 Profit calculations vs. pricing. (From Tom Giordiano, Executive MBA Program, University of New Haven, West Haven, Connecticut, 2007. Printed by permission.)

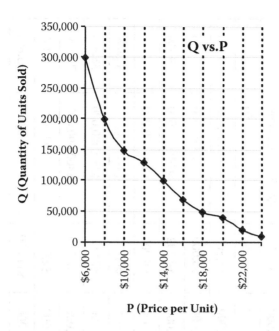

Figure 5.4   Quantity vs. price. (From Tom Giordiano, Executive MBA Program, University of New Haven, West Haven, Connecticut, 2007. Printed by permission.)

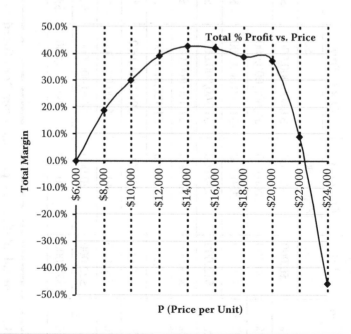

Figure 5.5   Total percent profit vs. price. (From Tom Giordiano, Executive MBA Program, University of New Haven, West Haven, Connecticut, 2007. Printed by permission.)

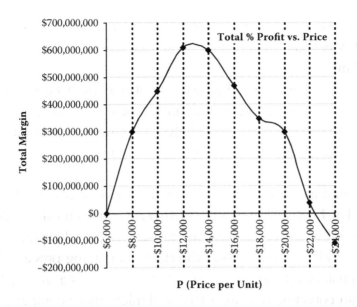

Figure 5.6 Total profit vs. price. (From Tom Giordiano, Executive MBA Program, University of New Haven, West Haven, Connecticut, 2007. Printed by permission.)

stronger, and we have a barrier to imitation, then we have even more potential for premium pricing. On the other hand, if we offer lower value, have lower brand power, and little to no barrier to imitation, we may be forced to lower the price. Next, we arrive at a price with respect to the market alternatives and compare this price to our profit model. We hope, of course, that market forces allow for the pricing that will generate the maximum revenue for the company. In this example, that pricing was $14,000 to $16,000. If we cannot achieve the maximum pricing desired, we begin to look at the other pricing options on the curves (Figures 5.5 and 5.6). If we can obtain a healthy profit margin with lower prices in line with the market forces, we can proceed to offer our new car to the market. Now if the desired profit cannot be obtained by the car as presently defined, more work will be required. The work may result in one or more of the following scenarios:

- Verification of the cost structure: If something major was overlooked, can the cost structure be reduced to obtain the desired profit?
- Cost reduction of the design: Can the design or manufacturing and procurement costs be reduced to achieve the desired levels of profitability?
- Creation of customer value: Is it possible to create a large increase in customer value to allow for a higher offering price and more demand?

- Reducing a very expensive feature(s): Is there a high-cost feature that does not contribute to customer value that can be reduced in level or totally eliminated?
- If profitability cannot be achieved, then it may be necessary to cancel the project. Remember that numbers, although not 100% accurate, can tell a rather accurate story, especially if experienced individuals are working through the cost and pricing scenarios.

The above tool is one of many options that drive decisions. Among the profit model that I defined, it is wise to also run through other calculations, such as return on investment (ROI), net present value calculations, Internal Rate of Return (IRR), etc., to help in the decision-making process. Firms should also consider opportunity costs. Perhaps there is a more profitable project that can consume resources that will allow more company profits instead of the current project in question.

We now arrive at the discussion of market size. Before any development ensues, it is essential that the target market is understood in terms of its potential size. The last thing to do is to offer a product to only realize that the product targeted a very small group (e.g., males aged 65 and above with an interest in electric trains). Although males aged 65 and above with an interest in electric trains is not a typical target for a development project, it clearly illustrates how small and constrained this market would be. The optimum situation is to target the largest customer group possible. Depending on your type of business, you may choose one type of customer group when defining your target market. In other cases, you may have the opportunity to select more than one customer group. There are a variety of classifications to group customers. First, I will define several segmentation groups individually to build the understanding:

Demographic: Grouping customers together by age, income, gender, family size, religion,race, nationality, primary language, education, health, generation, occupation, ethnicity, social class, etc.
Geographic: Grouping customers by area, such as regions of the country, world regions, country, state, city, climate, density, urban/rural locations, etc.
Psychographical: Grouping customers into cultural clusters, social sets, lifestyle, and personality type.

Behavior: Grouping customers by product usage (light, medium, heavy users), purchase behavior, brand loyalty (low, medium, high), and type of user.

Distribution: Grouping customers based on where they go to purchase your product, such as in store, online, or through the catalog.

Usage: Occasions, benefits sought, user status, usage rate, loyalty status.

The above forms some of the traditional marketing segmentations. For example, companies have targeted demographics for some time. Consider the health category. As soon as we reach the new year, dieting commercials and exercising plans are at the forefront of advertising. The companies offering such programs know that a large percentage of the population makes a so-called New Year's resolution to lose weight by dieting or exercising. New dieting programs and exercise contraptions enter the market and are pitched on television during the evening hours. After several weeks these advertisements begin to diminish, to only resurrect when summer is approaching, as people are again concerned about looking good at the beach. This is a perfect example of targeting potential customers based on the demographic of health, timing, and emotion.

In my opinion, the above segmentation groups are a good way to begin to look for the target market. It is possible to also look into larger categories. Such categories include those similarities that the above groups have in common. For example, what are the similarities that all of these groups can have in common? There are a few topics that come to mind to help in this determination. The first is needs-based segmentation. Needs-based segmentation is groups of customers that have the same basic need. Thus, we can combine multiple demographic groups in terms of these people having the same basic needs independent of race, religion, geographic location, etc. The same can be said for wants-based segmentation, where this would define a group of customers that have the same wants.

Another powerful method of segmentation is outcome-based segmentation. Outcome-based segmentation is the discovery of groups of people that have a set of underserved or overserved outcomes requiring new innovations. When we speak of these innovations, we are focusing on the desired outcomes when performing a specific task. In many cases, customers in all walks of life purchase products to help them complete various tasks. In many cases, these tasks can include various activities requiring high levels of skill to complete. Companies can devise solutions to these tasks by understanding what it takes to get these tasks done perfectly and create innovative solutions to these tasks to help the nonexpert reach the desired end result.

No matter which group of the above is to be targeted, companies must strive to link the features and benefits of their offerings to the largest number of target customers. If the offerings are dedicated to a small customer group, can the features and benefits be shifted to target a larger customer group with a common objective? Consider a company that makes low-sodium frozen foods targeting patients having heart disease. Is there a need for patients suffering heart disease to have a food that is low in sodium? Of course there is; however, does it make sense to target only these patients, or to perhaps adjust the offerings to suit such a larger market? Consider a 2010 National Health Interview Survey titled "Summary Health Statistics for U.S. Adults: 2010" from the CDC website. From this survey, Tables 1 and 2 estimate that the number of noninstitutionalized adults with diagnosed heart disease is 27.1 million. This translates to approximately 11.8% of noninstitutionalized adults with diagnosed heart disease. If we apply an awareness-trial-availability-repeat (ATAR)[5] type of projection, we can do our best to approximate a market size. The ATAR analysis is shown in Figure 5.7.

As we can see from the ATAR analysis, we begin with a possible market size of 27.1 million people, and based on a conservative analysis, we

Total possible target group	We begin with the total possible target group of patients with heart disease	27,100,000
Awareness	Percent of potential customers we could make aware of the product (e.g., advertising, effective packaging)	50%
Trial	Percent of aware customers who are willing to try product (have actual interest)	80%
Availability	Percent of distributers we can convince to carry product (grocery, mass, etc.)	50%
Repeat	Percent of those who are willing to try the product to actually purchase the product	50%
Forecasted	The total possible target group is multiplied by the corresponding percentages to obtain the forecast	2,710,000

Figure 5.7 ATAR analysis example 1. (From Tom Giordiano, Executive MBA Program, University of New Haven, West Haven, Connecticut, 2007. Printed by permission.)

can reach about 2.71 million of these people. Sounds like a vast number of people, but in the prepared food industry, the volumes should be much higher. Therefore, the question to ask is, are there any alterations that can be implemented and communicated to attract a much larger quantity of people? Perhaps an alternate product position is to target people desiring great-tasting healthy food (also applies to heart patients) that can be prepared in minutes with minimal cleanup and minimal impact to the environment. That certainly seems to appeal to a vast majority of the people capable of making a purchase decision. Therefore, assume that this particular food company endeavors to make the best-tasting and healthiest food in an innovative and low-cost package. It also performs independent lab tests to confirm that its food is in fact the healthiest compared to that of its competitors, and it also receives the seal from the American Heart Association. These attributes certainly provide the company with superior features and benefits. It can even go a step further and perform blind taste tests to tell the story of it great-tasting healthy food.

Now the question to ask is what is the potential market size for this offering? I surmise that after people graduate college and begin to work full-time, they begin to have less time to prepare their own food. Therefore, I estimate that people over 25 and under 65 years of age would be a potential target market. From the U.S. Census Bureau Quick Facts we can estimate the total possible market size:

Population, 2011 estimate: 311,591,917
Persons under 5 years, percent, 2010: 6.5%
Persons under 18 years, percent, 2010: 24.0%
Persons 65 years and over, percent, 2010: 13.0%

From these data, we can subtract persons under 5, 18, and over 65 to obtain roughly 176 million people above 18 and under 65 years of age. Next, we approximate roughly 10% of people 18 to 25 years of age to be about 31,159,191 people. Finally, this is subtracted from 176 million to obtain 144.8 million people for our potential market. We can now utilize this in our ATAR analysis. Note that I use the same percentages as the above example to better compare the target market. The ATAR analysis for our modified food product is illustrated in Figure 5.8. From the ATAR analysis in Figure 5.8, it looks like we can reach 14.5 million people (53 times more) than when we targeted patients of heart disease only.

Total possible target group	Adults ages 26–64	144,800,000
Awareness	Percent of potential customers we could make aware of the product (e.g., advertising, effective packaging)	50%
Trial	Percent of aware customers who are willing to try product (have actual interest)	80%
Availability	Percent of distributers we can convince to carry product (grocery, mass, etc.)	50%
Repeat	Percent of those who are willing to try the product to actually purchase the product	50%
Forecasted	The total possible target group is multiplied by the corresponding percentages to obtain the forecast	14,480,000

Figure 5.8 ATAR analysis example 2. (From Tom Giordiano, Executive MBA Program, University of New Haven, West Haven, Connecticut, 2007. Printed by permission.)

Of course, the example above is not intended to sell packaged food but to simply illustrate the idea that by adjusting the features and benefits, or by altering your message as to the communication of your features and benefits (product position), companies can target a large market of customers all sharing similar unmet needs or wants.

In conclusion, combining similarities to appropriate clusters of people can define a large target market compared to traditional, more focused segmentation. This should be performed only if it makes sense to the business model. For example, a company well known for its specialization of kosher food should consider the impact on its customers if it were to include other, nonkosher foods. Such a shift could drive away existing customers. This could be drastic to the firm. Thus, when looking for similarities, firms should ensure that the customer groups have the following in common:[6]

- Have a unique set of underserved or overserved outcomes that a large amount of consumers can relate to.
- Agreement of the target group on which outcomes are underserved or overserved, responding in the same manner to product and service features.

- Represent a sizable portion of the population.
- Are aligned with the core competency of the company producing the value proposition.
- Can be communicated easily through marketing and sales efforts.
- Share a common set of desired outcomes regarding the performance of a specific task.
- Have job-based segmentation as another method to identify new opportunities. Instead of a specific task to complete, job-based opportunities incorporate multiple tasks to complete a job or group of jobs that define a customer's desire end result.

Conclusion

Thus in conclusion, to deliver profitable innovations, companies must understand the concept of value. Value is generated for the company only when it can identify value propositions that will entice consumers to purchase the company's offerings. These are achieved by devising offerings targeting the important benefits that customers require. Companies must deliver these value propositions at an attractive and competitive price with respect to the value proposition or consumers will not be compelled to purchase these offerings. In order to achieve maximum profits, companies must have the lowest-cost structure possible and efficient operations. Finally, the target market should be defined as to allow for the largest market size possible, providing the company can meet the demand. Introducing one form of a barrier to imitation will create longer-term profits with a lower probability of imitation, the subject of the next chapter.

Chapter 6

Barriers to Imitation

In Chapter 5 we learned about delivering profitable innovations to targeted customers. We learned about a company's fixed and variable costs and how they play a role in the profit model. We learned more about customer value in the form of benefits companies must deliver. We learned about price elasticity and how pricing should reflect the value offered. Finally, we touched on pricing power, where companies can have greater pricing power if they possess some form of barrier to imitation.

In this chapter we will explore some of the various forms of barriers to imitation. Barriers to imitation, among other various items, are simply the leverage of a company's tangible and intangible assets. Tangible assets are in the physical form and include buildings and warehouse spaces, manufacturing equipment, product inventory, inspection equipment, packaging equipment, etc. These are the items that can be seen, touched, and related to rather easily by people. Intangible assets are those assets that cannot be physically touched. These assets are just as important for companies as their physical assets. Intangible assets are more difficult to imitate, as they are not as transparent as physical assets. These assets come in a variety of alternate forms and provide companies with a competitive edge when more are leveraged. Some examples of intangible assets are patents, trademarks, trade names, trade secrets, trade dress, and other various forms of goodwill.

Besides assets, there are other forms of barriers to imitation. Most of these typically require time to acquire and can be difficult for competitors to properly analyze, and therefore provide some level of difficulty of imitation. Some of these barriers include goodwill, such as brand power; these are the items that result in a company being worth more (if they were to be purchased by another company) than the worth of their assets. Other barriers, some attributed to goodwill, can also include customer understanding, customer relationships, supplier relationships, high-efficiency operations providing cost advantages, skill of people, business processes, firm's knowledge, understanding of technology, great vision of management team, distribution channels, customer lists, regulatory pioneering, economies of scale, and switching cost of the consumer. Can you think of any more? Now imagine how difficult it would be to research a firm's business process, customer lists, or the vision of its leaders. Thus, the more of these barriers a company builds, the more difficult it becomes for competitors to imitate.

Barriers to imitation can be split into two forms. These forms deserve separate attention so companies can understand how long it may take to acquire a certain barrier. The two forms of barriers to imitation are the long-term acquired and the short-term acquired. The long-term acquired is those barriers for which companies must be patient during the acquisition period. The acquisition of the long-term barriers is never ending, as they are always a subject for continual improvement and are the result of company efforts over time. The short-term acquired is those barriers that can be obtained rather quickly. These barriers are mostly in the form of intellectual property (IP) and can give companies advantages in the marketplace, especially if certain competitors do not understand intellectual property protection. I will first touch on the long-term acquired barriers so you can have a general understanding of these various barriers. It is beyond the scope of this book to dig deeper into these items, and countless books have already been written on them. If the reader is more interested in these topics, I suggest further study. In this book, I will focus more on the short-term intellectual property barriers, as I feel that many decisions makers do not have a good understanding of certain aspects of intellectual property. Therefore, I will focus on valuable discussions allowing for companies to utilize intellectual property as both an offensive and a defensive tool.

Below are the long-term barriers to imitation, followed by a small discussion of each.

Brand Power

Brand power is built over time and, as stated in Chapter 5, is related to position, awareness, consistency, and reminder. Position is the association with the perceived value the brand delivers in view of the customer. For example, growing up with Heinz ketchup,[1] I can relate to the value that Heinz delivers. I can remember from many years ago that Heinz positioned its company as producing the thickest ketchup. Heinz has made the public aware of its brand by television advertisements using the humor of the various gestures while waiting for the ketchup to pour out of the bottle. Heinz has always maintained this consistency in its brand and has never attempted to confuse the public by changing its recipe. Awareness is made by the iconic bottle identifying the brand, advertisements, graphics, logos, and the simple great quality that I can still recognize. By adhering to the latest trends and effectively communicating them, Heinz keeps reminding its customers about its brand sustaining the great name. For example, Heinz teaches the public on its website about the gluten-free advantages Heinz offers. Brand power is directly related to the perception of the product or service in the marketplace. A strong brand can provide a barrier to imitation and can also allow for premium pricing. Companies should always strive to be well perceived by their customers and the general public by always offering what customers expect and desire. By maintaining high levels of quality and consistency in their products or services, the public builds trust with a company and the brand becomes stronger.

Firm's Knowledge

Companies obtain a competitive advantage if they can accumulate areas of knowledge that rival their competitors. Having more knowledge of customer buying habits and unmet needs can allow companies to serve customers better than their competition. This can create a level of trust that would be difficult to break. Also, companies that have extensive understanding of certain technologies can provide themselves with a better advantage in terms of their offerings to customers. Customers do not buy for technology's sake, but if a technology allows for solving a customer's problem more effectively or allows for the easier production of a product, then leveraging a technology can provide a barrier to imitation when competitors cannot optimize the technology.

Customer Relationships

Good customer relationships can prevent your competitors from accessing these customers. When companies truly satisfy customers, distribution channels may not chance reduction of sales by allowing new comers to the game. Sometimes having that one salesman that is influential can provide a barrier to imitation. This alone will not suffice, but if your company has great products demanded by consumers, having the right sales force can only solidify the customer relationship.

Supplier Relationships

Having great supplier relationships can help companies get first-class treatment. It is best to have good relationships with a few key suppliers than to shop suppliers based on price alone. In some cases, owning a stake in the supplier can guarantee priority of work when developing new products. Suppliers can also provide design input and problem solving in terms of product quality and cost. In some cases, suppliers may be open to exclusivity agreements, meaning that they would sell the benefits of their technology to only your company for a period of time, allowing you to capitalize solely for initial market penetration.

High-Efficiency Operations

High-efficiency operations geared to providing the absolute lowest-cost advantages for companies can allow for maximum profitability. This is more valuable when competing on price-sensitive products, as having the absolute lowest-cost operations can provide profitability in commoditized markets.

Skill of People

This is simple: skilled people can make or break the performance of a company. Make sure you recruit top talent and give them the freedom to add value.

Processes

Proper product development processes, manufacturing processes, quality management systems, business processes, or any combinations of these can benefit companies. For example, applying Lean principles to product development can reduce the product development cycle, meet customer requirements better, and reduce rejects. Lean manufacturing can reduce scrap, reduce cost, and achieve lower levels of inventory.

Technology and Money

Jack Welch stated that General Electric would leverage products that require a vast amount of technology or money. This alone can prevent many competitors from entering a market.

Regulatory Pioneering

Some companies can leverage their competitors by influencing the various regulatory bodies within their industry. For example, the consumer product safety commission provides guidance on the testing and certification of children's products for compliance with the lead content limits. This was established in the Consumer Product Safety Improvement Act of 2008 (CPSIA). As stated on its website (http://www.cpsc.gov/about/cpsia/leadpolicy.pdf), the lead content law requires that the CPSIA provide that products designed or intended primarily for children 12 years of age and younger ("children's products") cannot contain more than 300 parts per million (ppm) of lead in any accessible part. We call this a 300 ppm lead content limit. This new lead content limit should not be confused with the commission's 90 ppm limit on lead in paint used on certain products such as furniture and children's toys. Let us assume that a toy manufacturer proves that the current limits mandated are unsafe for children. Let us also assume that this toy manufacturer has developed a newer and safer plastic resin having only 20 ppm of lead. By working with the Consumer Product Safety Commission (CPSC), this toy manufacturer can be instrumental in changing the regulations, thereby reducing the number of companies that can adhere to the new minimums. Of course, this is only a fictitious example, but it does explain the concept of regulatory pioneering.

Economies of Scale

The simple concept of selling more widgets means that the fixed cost is spread across more units. This allows for a lower-cost position in relation to competitors. This is why obtaining greater market share is beneficial. Companies should always strive to have the largest market share possible. Among other benefits, greater market share reaches more customers, allows for lower-cost production and raw material leveraging power, and builds awareness. Companies having products that can stand the test of time are perfect candidates for high-speed automation. By utilizing equipment to assemble and package products, companies can lower the cost of their offerings and reduce scrap due to operator error. See the example from Chapter 5.

Switching Cost of the Consumer

Positioning products where it would cost consumers too much money to switch to another brand is another type of barrier to imitation. Probably the best examples to discuss are the contracts that mobile phone companies provide. A customer walks into a mobile phone store looking for the coolest phone. He sees that the price tag is $600, but if he signs up for a two-year contract, he can get the phone for $50. Therefore, as he loves the phone so much, he signs the two-year contract. Six months later, a different mobile provider launches the next best mobile smart phone that is in high demand. The customer begins to think about what it would take to switch providers to have the ability to purchase the new phone. Upon his surprise, he learns that there would be a $550 charge to cancel the contract. Therefore, in most cases, the individual is forced to wait for his contract to end to avoid paying the charge. At that point, his mobile phone company still has a good chance of getting this customer to sign another two-year contract, providing it is offering the next best and coolest smart phone.

In addition to money providing a high switching cost for the customer, there can exist switching costs of skill and other inconveniences. For example, you learn how to operate a certain software package such as a computer-aided drafting program. It has taken you years to master this program. Therefore, after mastering one particular drafting program, the last thing you would want to do is learn another company's version. Thus, if companies can initially offer their products at great prices to get people using their products, they can begin to raise such prices as the switching cost due to the learning barrier prevents customers from switching to another brand.

Intellectual Property

Now we will discuss short-term acquired barriers, which comprise various types of intellectual property. Thus, we begin these discussions with the subject of patents.

Patents

What is a U.S. patent? To encourage the dedication of new and useful ideas to the public, first inventors are awarded a temporary monopoly for a specified time period for that disclosure. If the inventor of a concept is determined to be the first inventor of it, a patent may be granted to that inventor. A U.S. patent is a property right that allows the patent owner to exclude others from making, using, selling, offering to sell the invention throughout the United States, or importing that invention into the United States for a limited time in exchange for a full public disclosure of the invention. Also, if the invention is a process, the patent owner also has the right to exclude others from using, selling, or offering to sell the process and including products made by that process.

What does this mean? Basically it gives the patent owner the right to sue any entity for making, using, selling, offering to sell, or importing the patented invention in the United States. Note the phrase "exclude others"; this is often a misunderstood term that business executives do not grasp. Obtaining a patent on a particular device does not mean that the patent owner is free to manufacture and offer the sale of the subject matter contained in the patent. It only gives the owner the right to prevent others from making, using, offering to sell, etc., products that read on the patent claims. This will make more sense as we explore patent claims in detail later in this chapter.

In order to obtain a U.S. patent, a patent application must be filed with the U.S. Patent and Trademark Office (USPTO), where it will be examined to ensure that the subject matter presented is patentable. Patentable subject matter is those inventive concepts that have not yet already been invented by someone else or are not an obvious modification of an already existing device. In other words, if you were to try to obtain a patent for an already existing device, such as a common chair, the patent office would reject your claims for the chair, as it has already been invented by someone else in the past. The example of a chair rejection illustrates the use of a direct reference (i.e., substantially the same chair). A reference is usually a document in paper or electronic form that contains information describing a device.

This can be an earlier patent, earlier pending patent application, or even a sales brochure or article. A direct reference is a form of prior art (earlier patent, sales brochure, etc.) that is substantially the same as the device you are trying to patent. This can prevent the granting of a patent. To make matters worse, the patent office can reject a proposed invention with different references that are not the same as the proposed invention. This would be an obviousness type of rejection, and this gives the patent office the power to combine multiple references. For example, suppose an inventor studies the traditional paper clip and determines that a new type of paper clip can be invented that utilizes square ends instead of the common round ones. Now let us assume that there are no patents or any forms of public documentation that illustrate a paper clip having square ends. Let us also assume that the inventor files a patent application for this new paper clip. What would most likely happen is the patent office would reject the claims for the paper clip on the grounds that it would have been obvious to substitute square corners for round corners. Although the inventor thought of this unique design, it is not enough to warrant a patent.

What is patentable subject matter? U.S. law dictates that whoever invents or discovers any new and useful process, machine, manufacture, or composition of matter, or any new and useful improvement thereof, may obtain a patent. So to clarify, a process is a method of doing something. This can cover the process of assembling a consumer product or even the process of cleaning a gas grill, providing the process is new. A machine is self-explanatory and can include a new type of mail sorting machine or a novel machine that welds auto body panels to a chassis. An article of manufacture can fall into the class of a commercial or consumer product made available for sale, rent, or even for public use. A composition of matter can be a new formula for a cleaner or a new formula for transparent aluminum (no, this has not yet been invented). In addition, any improvements of these classes of items are also patentable. For example, Company A invents transparent aluminum that has the same strength as standard aluminum. Five years later, Company B invents a new formula for transparent aluminum that is 50% stronger. Company B can obtain a patent, providing its formula is new and is not an obvious combination of other known formulas. With this new improvement, Company B may license or sell the patent to Company A, or any entity, if desired. Company B may choose to sell transparent aluminum, providing it is not infringing on Company A's or another's patent rights. These options will make more sense when the subject of patent claims is discussed.

To help explain what patentable subject matter is, it is often helpful to explain subject matter that is *not* patentable. From the *Manual of Patent Examination Procedure* (MPEP) examples of subject matter not patentable under U.S. law are:

■ Printed matter: This would fall under copyright protection.
■ Naturally occurring article: A thing occurring in nature, which is substantially unaltered, is not a "manufacture." A shrimp with the head and digestive tract removed is an example.
■ Scientific principle: A scientific principle, absent any tangible structure, can be rejected as not within the statutory classes.

Types of Patents

We can now get into some specifics regarding patents. There are basically two types of patents. The first is a utility patent, and it protects the way an article works (the function or operation of the article). Utility patents cover a device, such as a consumer product, or a method of doing something, such as a process of packaging medicine. The second type of patent is a design patent, and it protects the way an article looks (the aesthetic shape of the article).

As stated above, in order to obtain a U.S. patent, a patent application must be filed in the USPTO. In most cases, the two most common types of patent applications are nonprovisional patent applications and design patent applications.

Nonprovisional applications are filed to obtain a utility patent (i.e., a product or a process). These applications for patents are examined and, if the claimed subject matter presented is patentable, can result in the issuance of a utility patent. The process for obtaining a utility patent takes about two to three years from the filing date of the application. Once issued, a utility patent has a term of 20 years from the filing date of the nonprovisional patent application. These types of patent applications are typically published 18 months from the filing date. The utility patent describes the device or method and ends in one or more patent claims. Patent claims are much like the property deed for your house; they describe the boundaries (limits) of the intellectual property in words. Although this book is not intended to cover all aspects regarding patents, some discussions are appropriate with respect to the parts of the patent application. Understanding these parts can help one to perform better and refined searches of patents and published patent applications, as these parts can be searched on an individual basis. Thus from the MPEP, the main parts of a patent/patent application are as follows:

- Patent number: Number assigned by the USPTO.
- Title: A brief but technically accurate description of the invention that should have less than 500 characters.
- Abstract: Allows the reader of the patent to determine quickly, from a cursory inspection, the nature of the invention.
- Inventor name: The inventor(s) named in a patent.
- Description/specification: The invention must be described in a clear and concise manner and must include the manner and process of making and using the invention in such full, clear, concise, and exact terms as to enable any person having ordinary skill in the field of the invention to make and use the invention. The specification must also include the best configuration of carrying out the invention. For example, if a device functions in a certain configuration (configuration A) but functions much better and is easier to manufacture in configuration B, where configuration B will be chosen for the commercial configuration, the patent must include the complete description of configuration B. This forces inventors to disclose the optimum configuration to the public at the time of the invention.
- Drawings: Black-and-white lined drawings that must include every aspect of the invention. The drawings must show each and every aspect of the claims for a nonprovisional patent application. Therefore, it is a good idea to ensure that drawings create a full disclosure of the invention when viewed on their own. I have found that if one can create and arrange drawings that describe the invention and operation without the use of words (like a storyboard), this ensures proper drawings. This also allows the examiner, the public, and those involved in possible future litigation to fully understand the invention as to remove any doubt that the inventor has properly possessed the invention at the time of conception.
- Claims: The specification shall conclude with one or more claims particularly pointing out and distinctly claiming the subject matter that the applicant regards as his or her invention. The claims define the property rights of the invention. Similar to a land deed, the claim or claims define the bounds of the invention and what is legally enforceable. This will be discussed in more detail.

Patent Claims

The claims of a patent are somewhat like the legal description in a deed because they describe the limits of the property. The claim or claims must particularly point out and distinctly claim the subject matter that is regarded as the invention. The claims define the scope of the protection of the patent. Claims are arranged by the structural description of the elements of the invention. For example, a chair can be claimed as having a flat base and three legs supporting the flat base. So in this case, the chair has four elements (three legs plus a base), with the further refined description that the base is supported by the three legs. So this claim will cover all chairs having a flat base and at least three legs supporting the flat base. This claim will also cover chairs having a flat base with four legs supporting the flat base. Confused? Just think, if the chair has four legs, you would reach three legs first, as you count to four. Therefore, from our previous discussion, a patent allows the patent owner to exclude others from making, using, selling, or offering to sell products covered by the invention. Therefore, assume the letters A, B, C, and D represent certain claim elements, such as the flat base and the legs. If a claim has elements A + B + C, a product having A + B + C + D would also infringe the claim since a patent excludes others from A + B + C. Let's call this patent rule 1. All executives must understand this basic concept. I'll repeat it: if a claim has elements A + B + C, a product having A + B + C + D would infringe the claim since a patent excludes others from A + B + C. Now if a product is to enter the market having elements A + B only, this would not infringe A + B + C. Thus, business executives may have some luck copying patented products by simply creating similar products having fewer elements than those contained in the patent claims. Of course, one must obtain the freedom to operate from an attorney to avoid any potential infringement issues.

To understand this with more clarity, we will run through a few examples of patent claims in reference to some drawing figures. These examples, although simple, will highlight some of the important aspects of patent claims to help in the understanding of property right violation (infringement). The first claim to discuss will reference the drawing in Figure 6.1. Before we begin, it is necessary to include some background information regarding patent claims. Patent claims are always numbered for reference. Patent claims must always introduce the elements of the claim, followed by further descriptive language. For example, the stool in Figure 6.1 has a flat base and three legs. Therefore, the patent claim will first introduce the base

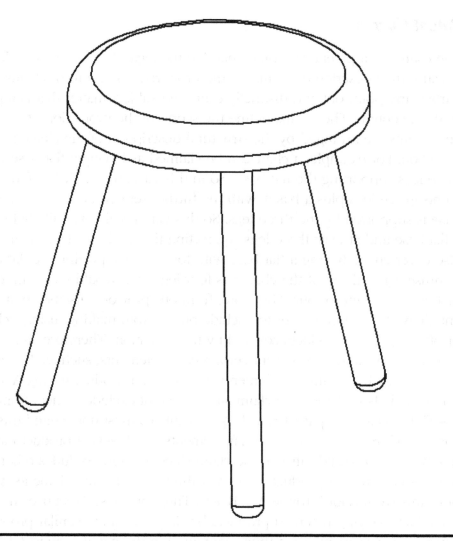

Figure 6.1 Three-legged stool. (From Anthony Sgroi Jr.)

and leg elements of the claim, and then add the descriptive language that the legs are connected to the base for supporting the base. The claim may be incomplete if the descriptive language is missing. For example, the argument can be made that simply having a flat base and three legs does not provide enough information to describe the stool in its entirety.

Below is the example of a claim directed to a three-legged stool:

Claim 1: A seating device, comprising:
a flat base, and
three legs supporting the flat base.

This claim covers any seating device containing a flat base and three legs; therefore, if another were to market a chair having a flat base and four legs connected to the flat base, this chair would infringe the stool since the chair has the flat base and at least three legs. If you recall, if a claim has elements A + B + C, a product having A + B + C + D would infringe the claim since a patent excludes others from A + B + C. Similarly, if a claim has elements A + B + C + D + E, a product having A + B + C + D + E + F would infringe the claim, since a patent excludes others from A + B + C + D + E. In the case of claim 1, A is the flat base, B is leg 1, C is leg 2, D is leg 3, and E is the connection of the legs to the base. Therefore, a chair having four legs would infringe, as A is the flat base, B is leg 1, C is leg 2, D is leg 3, E is the connection of the legs to the base, and F is leg 4.

The goal of a good patent claim is to add enough information to define the invention over the prior art, but not too much information as to restrict the invention. We can see this in more detail with reference to claim 2 describing a four-legged chair with backrest, as shown in Figure 6.2.

Claim 2: A seating device, comprising:
a flat base,
a backrest connected to the flat base, and
four legs supporting the flat base in an elevated position.

In this example, a three-legged stool would *not* infringe this claim (claim 2) since the chair claim (claim 2) excludes others having a backrest and four legs. The stool contains fewer elements than claim 2, and thus does not infringe claim 2 of Figure 6.1.

Now in this case, claim 2 only covers chairs having four legs, a flat base, and a backrest connected to the flat base. Therefore, this claim is too descriptive, and it would be more beneficial if this claim could be written in a form to cover the three-legged stool as well. We can write a new claim that covers more potential infringing products for better protection for the patent owner. First, we provide a few more definitions. Claims 1 and 2 are called independent claims. These claims do not refer back to any other claims and are descriptive when standing alone. In addition to independent claims, there are claims that do refer to other claims to provide more descriptive claim language. These claims are called dependent claims, and their main purpose is to add further restriction to the patent without adding to the independent claim, allowing for more patent coverage. Thus, we introduce claims 3 and 4.

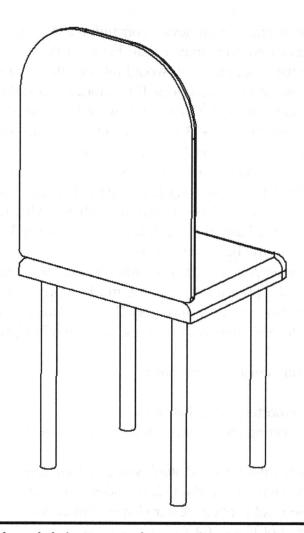

Figure 6.2   Four-legged chair. (From Anthony Sgroi Jr.)

Claim 3: A seating device, comprising:
  a flat base, and
  at least one leg connected to the flat base.

Claim 4: The seating device of claim 1 wherein the flat base further
  includes a backrest connected thereto.

Claim 3 is an independent claim that fully describes a chair having a flat
base and at least one leg. Now claim 3 will cover products having a flat base
and any number of legs. Therefore, the three-legged stool would infringe
this claim since the chair claim includes any seating device having a flat
base and at least one leg. A single-legged stool (bolted to a floor) would still

infringe claim 3. The addition of the backrest is added to claim 4 that refines claim 3, so that the main invention is still protecting the patent owner from many forms of chairs in multiple configurations.

This concludes the topic of utility patents. If you are unclear regarding utility patents, there are numerous books available. For more information regarding this topic, see *Patent It Yourself* by David Pressman.

The second type of patent that will be described is design patents. Design patents protect the aesthetic look of an article or the way something looks. The scope of a design patent is defined by the aesthetic look, as shown in the drawings. The claim for a design patent simply refers to the drawings, and the protection (aesthetic look) is covered by the drawings.

In order to obtain a U.S. design patent, an application must be filed with the USPTO. The process for obtaining a design patent takes about one year from the date of filing the application. An example of an article protected by a design patent is the look of the soda can developed by the Coca-Cola Company shown in Figure 6.3. As seen in Figure 6.3, patent coverage is limited by the drawings of the can.

The final type of patent application to be discussed is provisional patent applications. These types of patent applications are placeholders for a later-filed nonprovisional patent application. The filing fees are much lower than for nonprovisional applications. They do not require claims and are typically less expensive to prepare as well. Provisional patent applications are never examined until a nonprovisional application is filed that references the earlier filed provisional application. These types of patent applications cannot be used for design patent applications, and they expire in one year. Although they are not examined, the term *pat pending* (meaning patent pending) can be placed on products containing the subject matter in a provisional patent application. These applications can be the most inexpensive method of obtaining "patent pending" for a product idea. The requirements for a provisional patent application are the same as those for a nonprovisional patent application, except that provisional patent applications do not require a claim.

The Power of Patent Pending (a defensive tool)

As soon as any patent application is filed for a particular invention, the invention is patent pending. This allows for the term *patent pending, pat pend,* or *pat pending*, and the like, to be placed on the product or the

US00D357413S

United States Patent [19]

Kornick et al.

[11] Patent Number: **Des. 357,413**

[45] Date of Patent: ✶✶ **Apr. 18, 1995**

[54] **CONTAINER**

[75] Inventors: **Joseph M. Kornick; George Nukuto,** both of Chicago, Ill.

[73] Assignee: **The Coca-Cola Company,** Atlanta, Ga.

[✶✶] Term: **14 Years**

[21] Appl. No.: **12,248**

[22] Filed: **Aug. 26, 1993**

[52] U.S. Cl. **D9/503;** D9/518; D9/538

[58] Field of Search D9/518, 506, 500, 503, D9/504, 538, 539, 438, 537; 220/906, 669

[56] **References Cited**

U.S. PATENT DOCUMENTS

D. 224,640	8/1972	Mascia et al.
D. 226,176	1/1973	Bustedt et al.
D. 227,863	7/1973	Mascia
D. 228,229	8/1973	Mascia
D. 231,773	6/1974	Mascia
D. 248,544	7/1978	Saunders D9/503
D. 248,916	8/1978	Reynolds et al. .... D9/500 X
D. 271,281	11/1983	Abbott et al. D9/500
D. 291,659	9/1987	Powell .... D9/503 X
D. 310,025	8/1990	Foley

OTHER PUBLICATIONS

Sketch of Coca-Cola Bell Soda Fountain Glass–in use since approximately 1929.

Primary Examiner—Lucy J. Lieberman
Attorney, Agent, or Firm—Lynne R. O'Brien

[57] **CLAIM**

The ornamental design for a container, as shown and described.

DESCRIPTION

FIG. 1 is a perspective view of a container showing our new design;
FIG. 2 is a top plan view thereof;
FIG. 3 is a bottom plan view thereof;
FIG. 4 is a front elevational view thereof, the rear and side elevational views are the same; and,
FIG. 5 is a fragmentary cross-sectional view of the bottom thereof.

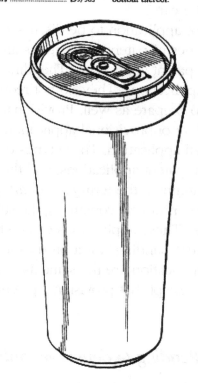

Figure 6.3   Example of a design patent. (From U.S. Patent and Trademark Office.)

packaging. This term can be powerful, as many executives do not understand the meaning of it. In many cases, some executives think that patent pending has the same meaning as the device being patented. This can create a barrier to imitation, as many executives would refrain from imitation when products or their packaging is marked patent pending. Patent pending or the like simply means that some type of patent application has been filed (i.e., provisional patent application, nonprovisional patent application, design patent application, etc.) for the specific device. It does not offer the patent owner any form of protection other than warning those that at some future time that a patent may issue on that particular device. Damages can be collected when the patent issues from the time that the patent application publishes. Therefore, if an infringing device is discovered, it may be possible to send a friendly letter to the proposed infringer. If the application is not published when a potentially infringing device is discovered, it may be best to request expedited publication of the application so the infringing clock begins to tick. If the application is a provisional patent application, a nonprovisional patent application can be filed soon after the infringing device is discovered with a request for expedited publication. Of course, always refer to an attorney when potential infringing activity is discovered, as the patent/application owner must be nonthreatening in all forms of communication when putting the potential infringer on notice. Any form of threat can invoke a lawsuit in the state of the proposed infringer, causing excessive costs to the patent/application owner. Therefore, never make the attempt to communicate with a potential infringer; leave this to an attorney. Also, if you want your attorney to be more threatening, always consider his or her legal advice regarding the language. Any threatening language can invoke a lawsuit triggered by declaratory judgment. This allows for the entity being threatened to bring a lawsuit to you in their home state. This will require you to defend yourself in the infringer's state. Like many legal disputes, whichever side has more cash to burn will always have a greater advantage.

The last subject I would like to touch on is the searching of patents. Before incurring large expenses on your idea, it is best to verify that your idea was not previously invented or discovered. Such verifications are printed publications of your idea, such as patents, patent applications, sales letters, product descriptions, etc. Some of the places to search are trade magazines and company websites. If searching for patents or published patent applications, there are a variety of places to start. The USPTO site or even Google Patent Search provides an easy to use searchable page. If searches cannot find prior invented devices, it may be worth seeking the advice of a patent attorney. If you intend to go to market with a specific product and you are fearful that you may potentially infringe a competitor, it may be necessary to get a freedom to operate from an attorney. A freedom to operate is a written opinion by an attorney that is based upon an extensive search of earlier patents and published patent applications that clears the offer to sell the device.

Trademarks

Trademarks and service marks identify the source of the goods or services to consumers. From the U.S. Patent and Trademark Office, a trademark is a word, phrase, symbol, or design, or a combination of words, phrases, symbols, or designs, that identifies and distinguishes the source of the goods of one party from those of others. Similarly, a service mark is the same as a trademark, except that it identifies and distinguishes the source of a service rather than a product. Thus, if a company develops a new product and conceives of a distinctive name, it is a good idea to trademark the name or the phrase that describes the product. The product, in addition to the distinctiveness of the name when subject to trademark protection, can provide a barrier to imitation. Over time, a good product and its trademark can build brand power. This brand power is linked to the trademark over time. Thus, a trademark can have both short-term and long-term benefits.

Trade Dress as an IP Tool

Trade dress protects the total image and visual appearance of an item that identifies the source of the item to consumers. Trade dress creates a visual impression that functions like a trademark (e.g., logo shape, color, etc.). Thus, trade dress overlaps some aspects of trademark (source identifier) and some aspects of design patents (visual appearance). Trade dress is intended to protect consumers from buying one product under the belief that it is another.

In order to qualify for protection under trade dress, the visual appearance of the item must be distinctive enough to the product line or entity it represents, where the uniqueness itself serves to distinguish the product from others. The uniqueness of the visual shape creates an association between that trade dress and a source in the mind of the consumer. For example, the Monster logo and colors of the can easily identify the energy drink. Other examples of trade dress are colors and shapes of pill bottles, the overall look of an automobile (i.e., the smart car), the distinctive round head shape of the Mobil gas pump, and the shape of a building, such as the Empire State Building.

Copyrights as an IP Tool

Copyrights cover any creative work or expression that is fixed in a medium. For example, a picture of the Golden Gate Bridge is a creative work that is fixed in a medium, namely, a photograph. A photocopy of that picture would be an infringement of the copyright. However, a different photograph of the Golden Gate Bridge, even if taken from the same location and lighting, would not be an infringement of the copyright. Companies should use copyrights as an IP tool for various company documents and artwork. Such items can include advertising and sell sheets, packaging, user's manuals, and product instructions. Most of a company's works can rely on state law copyrights. In some circumstances, namely, when that work will be licensed, it may be beneficial to register the work. For more information regarding copyrights, visit the U.S. Copyright Office at http://www.copyright.gov/.

Trade Secrets as an IP Tool

In addition to patenting an article of manufacture such as a machine, process, composition, etc., other forms of protection are available. In comparison to patents, which have a finite time of protection, trade secrets offer unlimited durations of protection. As long as the owner of the secret information ensures the attempt to keep that information a secret, the time period is unlimited in duration. The methods of secrecy can include secure areas, employment agreements, rooms allowing only authorized personnel, security guards, etc. These methods can be less expensive than patents, but require infrastructure to maintain the secrecy. Trade secrets should not be utilized for those items that can be reversed engineered. For example, if there is a trade secret for the assembly of a product sold in the public domain, anybody capable of reverse engineering the product is free to copy the product. This type of product should be patented if protection is desired. On the other hand, if there is a composition of matter difficult to reverse engineer, then it would be proper to utilize trade secrets instead of patents. If you recall, patents have a limited duration and the inventor must fully disclose the composition and the manner of making and using it. This is the reason why Coca-Cola does not patent the formulas for its soft drinks.

There are three essential requirements of a trade secret. The first is the information being kept secret must be commercially valuable. The second is the information must be novel, similar to patents; this means that the information has not already existed in the public domain. The third is there must be reasonable efforts to maintain the secrecy of the information.

Conclusion

To conclude, we have both long-term and short-term barriers to imitation. Long-term barriers include some intellectual property barriers and other forms of barriers that we can classify as goodwill for the purposes of this chapter. The long-term barriers are items that can be worked on immediately but will not be acquired for some time. Nevertheless, companies with vision must begin to position themselves to obtain some of these long-term barriers. Begin working with customers to first understand them and deliver what they want. This will help define your brand and build more awareness. Seek out the best suppliers and form partnerships with them. Boost efficiency in your operations. These are just some of the items to start on with respect to the long-term barriers. Study the above items and others, as this is a continual improvement process. Finally, become knowledgeable in the areas of intellectual property. Be the first in your firm to understand patents and how they can be use as both a defensive tool and an offensive tool. Offensive is simply marking your products as patented with the patent number or patent pending. This in some cases will deter imitators, as they may not want to drift into the waters of patented or patent pending products. Defensive is enforcing your patents. If you have a great set of offerings, you may begin to build a quality patent portfolio. When infringing devices are discovered, a friendly letter offering the license of your patent is one way to put the potential infringer on notice. This may result in the potential infringing activity being stopped.

No matter the type of barriers you may choose to use, having more will provide a higher barrier to imitation. Once executives understand these barriers, they will have the ability to judge them rather quickly. As with some barriers to imitation, they can only delay imitation for a finite time period. Competitors with resources and know-how can find a way to build their own brand power or work around certain patents. Thus, ensure that when you enter the market, your products meet customer expectations at the proper prices to properly penetrate the market. Your barriers of imitation should provide you with the time necessary to properly penetrate your market. Once penetrated, keep innovating with respect to your products or services. This will keep your customers coming back to your offerings and your competitors constantly wondering.

Chapter 7

Applications of Graphical Strategy Tools

In a previous chapter we defined the four parameters of the strategy icon. We learned how the icon displays the levels of the four parameters, creating a visual display of the competitive landscape in use with the visual strategy map (VSM). The icon displays the benefit levels, opportunity levels, cost position, and barriers to imitation. Later, detailed discussions were provided to solidify the derivation of the visual strategy map. These topics included opportunity identification, idea generation, customer value, profit models, and finally, detailed discussions of the various barriers to imitation.

In this chapter, we will expand on the previously presented visual tools introduced earlier in this book. In the discussions that follow, the reader will learn how to customize the visual strategy map according to the principles of this book. Later, alterations of the visual tools will be illustrated so that the reader can apply the principles of this book to their favorite business framework. This will be illustrated by the use of several examples: strengths, weaknesses, opportunities, and threats (SWOT) analysis, balanced scorecard approach, and disruptive innovation model. The reader is encouraged to review the derivation of the strategy icon and the visual strategy map previously presented.

The strategy icon was introduced in Chapter 1 and is reproduced in Figure 7.1. This graphic includes four quadrants providing specific information communicated by a predefined shading convention. Thus, the four quadrants and their associated shading display five dimensions of information. The grayscale shading convention is reproduced in Figure 7.2.

Figure 7.1   The strategy icon. (From Anthony Sgroi Jr.)

Strategy Icon (Grayscale Key)

Strategy Parameter	Symbol	Black Shade Indicator	Gray Shade Indicator	White Shade Indicator
Benefits	Lightbulb	High-benefit level	Medium-benefit level	Low-benefit level
Cost position	Money bag	Low-cost position	Medium-cost position	High-cost position
Opportunity	Partially filled circle	High opportunity	Medium opportunity	Low opportunity
Barriers to imitation	Padlock	High barriers to imitation	Medium barriers to imitation	Low barriers to imitation

Figure 7.2   Quadrant shading for the strategy icon (grayscale). (From Anthony Sgroi Jr.)

Modifications of the graphical tools begin with the alteration in the display of the strategy icon. For example, instead of using a gray shading scale, a color scale can be substituted. This can bring more life and ease in the display of the icon. Alternatively, a number scale can also be used to better display the levels. Using a number scale would also provide increased flexibility for comparing slight differences in levels. For example, if we chose a range of 1 through 12, we now have several additional data points to better distinguish the levels instead of the three levels as dictated by the grayscale.

Turning back to the color shading option, we can choose a convention where green indicates a high benefit level to the customer, yellow indicates a medium benefit level to the customer, and red indicates a low benefit level to the customer. For the number scale, we can define any range we prefer. Therefore, by example, we can choose a range of 1 through 12 to define our scale. From our color and range definitions, we can tabulate these levels and also include our previous grayscale convention for comparison. This is detailed in Figure 7.3.

As seen in Figure 7.3, green corresponds to black, yellow corresponds to gray, and red corresponds to white. This is a straightforward comparison. For the numbering scale, we have defined a subrange within each parameter comprising four numbers. This allows more room for comparison of certain specific parameters of the icon. For example, Company A provides certain high levels of customer benefits that would be best represented as an industry maximum. Thus, Company A receives a value of 12. Company B provides very high levels of the same benefit but not quite as high as Company A. On a comparative basis, it would not be proper to define the benefit levels of Company B as medium. Thus, a value of 10 can be used to compare Company B to Company A, allowing for a more accurate comparison.

Strategy Icon Parameters

Any Chosen Parameter	Color Scale	Grayscale (Black and White)	Alternate Numbering Scale (1 to 12) Ranked
High	Green	Black	12, 11, 10, 9
Medium	Yellow	Gray	8, 7, 6, 5
Low	Red	White	4, 3, 2, 1

Figure 7.3 Quadrants for the strategy icon (color and number scale). (From Anthony Sgroi Jr.)

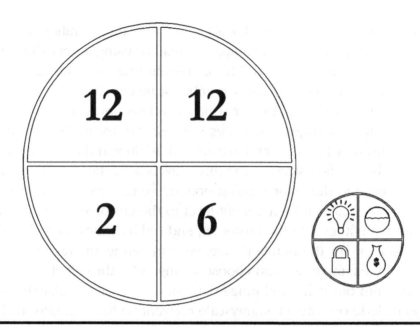

Figure 7.4 Strategy icon using number scale and icon key. (From Anthony Sgroi Jr.)

The number can be a subscript in the quadrant, or can encompass the entire quadrant using a key to define the icon's parameters. Figure 7.4 illustrates such an example of this arrangement. In this example, the icon is communicating high benefits and high levels of opportunities. The barriers to imitation are quite low and the cost position is medium. To the right in Figure 7.4 is the key indicating the parameter for each quadrant.

The reader will recall that in our previous example of the visual strategy map, we utilized a single strategy icon to describe each company. This was used in the eatery example in Chapter 1. In our next variation, we will utilize a specific strategy icon for each feature along the entire competitive landscape. This will provide specific strategic information with respect to each feature for a more detailed analysis. This example will utilize a key for the strategy icon and a grayscale shading approach. Since the key is present, each icon will lack the specific graphics and will be reduced in size for a better fit.

The visual strategy map is now described in detail by reference to Figure 7.5. In this example, we are communicating the potential future state of a company based on running through the entire strategy transformation process. The strategy transformation process will be discussed in detail in Chapter 9.

Along the horizontal axis are a series of features that form a product's offerings. In this example, we are assuming that the product consists of

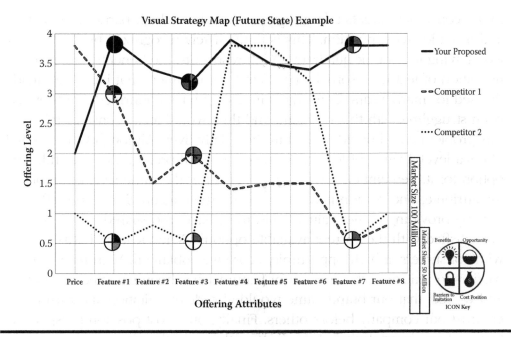

Figure 7.5   Visual strategy map example. (From Anthony Sgroi Jr.)

eight features or offering attributes. Along the vertical axis, I have created a scale that ranges from 0 to 4. The VSM contains three distinct curves. The solid line illustrates the mapping of our new proposed product strategy. In this example, we are comparing our proposed product to those of two competitors. The product of Competitor 1 is denoted by a hollow dashed line, and the product of Competitor 2 is denoted by a solid dashed line. Based on customer feedback, the dominant features of this offering are features 1, 3, and 7. Therefore, the VSM includes a strategy icon at the corresponding data point for each curve with respect to features 1, 3, and 7. With respect to feature 1, our product offers a high level of this feature, as its offering level on the vertical axis is nearly 4. Competitor 1 offers some level of this feature (about 3), as denoted on the vertical axis. On the other hand, Competitor 2 offers low levels of feature 1 (approximately 0.5). The curves as defined along the horizontal axis and vertical axis offer two dimensions of information as depicted by the 2-D map. We can make the argument that there exist three dimensions of information (price, offerings, and their associated levels). With the addition of the strategy icon, we are provided with more data that help communicate the strategy in addition to helping executives make strategic decisions. The strategy icon adds four additional components of strategic information with their associated levels. By reference to feature 1, we can verify that our proposed product offers high value-added benefits to the consumer, targets a large opportunity, has a high barrier to imitation, and has a low-cost position. This is immediately recognized by the strategy icon having four black quadrants. With respect to the benefits, our configuration of feature 1 solves a problem for consumers that has been unaddressed for many years. Consumers in testing have confirmed that they have been struggling with this problem, and they would feel a sense of relief if this problem could be addressed in their daily lives. Although Competitor 1 offers a level 3 value of feature 1, consumers still prefer a better fulfillment option for it. Remember, if two companies offer the same level of an offering attribute, one version may be easier for the consumer (or more efficient), thereby providing higher value. Consumers have also shared that they are not satisfied with the current available options. When feature 1 was tested with consumers, a high opportunity score was obtained. With respect to barriers to imitation, the concept of feature 1 has been patented recently, and we feel that our brand name would also deter imitation, as consumers trust our company before others. Finally, on a cost position perspective, feature 1 has been designed as an integral part of the product's housing, and thus does not add any significant cost for its manufacture. In conclusion, the image of an all-black strategy icon communicates the situation without the requirement of a vast number of words.

With respect to feature 1, we can state the following for Competitor 1 and its position on the VSM. As compared to our feature 1, Competitor 1 offers lower levels of value with the configuration its feature 1. In fact, our version of feature 1 better satisfies customers in two dimensions. The first dimension is simply our company offers more of feature 1 than Competitor 1, as indicated by the level of the curves on the VSM. As long as we are not adding too much of feature 1, driving the cost too high, we are in a good position. The second dimension is that our feature 1 better suits the customer's need, and thus provides more targeted value (benefits), denoted by the solid black upper left quadrant in the strategy icon.

Competitor 1 offers medium value, denoted by the gray-shaded upper left quadrant. In terms of the upper right (opportunity) quadrant, all quadrants for all strategy icons are shaded black, indicating that feature 1 provides the same opportunity for all companies in this example. However, there can be circumstances where the VSM does not have uniform opportunity quadrants regarding an opportunity. For example, let us assume that one competitor does not have the technology or know-how to offer a specific feature. This would indicate a smaller opportunity for that particular company. It is up to the user of the VSM to choose a convention that works for them.

Competitor 1 does not offer any barrier to imitation, as indicated by its low brand power, lack of intellectual property, and other lacking assets, allowing us to market this feature at will. This is communicated by the white lower left quadrant of the strategy icon.

In terms of the cost position of offering feature 1, we can see that the lower right quadrant is pure white, indicating that this feature is very costly for Competitor 1. This makes sense as to the reason why its offering price is at such a high level (nearly 4). Based on the analysis of its product, Competitor 1 seems to have overdesigned its version of feature 1. The analysis showed that the product is overdesigned and utilizes high-cost materials.

With the discussions of Competitor 1 in mind, we can briefly run through the curve and strategy icon for Competitor 2. Competitor 2 offers very low levels of feature 1, as is indicated by the 0.5 level. In addition, the little offered by Competitor 2 provides no consumer value and is denoted by the white color of the upper left quadrant of the strategy icon. In this example, and as explained with respect to Competitor 1, the opportunity levels are the same for all three companies, as shown by the black upper right quadrant. The lower left quadrant is white for Competitor 2, indicating that there is no barrier to imitation. This was confirmed through our analysis of Competitor 2. Competitor 2 does not produce any searchable intellectual property, and we could not find any leverage that Competitor 2 can impose on distributors and consumers. With respect to cost position (lower right quadrant of the strategy icon), it has been determined that the cost for Competitor 2 to deliver feature 1 is somewhat medium. Although, Competitor 2 offers little of feature 1, the way Competitor 2 delivers feature 1 does bear a cost. Our analysis illustrates that Competitor 2 bears medium levels of cost due to material selection and number of parts used. However, Competitor 2 does have lower-cost positions for the remaining features, and this indicates that its offering price can be maintained at such low levels. Similar discussions can be made for features 3 and 7.

The VSM also includes the aforementioned market size gage (MSG). In this example, the VSM illustrates the MSG in a vertical position, showing a total market size of $100 million annual sales. It is believed that the new strategy can obtain $50 million in annual sales one year after the strategy is introduced. It should be noted that additional bars can be included to communicate the market shares of the competitors. Thus, Competitors 1 and 2 would each have a bar. If this were to be included, the market size gage would include four total bars. The first bar would represent the market size, the second bar would represent the potential future share of our company, and the remaining two bars would communicate the share of the competitors.

To the right of the MSG is the icon key. This allows the reader of the strategy to verify the information located in the icon's quadrants. If using a large plot in color (or optional grayscale), each strategy icon can include all graphics in each quadrant, as this will be easier to read on such a large plot. However, if you are forced to use smaller prints in black ink, the icon key and the strategy icons shown in Figure 7.5 will suffice. The icon key includes the descriptive terms for the quadrants to keep the reader apprised of each. Finally, a legend is included illustrating the line style for the respective strategy. In this example, due to black ink, the lines are given alternate styles to differentiate each strategy. Again, if using color, solid color lines can be substituted for segmented styles. From the VSM, as we will see in a later example, a good strategy should make sense and stand apart from the rest. Standing apart is verified by producing a different curve that stands apart from the competitor's. In addition, based on the offerings and their levels of focus, a descriptive tagline should be possible that allows for easier communication of one's strategy. The ability to draft a quick tagline from the strategy ensures that the strategy has meaning. A tagline is a phrase that describes the strategy using as few words as possible.

It should be noted that the reader is free to elaborate upon the use of the VSM. For example, one could utilize multiple shades of gray that span from white to black, proving added depth to the strategy icon. The options with respect to variations are numerous. Again by example, in the visual strategy map future state (VSMFS), as shown in Figure 7.5, I have included three distinct strategy icons for each curve, producing nine total icons. It can be entirely possible to only utilize icons for a single feature, providing this is the main strategic feature. One can also define one strategy icon for each curve. Finally, a convention can be created where any feature from a competitor that is not a threat does not require any strategy icon. It is up to the reader to determine which method will best communicate the strategy.

It is the ultimate goal of this icon to provide added information to the visual strategy map. It has also been defined so that when all four quadrants of the icon are colored green (black for grayscale), the company will achieve maximum benefit from the strategy. Of course, this does not mean that some portions of the icon being yellow (gray for grayscale) or red (white for grayscale) would define a poor strategy. The company's strategy can comprise several offerings (product features, company offerings, etc.), where one offering may be the key portion of the strategy and others are supporting must-have additions to the overall strategy. The decisions as to what to include in a company's strategy are based on sound business judgment by those qualified in their respected fields of endeavor. The inclusions of various offerings will vary from one company to the next, and of course will vary across different industries.

We now understand that our icon helps to communicate various attributes with respect to the offerings for various companies. If you recall, the offerings can be the features the entire business offers. In other cases, the offerings can represent a series of products a company markets. In still other cases, the offerings can represent one of several divisions of a company. Finally, the offerings can be a single set of product features of one strategic product. Think about the Swiffer WetJet offered by the Procter & Gamble Company. This product can have two sets of strategies: one set describing the device that houses the cleaning solution and another set describing the features of the disposable pad. However, if desired, both the device and the disposable pad can be included in the strategy. It is up to the entrepreneur to determine the optimum configuration of the strategy.

We now turn our discussions to the application of alternate frameworks. The discussions to follow will focus on this approach, referencing the strategy icon. Once each respective icon is discussed, it can be used with the visual strategy map in any configuration, as previously described. Our first example will utilize the SWOT analysis.

SWOT Analysis

The SWOT analysis is a classic analysis businesses use in their planning process. The term is an acronym for:

- S = Strength: These are the strengths of the company.
- W = Weakness: These are the weaknesses of the company.
- O = Opportunity: These represent opportunities for the company.
- T = Threat: These are the threats of the company.

For a company's strategy to be aligned, it must strive to match its resource strengths to the best market opportunities and erect defenses against external threats and weaknesses. This can be better understood by discussing each SWOT parameter individually.[1]

Strength

A strength is something a firm does well or an attribute that enhances its competitiveness. This can include:

- Valuable skills, competencies, or capabilities, such as internal processes, technology, and knowledge of customer.
- Valuable physical assets (i.e., equipment/software)
- Valuable human assets, such as highly skilled and motivated people
- Valuable organizational assets (tangible and intangible)
- Having a strong core competence (What are you known for? Are you the best at what you are known for?)
- Differentiated value-added offerings
- Strong financial position
- Strong reputation (high brand equity)
- Cost advantage over rivals
- Strong advertising and promotions
- Product/service innovation capabilities
- Good supply chain management capabilities
- Superior customer service

Weakness

A weakness is something a firm cannot do well and places the firm at a disadvantage relative to rivals. These can be lacking some of the important strengths as listed above. Below is a short list of the common weaknesses companies should begin correcting:

- Unsatisfied customers
- Inferior skills or expertise
- Lack of important assets (physical, organizational, intangible assets)
- Poor understanding of markets

Opportunities

This topic was discussed in Chapter 3. Opportunities should be in alignment with a company's strengths (financial and internal capabilities) to achieve sustainable long-term growth. The opportunities should also be aligned with the competitive advantage of the company. The most important opportunity is, of course, market opportunities. This was the difference in the importance and satisfaction scores discussed in Chapter 3.

Threats

Threats are present for all companies. At any given moment, a competitor can introduce a new product that can pose a threat. In addition, a substitute product from a company never considered can threaten any business. Companies must ensure that their offerings are sustainable. Some of the potential threats are:

- Emergence of cheaper/better technologies
- Introduction of better products by rivals
- Entry of lower-cost foreign competitors
- Rise in interest rates
- Unfavorable demographic shifts
- Adverse shifts in foreign exchange rates

Companies that prefer using a SWOT analysis can illustrate the results using the icon approach. This is illustrated in Figure 7.6. For the example in this book, the icon in Figure 7.6 will be called the SWOT icon. For purposes

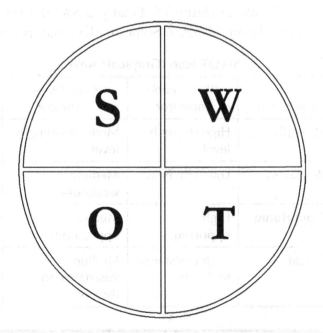

Figure 7.6   SWOT icon. (From Anthony Sgroi Jr.)

SWOT Icon Parameter Convention

Any Chosen Parameter SWOT	Color Scale	Grayscale (Black and White)	Alternate Numbering Scale (1 to 12) Ranked
High	Green	Black	12, 11, 10, 9
Medium	Yellow	Gray	8, 7, 6, 5
Low	Red	White	4, 3, 2, 1

Figure 7.7 SWOT icon shading and number scale. (From Anthony Sgroi Jr.)

of simplicity, the SWOT icon will have a letter in each quadrant. Each letter will represent each parameter of the SWOT analysis. If desired, a series of graphics can be used. Similar to the strategy icon, the SWOT icon can utilize a shading or numeric scale. These options are illustrated in Figure 7.7. Thus by example, we can represent the results of the SWOT analysis in grayscale via Figure 7.8.

With the above convention, the SWOT icon can be used in the visual strategy map in any desired method discussed. For example, SWOT icons can be used to describe the general offerings of the company and its competitors. Alternatively, the reader is free to use a SWOT icon for each feature of the offerings, as shown in Figure 7.5. Finally, a SWOT icon can be used to indicate certain key offering features. Some readers may not prefer the use

SWOT Icon (Grayscale Key)

Strategy Parameter	Parameter	Black Shade Indicator	Gray Shade Indicator	White Shade Indicator
S	Strength	High strength level	Medium strength level	Low strength level
W	Weakness	Low weakness	Medium weakness	High weakness
O	Opportunity	High opportunity	Medium opportunity	Low opportunity
T	Threat	High Resistance to threats	Medium Resistance to threats	Low resistance to threats

Figure 7.8 Quadrant shading for the SWOT icon (grayscale). (From Anthony Sgroi Jr.)

of the SWOT analysis. Therefore, another example is provided that may be more in line with the reader's preferences.

Balanced Scorecard Approach

The balanced scorecard[2] is a planning and management system that is used to align business activities to the vision and strategy of the organization. It also guides organizations to invest in certain key strategic measures. It was originated as a performance measurement framework that added strategic nonfinancial performance measures to traditional financial metrics to give executives a more balanced view of organizational performance.

It was conceived to provide emphasis on other various measures instead of pure financial measures. Although it retains financial measures, it also includes certain key measures necessary for long-term success. In addition to financial measures, the balance scorecard (BSC) also includes customers, internal business processes, and learning and growth measures. The reader can verify the strong similarities of Lean. The creators of this framework discovered that measuring financial performance solely is not adequate for guiding and evaluating the journey that companies must make to create future value through investment in customers, suppliers, employees, processes, technology, and innovation. This framework is illustrated in Figure 7.9. Each measure is discussed below.

Learning and Growth Perspective

Similar to a Lean principle, this perspective includes employee training and corporate cultural attitudes related to both individual and corporate learning. As companies experience rapid technological change, it is becoming necessary for them to be in a continuous learning mode. Learning results in the creation of reusable knowledge. This knowledge must be readily available to drive rapid product development and minimize waste.

Just as taught by Lean, the creators of BSC understood that learning is more than training. They realized that organization learning includes mentors within the organization, as well as the ease of communication among workers that allows them to readily get help on a problem when it is needed.

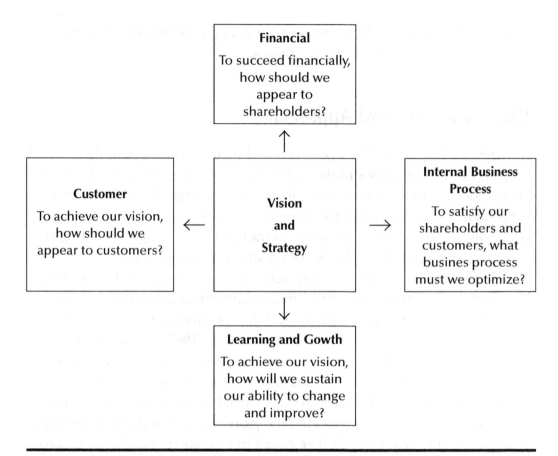

Figure 7.9 Balanced scorecard framework. (Adapted from Robert S. Kaplan and David P. Norton, "Using the Balanced Scorecard as a Strategic Management System," *Harvard Business Review,* January–February 1996, 76.)

Business Process Perspective

This perspective refers to internal business processes. Such processes that can be measured are customer satisfaction levels, number of new products launched per year, and on-time delivery. Companies must improve their processes of deriving customer value and driving out waste, another principle of Lean. Creating metrics for these activities can help drive success.

Customer Perspective

As discussed in an earlier chapter, customers must be at least satisfied to repurchase. Higher levels of customer satisfaction will result in delighted customers. Companies must ensure that they are timely delivering value to customers with minimal waste in terms of meeting their needs and wants.

Financial Perspective

The creators of the BSC do not disregard the traditional need for financial success and data. Of course, businesses operate to create and distribute wealth to their shareholders. This is indicative of the financial success of a business.

So what does this mean? Basically, the BSC places emphasis on all four measures. This simple message is that divesting in certain key functions to drive better short-term financial results is wrong for the long-term success of the company. Divesting can cause inefficient processes, lack of customer understanding, and low knowledge capture. If processes are inefficient, customer research is halted, and company learning is stalled, this may pose a future threat for the company. Sure, divesture of these activities will show short-term cost savings, but the company can be put in a position where it cannot recover from a new threat later on. For more on this topic, see *The Balanced Scorecard: Translating Strategy into Action* by Robert S. Kaplan and David P. Norton (Harvard Business School Press, 1996).

Similar to the SWOT framework, the framework for the BSC can also be used as an icon in the visual strategy map. One such example is illustrated in Figure 7.10 and is dubbed the BSC icon.

In this example, the letters indicate the BSC measure and can have a similar convention as per the previous examples. The BSC icon can also be used to evaluate the effectiveness of the company's strategy in relation to its

Figure 7.10   BSC icon. (From Anthony Sgroi Jr.)

BSC Icon (Grayscale Key)

Strategy Parameter	Parameter	Black Shade Indicator	Gray Shade Indicator	White Shade Indicator
F	Financial perspective	High focus on financial measures	Medium focus on financial measures	Low focus on financial measures
C	Customer perspective	High focus on customer satisfaction	Medium focus on customer satisfaction	Low focus on customer satisfaction
P	Business process	High emphasis on efficiency	Medium emphasis on efficiency	Low emphasis on efficiency
L	Organizational learning	High organization learning	Medium organization learning	Low organization learning

Figure 7.11 Quadrant shading for the BSC icon (grayscale). (From Anthony Sgroi Jr.)

competitors. The convention for the BSC icon is illustrated in Figure 7.11 for the grayscale option. As a note, the previously described color and numeric convention can be substituted for the grayscale option.

Of course, it is desirable to have a totally black BSC icon as defined by the convention in Figure 7.11.

Disruptive Innovation

The traditional approach to company growth comes in the form of sustaining innovations. Sustaining innovations are product improvements fulfilling more of the sophisticated needs of the market. These improvements represent higher-performance attributes most valued by the industry's most demanding customers. This can begin to promote risks for certain companies. At some point, the introduction of constant sustaining innovations can eventually overshoot customers' needs over time. This is the result of companies' offerings being too expensive or too complicated for most of the customers within their market to handle. This is a direct result of companies innovating faster than the changing needs of their customers.

Companies that focus on sustaining innovations charge higher prices for their innovations. Greater profits are enjoyed, as companies target the more demanding segments of their markets.

This can promote a problem for the innovator. At some point, when the market is saturated with high-end sophisticated, complicated, and expensive products, companies run the risk of being disrupted. Such disruption comes in the form of disruptive innovation. This term was introduced by Clayton Christensen and is thoroughly discussed in his books titled *The Innovator's Dilemma* and *The Innovator's Solution*. Disruptive innovation allows for cheaper and simpler products to enter the market, targeting lower-demanding customers. Since these products target the lower-tier customer base, companies engaged in sustaining innovations often ignore these offerings until they take hold in the market. Unfortunately, at some point it may be too late for sustaining innovating companies to recover from the rapid loss of their customers, now seeking simpler and lower-cost products.

Christensen identified two types of disruptive innovation. The first is called new market disruptions and the second is coined low-end disruptions. Each is discussed in detail below.[3]

New Market Disruptions

New market disruptions target lower-performance needs of customers. However, at the same time, they target simplicity and improved convenience. Thus, these innovations strive to give customers simplicity and convenience. These disruptions target nonconsumption-type customers. These are the customers that do not buy specific products, as they typically lack the money for purchase or skill to use such products. Therefore, these disruptions target new customers where the incumbent leaders feel little threat in the beginning stages of disruption. Canon's desktop copier is an example of this. When first introduced to the market, the makers of large corporate high-speed photocopy equipment were not threatened, as the quality and speed were inferior. However, in time, as quality improved, the new convenience became good enough to pull customers into a new value network. This type of disruption does not invade the mainstream market. Instead, it slowly pulls customers out of the mainstream value network into the new one.

There are two questions to ask to determine if an ideal has a new market disruptive potential. For new market disruption, at least one of these questions must be answered with a yes for confirmation. Two would build a stronger case:

1. Is there a large population of people who historically have not had the money, equipment, or skill to do this thing for themselves, and as a result have gone without it altogether or have needed to pay someone with more expertise to do it for them?
2. To use the product or service, do customers need to go to an inconvenient, centralized location?

Low-End Disruptions

Low-end disruptions target overserved customers in the low end of the mainstream market. These disruptions have performance attributes that are good enough for the low-end users of the mainstream market. The two questions that must be confirmed for this type of disruption follow:

1. Are there customers in the low end of the market who would be happy to purchase a product with less (but good enough) performance if they could get it at a lower price?
2. Can we create a business model that enables us to earn attractive profits at the discount prices required to win the business of these overserved customers at the low end?

The questions above are called the litmus test. Once an innovation passes the new market or low-end test, there is still a final (third) question that must be confirmed for the litmus test:

3. Is the innovation disruptive to all of the significant incumbent firms in the industry? If it appears to be sustaining (sustaining innovation and not disruptive) to one or more significant players in the industry, then the odds will be stacked in that firm's favor, and the entrant is unlikely to win.

We can utilize the disruptive innovation model in the visual strategy map as in our previous examples. This can serve as a model for the disruptor. As the disruptor, we would want to create an icon that can indicate the likelihood of disruption as per the discussion above. By use of the litmus test, we can define three distinct parameters. The first is the sustaining innovation model denoted by the letters SI, the second is the new market disruption model denoted by NM, and the third is the low-end disruption model denoted by LE. In this case, we can call the icon the disruption icon. This icon is displayed in a nonshading format in Figure 7.12. We can also define

Figure 7.12 Disruption icon. (From Anthony Sgroi Jr.)

a shading convention for this model, where a shading convention of the icon is shown in Figure 7.13.

With use of the convention as depicted in Figure 7.13, we can now discuss the possibilities for disruption using an example. First, the disruptor would target a series of companies engaged in pure sustaining innovation work. This would be displayed by a single shaded SI parameter. The shading (black, gray, white) would depend on the intensity of their sustaining innovation development. They would of course have zero levels of new market disruption (NM) or low-end disruption (LE).

Next, the disruptor would be required to figure out which parameter it would target for disruption. If it is an ultra-low-cost manufacturer, it may consider low-end disruption. On the other hand, if it can create a very convenient and easy-to-use product where high skill was required in the past, it may consider new market disruption. In either case, the disruptor must pass each phase of the litmus test. In this example, our disruptor will target over-served customers using low-end disruption.

Finally, we need to consider the market potential. We can use a convention similar to the market size gage, as previously presented. In this example, the total market would comprise the mainstream market. We would then

Disruption Icon (Grayscale Key)

Icon Parameter	Parameter	Black Shade Indicator	Gray Shade Indicator	White Shade Indicator
SI	Sustaining innovation	High levels of sustaining innovations	Medium levels of sustaining innovations	Low to no levels of sustaining innovations
NM	New market disruption	High probability of disruption	Medium probability of disruption	Low probability of disruption
LE	Low-end disruption	High probability of disruption	Medium probability of disruption	Low probability of disruption

Figure 7.13 Quadrant shading for the disruption icon (grayscale). (From Anthony Sgroi Jr.)

have three possible market shares to consider. The first is the share that represents those customers willing to pay for added performance. These are the customers of sustaining innovation. The second is the customer base comprising the overserved customers. These are the targets of low-end disruption. The third is the nonconsumers. These are the customers seeking convenience and solutions to skill barriers. These are the targets of new market disruption. Once this market size and the relative shares are determined, we must ensure that the disruptor of choice aligns to a market of sufficient size or share. This would identify if there is a good opportunity for disruption.

Therefore, in our example we have successfully passed the litmus test for low-end disruption. There is one significant incumbent heavily engaged in sustaining innovation. The market size is represented by $100 million in annual sales. It has created such high levels of features and complexity that the market is substantially overserved. Estimates are that 60% of this customer base are overserved, 25% are willing to pay for sustaining innovation, and the remaining 15% desire added convenience. The current incumbent has a product of eight features as a result of years of sustaining innovations. Therefore, an introduction of a low-end disruptive product should go unnoticed by the disruptor. In this example, the disruptor can successfully target the overserved customers using only four features. By having only four features, the disruptor can sell its product at half the price of the incumbent.

Figure 7.14 Disruption icon (incumbent). (From Anthony Sgroi Jr.)

From the above discussion, the disruption icons for the incumbent and the disruptor are shown in Figures 7.14 and 7.15, respectively.

Finally, we can create a visual strategy map using the disruption model. The final result based on the above discussion is shown in Figure 7.16. From this figure, we can verify that the proper model for illustrating the potential for a low-end disruption is present. First, the incumbent offers eight features at a high price. The market size is only 25% of the share of the total market. This represents the number of people most likely to be willing to pay for high levels of features and performance. The modified market size gage includes the letter identifiers for aligning the market share to the type of innovation. This helps us to immediately identify the disruptor's potential market share for low-end disruption (LE). From the map, we can verify that this size is approximately 60%. This represents a viable market size. The low-end disruption is also evident on the reduced number of features (4 from 8), and they are also offered in lower levels. This is represented by the two curves. Finally, the disruption icons also align each company's innovation strategy. The incumbent is focused on purely sustaining innovation activity. The disruptor is focused on low-end disruption. It would seem likely that the incumbent will ignore the initial activities of the disruptor.

Figure 7.15 Disruption icon (disruptor). (From Anthony Sgroi Jr.)

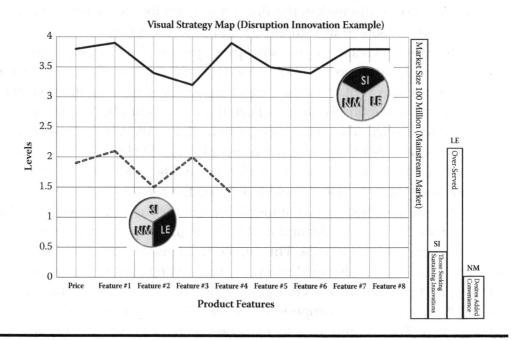

Figure 7.16 Visual strategy map (disruption innovation example). (From Anthony Sgroi Jr.)

Conclusion

This chapter taught variations of visual management. We began by modifying the use of the strategy icon. Later, we used the principles of visual management to incorporate some of the popular frameworks used in business. The reader is encouraged to modify these visual tools to his or her liking using the logic presented in this chapter, if desired. In the chapters to follow, we will revert back to the initial strategy icon introduced earlier. The parameters (benefits, cost position, opportunity, barriers to imitation) will aid in the analysis of ranking offerings.

Chapter 8

Ranking Offerings

In the last chapter we looked at various alterations of visual management. We learned how to alter the strategy icon to provide more depth of information. Later, we learned about a few popular business theories and applied the concept of visual management to them. In this chapter, we will maximize value and minimize waste by introducing techniques to rank and prioritize offerings generated from our idea generation process.

After going through the techniques in the chapter for idea generation, you should have a variety of possible idea choices. The question is, how can you quickly decipher through a large list of ideas or at least arrange them so they make sense? This will be the main focus for this chapter. Eliminating weak alternatives early that do not have the potential to create value for the customer and company is a function of Lean. Once this chapter is fully understood, you will have the background necessary to bring your strategy together in visual form. In Chapter 10, I will again run through the ranking process using a detailed example. This will facilitate learning and will complement the strategy transformation process that will also be illustrated in detail.

The strategy icon will serve us in this chapter. I will utilize each quadrant of the icon on an individual basis. From each quadrant, each symbol will represent one of four offering dimensions. As previously discussed, the first is value, value in the form of customer *benefits*; the second is *opportunity*; the third is *barriers to imitation*; and the fourth is the *cost position* of the offering. These offering dimensions will first be considered individually, and then combined with user-defined weights for overall ranking. The intriguing part is that this ranking system will allow the reader to customize the parameters of the rank (similar to a weighted average) as to what he or she deems important to his or her type of business. For example, one manager may determine that customer value (benefits) and offering costs are the most important items for ranking, whereas opportunity and barriers to imitation are of low priority. Thus, in the ranking matrix that will follow, the user can reflect this decision and obtain rankings that apply less weight to those dimensions (opportunity and barriers to imitation) that are not key.

Ranking of ideas first begins with the understanding of customer value. Of course, this is why any entity is in business. It should be focusing on those offerings that a vast number of customers require that add value to the purchaser. This chapter will run through techniques that will allow companies to evaluate potential offerings in terms of the value they deliver from a customer perspective. These evaluations will provide you with much needed information so you can begin to understand which offerings to include and which to discard. This dimension should be quantified with the customer in mind. Business executives should refrain from assuming they totally understand the customer. Therefore, it is best to have customers evaluate potential offerings. This helps business executives face the facts and eliminates the waste of wishful thinking.

In terms of opportunity, you should have captured some of this information from Chapter 3. With this in mind, you may have the data necessary to estimate the opportunity levels of some new potential offerings. If you have derived a completely new type of offering, you can always ask customers new questions about the importance and satisfaction for new opportunity calculations.

The last two dimensions (barriers to imitation and costs) can be done internally, if desired. Of course, these activities can be worked on with the assistance of external resources, such as the expertise of an intellectual property attorney when looking at various components of barriers to imitation. These dimensions should always play a role in the decision-making process. Executives should consider which dimensions are the most important. Since we are dealing with more than one dimension, there is a relative importance (e.g., one being equally important or twice as important as another). For example, is the cost position of the offerings just as important as customer value? If the answer is yes, then the dimension of cost position will have the same weight as customer value for the purposes of decision making. Not clear? Stated another way, assume that customer value is the most important aspect in the ranking for a specific offering. We can then assign any arbitrary number to that aspect, such as the value of 10. If cost position is just as important as customer value, we can also assign a value of

10 to reflect the equal level of importance. To continue, let us say that in this example the opportunity is 80% as important as customer value and the cost position; this would result in opportunity receiving a value of 8. Finally, if we conclude that barrier to imitation is half as important as customer value, then it would be assigned a value of 5. With this convention in mind, we can put these criteria in a matrix and begin to evaluate the overall rankings of each potential offering. With these values in place, we can obtain a score that is compared to a predefined "perfect score" and obtain final results in the form of a single number or percentage with respect to that perfect score. This would allow us to sort the final number for prioritization. As a final note, the reader is free to add other dimensions to the ranking process. For example, market size can be added, if desired. On the other hand, the reader is free to discard one or more offering dimensions.

To begin, we first define a series of offerings that make sense for our business. Remember that new offerings must add value to customers. We can judge the opportunities of new offerings by reference to earlier opportunity score calculations, as discussed in Chapter 3. From the most abundant set of opportunities, we can define a series of offerings. To generate ideas for new offerings, refer to Chapter 4 that illustrates idea generation techniques. These offerings can form the basis of your business model, such as the main attributes of your favorite airline. On the other hand, they can be the features of a single strategic new product. This will depend heavily on the type of business, the competitive situation, the choices you intend to make, the level of competition, etc. Regardless of your situation, you first must define a series of offering features that can be easily communicated to current and potential customers. Once this is achieved, and depending on how well you know the needs and wants of the targeted customers, you may already have a good understanding of the value these specific features will provide. It is always a good idea to run the new ideas through the product fulfillment map as a first filter. This can help you find early shortcomings if they are present with respect to new ideas. If you do not have a good understanding of the type of value certain offerings bring, you will have to ask targeted customers in such a way that you can determine what value the offerings bring, their type of value (i.e., must-have requirements, one-dimensional requirements, and attractive requirements), and how important they are.

I will run through one of a few techniques for obtaining customer feedback. If you recall from Chapter 3, we introduced three customer requirements followed by a discussion of each. These requirements[1] are shown

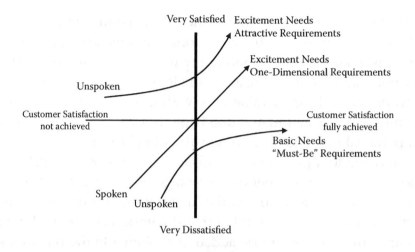

Figure 8.1   The three customer requirements. (Adapted from Elmar Sauerwein, Franz Bailom, Kurt Matzler, and Hans H. Hinterhuber, "The Kano Model: How to Delight Your Customers," Preprints Volume I of the IX International Working Seminar on Production Economics, Department of Management, University of Innsbruck, February 1996. Printed with permission.)

in graphical form in Figure 8.1. The first were the must-have or must be requirements. There are certain must-have requirements that must be included in your offering or customers will not be satisfied. The absence of one or more must-have requirements can lead to high levels of customer dissatisfaction. The second type of requirements is the one-dimensional requirements. These requirements provide more satisfaction to customers in proportion to the levels offered. The final are the attractive requirements, and these types of requirements make customers extremely satisfied and are important in highly differentiating your offerings.

To determine the type of requirements for the generated ideas, there is a technique called the Kano questionnaire. It allows one to evaluate the type of requirement based on the answers provided. In order to utilize the questionnaire, it is first essential that the criteria being considered are put into a question form. What differentiates the Kano technique from others is with this technique, each potential offering or feature is evaluated using two questions. The first asks the functional form of the question, meaning how one would feel if the particular feature was present. The second asks the dysfunctional form of the question, meaning how one would feel if the particular feature was *not* present. The combination of the answers with a well-thought-out table allows for a quick determination as to the type of requirement. For accuracy, the questionnaire should be given to several

Questionnaire Template

Potential Feature/Requirement: Enter potential requirement here

Enter the function form of the question relating to the potential requirement. *(Functional form of the question)*	1. I like it that way. 2. It must be that way. 3. I am neutral. 4. I can live with it that way. 5. I dislike it that way.
Enter the dysfunction form of the question relating to the potential requirement. *(Dysfunctional form of the question)*	1. I like it that way. 2. It must be that way. 3. I am neutral. 4. I can live with it that way. 5. I dislike it that way.

Answer each question independently by circling the appropriate answer.

Figure 8.2   Questionnaire template. (Adapted from Elmar Sauerwein, Franz Bailom, Kurt Matzler, and Hans H. Hinterhuber, "The Kano Model: How to Delight Your Customers," Preprints Volume I of the IX International Working Seminar on Production Economics, Department of Management, University of Innsbruck, February 1996. Printed with permission.)

individuals representing the target market. The results will be tabulated so that the majority data can determine the type of requirement. This will be made clear with more discussions to follow. Of course, more examples will be provided in this and in later chapters.

The questionnaire template[2] for a single feature is shown in Figure 8.2. Thus, for each feature, the participant will choose one answer for the functional form of the question and one answer for the dysfunctional form of the question.

These two answers will be processed through the Kano evaluation table[3] illustrated in Figure 8.3. The answers for each (functional form and dysfunctional form) are mapped using the Kano evaluation table for the determination of the requirement type.

For example,[4] consider a ski manufacturer that has developed a new feature for a ski that has the ability to grip well on hard snow. This feature would then be converted into a functional and a dysfunctional form of a question and placed into the questionnaire block as shown in Figure 8.4 and distributed to representatives of the target market. From Figure 8.4, we can see one's individual's responses. This particular individual stated that he or she liked the fact that the skis could grip hard snow, but was neutral on if the skis could *not* grip well on hard snow.

These answers are then processed through the Kano evaluation table, where the requirement is determined based on the intersection of the

Kano Evaluation Table

Evaluation of Customer Requirements		Locate column associated with negative form of the question ↓ ↓ ↓ ↓ ↓				
		1. Like	2. Must be	3. Neutral	4. Live with	5. Dislike
Locate row associated with positive form of the question	1. Like ➡	Q	A	A	A	O
	2. Must be ➡	R	I	I	I	M
	3. Neutral ➡	R	I	I	I	M
	4. Live with ➡	R	I	I	I	M
	5. Dislike ➡	R	R	R	R	Q

A = attractive, M = must be, R = reverse, O = one-dimensional, Q = questionable, I = indifferent.

Figure 8.3 Kano evaluation table. (Adapted from Elmar Sauerwein, Franz Bailom, Kurt Matzler, and Hans H. Hinterhuber, "The Kano Model: How to Delight Your Customers," Preprints Volume I of the IX International Working Seminar on Production Economics, Department of Management, University of Innsbruck, February 1996. Printed with permission.)

applicable row and column. This is illustrated in Figure 8.5. From Figure 8.5, the "neutral" rating of the dysfunctional column intersects the "like" rating of the functional row, indicating an attractive requirement. Thus, the ski gripping well on hard snow is an attractive requirement.

From Figure 8.5, we can see the possible results that can be generated from the Kano evaluation table. The letters in the Kano generation table are:

- A = Attractive requirement (previously discussed).
- M = Must-have requirement (previously discussed).
- O = One-dimensional requirement (previously discussed).

Potential Feature/Requirement: Edges of Skis Gripping on Hard Snow

If the edges of your skis grip well on hard snow, how do you feel? (Functional form of the question)	① I like it that way. 2. It must be that way. 3. I am neutral. 4. I can live with it that way. 5. I dislike it that way.
If the edges of your skis do not grip well on hard snow, how do you feel? (Dysfunctional form of the question)	1. I like it that way. 2. It must be that way. ③ I am neutral. 4. I can live with it that way. 5. I dislike it that way.

Figure 8.4   Functional/dysfunctional question for a product feature. (Adapted from Elmar Sauerwein, Franz Bailom, Kurt Matzler, and Hans H. Hinterhuber, "The Kano Model: How to Delight Your Customers," Preprints Volume I of the IX International Working Seminar on Production Economics, Department of Management, University of Innsbruck, February 1996. Printed with permission.)

- I = Indifferent: This does not result in satisfaction or dissatisfaction when fulfilled or not; these attributes should be avoided.
- R = Reverse attribute: This indicates that the feature or attribute leads to absolute dissatisfaction and should be avoided.
- Q = Questionable: Participant may have been confused by the question; check wording and repeat.

Once the reader understands this approach, it can be used to evaluate the list of potential features derived from idea generation. This evaluation process requires few participants. Based on a previous study by the American Marketing Association, it has been determined that only 20 to 30 customer interviews in a particular segment will suffice in determining approximately 90% to 95% of all possible product requirements. Therefore, it is a good idea to utilize at least 20–30 participants for all of the potential features. This will allow one to place all of the results in a table where the majority can dictate the requirement type. This can be seen in Figure 8.6, where the results of 30 participants have been tabulated. Thus with respect to the edges of the skis gripping on hard snow, we have 15 (50%) of the participants that resulted in a must-have requirement. Serviceability resulted in an attractive requirement as 17 participants indicated, and ease of turn resulted in a one-dimensional

Evaluation of Customer Requirements		Locate column associated with negative form of the question ↓ ↓ ↓ ↓ ↓				
		1. Like	2. Must be	3. Neutral	4. Live with	5. Dislike
Locate row associated with positive form of the question ➡	1. Like ➡	Q-	A	Ⓐ	A	O
	2. Must be ➡	R	I	I	I	M
	3. Neutral ➡	R	I	I	I	M
	4. Live with ➡	R	I	I	I	M
	5. Dislike ➡	R	R	R	R	Q

A = attractive, M = must be, R = reverse, O = one-dimensional, Q = questionable, I = indifferent.

Figure 8.5 Utilizing the Kano evaluation table. (Adapted from Elmar Sauerwein, Franz Bailom, Kurt Matzler, and Hans H. Hinterhuber, "The Kano Model: How to Delight Your Customers," Preprints Volume I of the IX International Working Seminar on Production Economics, Department of Management, University of Innsbruck, February 1996. Printed with permission.)

requirement per 15 participants. This concludes the method in how to determine the requirement type.

The next step is to prioritize each potential offering, beginning with customer value. This allows executives to find those offerings most preferred by customers, and hence highlights which are more valuable. A high-priority offering will have more customer value-benefits than a lower-priority offering. This is also apparent by higher importance scores. This information allows executives to make trade-offs. For example, if one particular feature is extremely expensive to include or falls close to a competitor's patent, and this feature is of low priority, executives can ignore it. Thus, for eliminating poor alternatives, it is important to know which potential features are more or less important to customers. Similar to the type of requirements

Product Requirement	A	O	M	I	R	Q	Total	Category
Edges gripping on hard snow	4	7	15	2	1	1	30	M
Service	17	6	1	4	1	1	30	A
Ease of turn	5	15	7	2	0	1	30	O
Scratch-resistant surface								
Etc.								

It is more useful to put the above in terms of percentages. Simply divide each above number by the total number of surveys and multiply by 100; this will yield the results in % (see below).

Edges gripping on hard snow	13.3	7	50	6.67	3.3	3.3	100%	M
Service	56.7	20	3.3	13.3	3.3	3.3	100%	A
Ease of turn	16.7	50	23.3	6.7	0	3.3	100%	O

Figure 8.6 Results of 30 participants. (Adapted from Elmar Sauerwein, Franz Bailom, Kurt Matzler, and Hans H. Hinterhuber, "The Kano Model: How to Delight Your Customers," Preprints Volume I of the IX International Working Seminar on Production Economics, Department of Management, University of Innsbruck, February 1996. Printed with permission.)

(one-dimensional, must-have, attractive), the prioritization of offerings should also be determined by the customers representing the target market. Therefore, when administering the questionnaire, it is proper to include a relative importance chart[5] for the participants to fill out. This is crucial if you are not intending to have importance and satisfaction scores rated. Such an example is illustrated in Figure 8.7. Figure 8.7 complements our example in this chapter. The chart is based on a scale from 1 to 7, where 7 indicates a high level of importance. The value of 1 would indicate that the particular feature is not required or important at all. From the answers obtained, the most common ratings can be grouped together to arrive at a total rating for a particular offering/feature, as shown in Figure 8.7.

To generate the final grouped features shown in Figure 8.7, we need to evaluate the individual scores for each feature. We can illustrate the use of the relative importance for a single feature based on answers from 30

Relative Importance

How important are the following features? Rate each on a scale of 1 to 7.							
	Totally Unimportant				*Very Important*		
	1	2	3	4	5	6	7
Edges gripping on hard snow					X		
Service							X
Ease of turn				X			
Ski color		X					
Etc.							

Figure 8.7   Relative importance example for various product features. (Adapted from Elmar Sauerwein, Franz Bailom, Kurt Matzler, and Hans H. Hinterhuber, "The Kano Model: How to Delight Your Customers," Preprints Volume I of the IX International Working Seminar on Production Economics, Department of Management, University of Innsbruck, February 1996. Printed with permission.)

participants. By reference to Figure 8.8, the values from 30 people are illustrated for the feature of the skis gripping on hard snow. The most common rating number from the survey is 5 (11 total responses). Therefore, we can use the approach of choosing the rating number having the majority choice for the final rating number. If it seems that the data are too overlapping, one may require some statistical analysis to better make sense of the data. If a statistical analysis cannot make sense of the data, you may want to revisit the feature to ensure that it makes sense to the consumer. You should also ensure that you are conveying the information properly. If the participants do not understand the question, they cannot provide an accurate answer. It is up to the reader of this book to break down the data that work best for a proper analysis to fuel decision-making discussions.

With the results of our analysis, we now have a better understanding of the value certain offerings can bring to customers. Basically, the offerings near the "very important" ratings are going to provide higher customer value. The versions having a lower rating may be boosted up if they are a one-dimensional requirement. If this is the case, you may want to verify if that particular feature is a hidden gem. A hidden gem would result in a "very important" rating providing the levels are increased. This concludes the value or benefits offering dimension.

Feature

	Totally Unimportant						Very Important
Participant	1	2	3	4	5	6	7
John Doe 1					5		
John Doe 2				4			
John Doe 3					5		
John Doe 4		2					
John Doe 5							
John Doe 6					5		
John Doe 7						6	
John Doe 8	1						
John Doe 9			3				
John Doe 10					5		
John Doe 11						6	
John Doe 12	1						
John Doe 13		2					
John Doe 14					5		
John Doe 15						6	
John Doe 16					5		
John Doe 17			3				
John Doe 18					5		
John Doe 19						6	
John Doe 20					5		
John Doe 21			3				
John Doe 22				4			
John Doe 23					5		
John Doe 24						6	

Edges Gripping on Hard Snow

Figure 8.8 (continued)

Feature (continued)

Edges Gripping on Hard Snow							
	Totally Unimportant						*Very Important*
John Doe 25							7
John Doe 26					5		
John Doe 27				4			
John Doe 28	1						
John Doe 29			3				
John Doe 30					5		
Totals	3	2	4	4	11	5	1

Figure 8.8 Relative importance of a single feature. (Adapted from Elmar Sauerwein, Franz Bailom, Kurt Matzler, and Hans H. Hinterhuber, "The Kano Model: How to Delight Your Customers," Preprints Volume I of the IX International Working Seminar on Production Economics, Department of Management, University of Innsbruck, February 1996. Printed with permission.)

It should be noted that the relative importance is another method of obtaining importance ratings from targeted customers. The questionnaire can include importance and satisfaction questions as per the format in Chapter 3. It is the object of this book to include optional alternative methods to enhance learning that may better appeal to certain readers.

We now direct our discussion to the opportunity offering dimension. If you recall, opportunity scores were calculated based on obtaining importance and satisfaction scores for a specific product feature or general offering. From your analysis, you should already have some opportunity scores. However, you may have generated new offering feature ideas from the idea generation chapter that requires rating. Thus, you also need to know the importance and satisfaction for any new offering(s). This will allow you to calculate the opportunity scores for the new potential offerings. If you require new ideas to be rated by customers, simply include this in your questionnaire when you administer the above items to customers that will represent your target market. By asking about the importance and satisfaction for the new potential offerings, you can calculate the opportunity scores. At this point, you will have solid customer data with respect to value and opportunity. You now need to explore the remaining two offering dimensions.

With respect to barriers to imitation, business leaders need to ask themselves if they are willing to invest in some level of barrier to imitation. In some cases, the products being offered may have a short shelf life and will be replaced rather quickly. This may allow for minimal barrier to imitation levels. On the other hand, the products may be sold on the market for a number of years. This would warrant higher levels of barriers to imitation. This decision is left to the business leader to decide. In Chapter 6, I discussed the various barriers to imitation. These barriers should be considered, as preventing imitation is highly desired, especially if cost allows these barriers.

The final offering dimension to consider is the cost position of the offering. Business leaders can work with the various disciplines of the company to determine the cost of the new offerings. Once determined, the cost positions can be assigned to each new idea (potential new offering).

From the analysis, we can now begin the ranking by applying the results and a user-defined scale to the offering dimensions. The offering dimensions are those parameters defining the quadrants on the strategy icon (benefits, opportunity, cost position, and barriers to imitation). I will describe a ranking system that utilizes all four offering dimensions with equal and unequal weights. Thus, for simplicity, let us begin with all four offering dimensions being equally important. Therefore, we can assign each offering dimension with any chosen weight factor. For this example, I choose the value of 10 for the relative weight of each offering dimension. That means that each feature to be analyzed can receive a maximum score of 10. If each of the four offering dimensions can receive a maximum score of 10, the total perfect score would be 40 (10 + 10 + 10 + 10). If we base the scores on a percentage basis (or decimal equivalent), a maximum score of 10 (100%) would receive the decimal equivalent of 1.0. Thus for 50%, the decimal would be 0.5, for 30% the decimal would be 0.3, etc. To bring this concept to life, I have created the offering ranking matrix illustrated in Figure 8.9. The offering ranking matrix of Figure 8.9 is arranged with the four offering dimensions having a maximum achievable score of 10 for each dimension, as indicated under the corresponding symbol.

As illustrated in Figure 8.9, I have input the values for four offering features. The first (offering 1) provides 80% of the benefits desired by consumers of the target market as taken from the previous value analysis (importance scores, results of the product fulfillment map, general assessment of utility and emotion, etc.). The opportunity is 50% of the maximum

Offering Dimensions

	Value (Benefits)	Opportunity	Barrier to Imitation	Cost Position of Offering	Total Score	% of Perfect Score
Enter the Relative Weights for Each Dimension →	10	10	10	10	40	N/A
Offering Attributes (Enter Decimal %) ↘						
Offering #1	0.8	0.5	0.7	0.2	22	0.55
Offering #2	0.7	0.4	0.2	0.7	20	0.50
Offering #3	0.1	0.5	0.7	0.9	22	0.55
Offering #4	0.9	1	0.5	0.9	33	0.83

Figure 8.9   Offering ranking matrix of equal weights. (From Anthony Sgroi Jr.)

10. The barrier to imitation is also high, with 70% out of 100%. This is reflected by a series of patents protecting the feature of offering 1. The last part is the cost position. Offering 1 is costly to produce and thus receives 20% out of 100%. When these are all added, the total score is 22 (0.8 × 10) + (0.5 × 10) + (0.7 × 10) + (0.2 × 10). This is calculated as a percentage of the total perfect score of 40 and computes to 55%, or 0.55 (22/40). The remaining offerings (2 through 4) are also shown. From the matrix, it is clear that offering 4 is optimum, as this calculates to 83%; second is offerings 1 and 3 having 55%, followed by offering 2 with 50%. Depending on your situation, the choice may be simple to decipher through. For example, when comparing offerings 1 and 3 only at 55%, we can decide rather easily that offering 1 provides more customer value (benefits) than offering 3, but at a much higher cost. If the cost is still at acceptable levels, then the decision is rather easy. More importantly, there may be opportunities to lower the cost of offering 1.

We can also apply unequal weights to one or more of the offering dimensions. For example, let us assume that in our example, cost is the major driver. We determine that all customers of the target market are driven by cost, and that the other dimensions are not as important. I am stating this example in the extreme to illustrate how the offering ranking matrix functions. Thus, let us assume that cost is four times as important as the remaining three offering dimensions. Therefore, by reference to Figure 8.10, the reader can see the new relative weight for cost position at a 40 (4 × 10) maximum possible value. With the same input values (%) as in Figure 8.9,

Offering Dimensions

	Value (Benefits)	Opportunity	Barrier to Imitation	Cost Position of Offering	Total Score	% of Perfect Score
Enter the Relative Weights for Each Dimension ⟶	10	10	10	40	70	N/A

Offering Attributes (Enter Decimal %) ⟶

	Value (Benefits)	Opportunity	Barrier to Imitation	Cost Position of Offering	Total Score	% of Perfect Score
Offering #1	0.8	0.5	0.7	0.2	28	0.40
Offering #2	0.7	0.4	0.2	0.7	41	0.59
Offering #3	0.1	0.5	0.7	0.9	49	0.70
Offering #4	0.9	1	0.5	0.9	60	0.86

Figure 8.10   Offering ranking matrix of unequal weights. (From Anthony Sgroi Jr.)

notice how the final decimals change, as shown in the percent of perfect score column in Figure 8.10. In this case, offering 4 is now optimum, followed by offering 3, then offering 2, and finally offering 1. Thus, the offering ranking matrix can be customized by the decision makers to receive the most accurate rating possible that better aligns to one's situation.

It should be noted that in the above examples, I have only illustrated four offerings in the matrix. Of course, it is more likely that the reader of this book will have more than four possible offerings. Thus, the entire list can be analyzed and later sorted by a spreadsheet tool beginning with the highest value. This will allow easier decision making. Once completed, the results in the offering ranking matrix doubles as knowledge retention and can be reused later when needed.

Conclusion

This chapter concludes the discussions of the parts necessary to transform a strategy. Chapter 9 will describe the strategy transformation process, which brings all of the previous chapters together. The process includes both the evaluation and transformation of a strategy. In Chapter 10, a complete example will be presented to illustrate the entire strategy transformation process.

Chapter 9

Strategy Transformation Process

In this chapter, the strategy transformation process will be discussed. The process will bring together all of the tools and discussions previously presented. Since the many details of the strategy transformation process have been fully described in previous chapters on an individual basis, this chapter will discuss the process at a higher level. It is the intention of this chapter to prepare the reader for a detailed example utilizing the entire strategy transformation process.

Strategy always begins with the understanding of the current state. Companies must understand their competitive position within the marketplace compared to their competitors and the perception of the industry itself. Not until the current state is understood can a company begin to explore an optimized strategy. This process begins with the listing of the offerings for your company, your competitors, and the general factors of the industry, if applicable. The offerings are best listed in such a way that companies can begin to analyze them in terms of the value (benefits) they deliver to customers. In addition, the list should include the cost levels (low, medium, high) for the offerings. This logic is sound when you think of the concept that companies must bear a cost to deliver benefits to customers. This allows for a quick analysis as to the validity of the offering. For example, if the benefit level is low and the cost level is high, this should raise a flag to those trying to define the current state that something is wrong with the current strategy. As a note, the benefits and cost are two components represented in the strategy icon.

Cost-to-Benefit Grid

Grid Title (i.e., your company, competitor, industry factors)			
Customer Offerings and Impacting Factors	*Benefit Level of the Offerings (low, medium, high)*	*Company Cost of the Offering (low, medium, high)*	*Offering Level (user-defined scale, i.e., 1–4)*
Customer purchase price			
Offering 1			
Offering 2			
Offering 3			
Offering 4, etc.			

Figure 9.1　Cost-to-benefit grid. (From Anthony Sgroi Jr.)

To begin capturing the offerings, I prefer to first arrange them in list form. The list format is shown in Figure 9.1 and is denoted as the cost-to-benefit grid. The cost-to-benefit grid captures all of the offerings along the left column, beginning with customer purchase price. The offerings are then inserted beneath customer purchase price to allow for the capturing of the benefits, costs, and offering levels. To begin, managers begin listing the offerings of their company in a cost-to-benefit grid. Once completed, the offerings of the competitors are tracked in a separate cost-to-benefit grid. Finally, any contributing industry factors that influence the strategy can also be tracked in a separate cost-to-benefit grid, if necessary.

To begin, the offerings contained in each cost-to-benefit grid can be subject to some discussion for the determination of their associated offering levels. Later, after the levels are assigned, the offerings can be grouped according to high or low levels as per the offering level (last column). This will help to avoid choppy curves. Be sure to include other important factors that impact your business. Impacting factors are those unspoken items that have an effect on a business or industry. For example, recall the car dealership example discussed earlier. We know the difficulties and games car dealers play when trying to shop for a car. Have you ever spent two hours with the salesman and "manager" reading the "paper offer" 10 times? They go back and forth saying this is the best they can do and they are losing money when you know they are still obtaining a healthy profit. This causes frustration and many times also lost sales. These difficulties seriously impact present and future sales, and therefore should be included as an impacting industry factor.

If you are having a difficult time defining the offerings or the impacting industry factors, refer to the following short list:

- Consider those offerings that a company or industry provides to customers that satisfy a need or want.
- Consider those offerings contributing to the customer purchase decisions.
- Consider those offerings that you or the players in your industry invest in.
- Consider those offerings most common in your industry.
- Consider those offerings subject to advertisement.

Once you have an accurate discussion on the listed offerings, an offering level scale (i.e., 0–4) is defined. You will begin to define relative ratings based on the comparison of the levels for the combined offerings and prices within your scale. Refer to all cost-to-benefit grids for this exercise. The method of defining price levels and offerings levels was explained in detail in Chapter 2. Begin by assigning a number for the customer purchase price and record this rating (level) in the appropriate cell for each cost-to-benefit grid. Next, assign the numerical values for the offering levels for each grid. Finally, finish the grids by inputting the benefit and cost levels (low, medium, high) for the remaining cells. This may take several iterations; therefore, keep working through the offerings until the prices, offerings, industry factors, and levels seem accurate on a relative basis.

By now you have already captured some information regarding two of the four quadrants of the strategy icon. At this point, you can begin to create the visual strategy map of the current state if desired. However, you may choose to first complete the entire strategy icon and market size gage since the visual strategy map (current state) is ultimately desired and requires the completion of these items. The complete analysis of the four quadrants of the strategy icon and the market size gage may require some work to form an accurate understanding of the current state. However, the addition of these items will create more of a complete picture of the current strategy. To help, you can define the strategy icon using the icon generation grid shown in Figure 9.2. This can help you perform an analysis as to the levels for each parameter of the strategy icon. Of course, you may require a separate icon generation grid from each applicable offering, or you may choose to use one icon generation grid for the entire strategy. This is dependent on the offerings being considered and your judgment.

Company or Offering Name: Icon Generation Grid

Icon Parameter	Parameter Level	Discussion
Benefits	Low-medium-high (color or numeric scale)	Enter discussion here
Opportunity	Low-medium-high (color or numeric scale)	Enter discussion here
Barrier to imitation	Low-medium-high (color or numeric scale)	Enter discussion here
Cost of offerings	Low-medium-high (color or numeric scale)	Enter discussion here

Figure 9.2 Icon generation grid. (From Anthony Sgroi Jr.)

Now the analysis of the strategy icon can begin. With respect to the value or benefits (upper left quadrant) of the strategy icon, the use of the product fulfillment map makes sense to employ. With this tool, the value being offered (or lack thereof) can be found by running the various offerings through the map. In addition, if importance scores were initially obtained, they can be used to determine the benefit levels of offerings.

Next is the understanding of the opportunities (upper right quadrant of the strategy icon) that the current offerings provide. This is best accomplished via the ranked opportunity score calculation where the ranked difference of importance and satisfaction is computed. The product fulfillment map also displays some level of opportunity. If managers understand the customer very well, they may have the necessary information to determine the current importance and satisfaction levels. If they cannot gage this, it may be necessary to have targeted consumers run through the importance and satisfaction aspects of the current offerings. As a note, running through the product fulfillment map with targeted customers can provide opportunity information as to what is currently underserved (not offered) or over-served (too much being offered).

The next item for analysis is barriers to imitation (lower left quadrant of the strategy icon). This analysis can be a simple cursory view of the many possible barriers or can be a detailed analysis, if desired. This may require some form of judgment. For example, how much barrier to imitation will brand power provide? With respect to intellectual property barriers, you may choose to run through this process internally. However, if desired, a patent attorney can be of assistance for a more detailed picture. Ensure that you gage your current barriers to imitation in addition to your competitor's. Revisit the barrier to imitation Chapter 6 to refamiliarize yourself with this subject matter.

Finally, the cost position (lower right quadrant of the strategy icon) of the strategy is analyzed. Companies should have a good understanding of their cost structure, which could allow for a rather quick exercise. However, some research may be necessary with respect to the cost position of the competitor's offerings. This is best done by the study of the offerings and the study can include number of components for their products, country or origin, shipping costs, market prices, etc. Read Chapter 5 to refamiliarize yourself with the possible cost considerations to help you through your analysis.

Finally, the last component to consider is the market size gage (MSG). With respect to your company and your competitors, first you must determine the overall size of your current market. This can be in the form of annual sales dollars or annual units sold. It is up to the company to choose the unit desired. The next item to determine is the market share that your company currently has. This allows you to first understand the total market size, and second to understand how much of that market you have. This information is handy to have since you always want to know when you are approaching the maximum market size, as this may be a trigger to revisit your strategy. Also, having the current market size will allow you to compare the new potential market size of your new strategy to your current strategy. Of course, you may or may not want to strive for a larger market size. Having a larger market size does not necessarily guarantee a high penetration. Therefore, you may realize that if you target a smaller total market size but are able to get more penetration, you may be in a better position. As a note, the respective market shares of the competitors can also be included if desired. Refer to Chapter 1 for reference to adding the respective market shares of the competitors to the market share gage.

I find it easier to first begin defining the 2-D map, and after the map is complete and accurate, insert the strategy icon(s) and market size gage into it to create the current state visual strategy map. The 2-D map is simply the graphical depiction of the combined cost-to-benefit grids. Simply insert each offering/factor on the bottom of the 2-D map and record each offering/factor level on the left vertical portion of the map. From the intersection of each offering/factor to its corresponding level, a point can be inserted for each, forming the basis for a curve. Repeat this step for all cost-to-benefit grids. You may be required to shift offerings around to make the smoothest set of curves possible.

To complete the map, insert the strategy icons and the market size gage to complete the visual strategy map current state. This will capture the present strategy for your company compared to your competitor's. If desired, a separated strategy icon can be used for the entire curve of a company, or certain selected key offerings. This decision depends on the offerings contained in the map and is decided on a case-by-case basis.

Once the final curves are obtained, you can analyze them where you can verify if there is an area of focus for your company. A proper area of focus is those offerings that collectively add up to customer benefits ultimately providing customer value. If high levels of offerings are present that do not add benefits (value), then waste may be present. Now study the curves of the competitors. Do the competitors have the same curve as yours? If the curves are the same, this indicates a similar strategy with no differentiation. If the curves are different, this would indicate a different or unique set of offerings. If you find that your current curve is unique, you may be in a decent position. Finally, can your strategy be described by few words? If this is the case, the offerings for your company are clear. If not, continue to read on. Once the current state is complete, we will study and modify the strategy to ultimately create an optimum future strategy. This future strategy will be communicated in a visual strategy map (future state) and should define a unique strategy when completed.

Once the visual strategy map current state (VSMCS) is drawn, the current strategy is analyzed using the product fulfillment map. An early benefit of the product fulfillment map is that companies can learn very quickly where they can add customer value. It may be entirely possible that some companies discover key unmet needs during this analysis. If this is the case, any new potential offerings can be rerun through the product fulfillment map for an updated analysis. With use of the product fulfillment map, the current state can be captured, including all of your current offerings, your fulfilled items, and your unfulfilled items that you currently deem important at this time. This is captured in a current state grid and is shown in Figure 9.3.

Ideas for transforming your strategy to an optimum strategy can be generated using the concepts from Chapter 4. As previously discussed, strategy modification can come from multiple sources. The first is the information just learned by running through the product fulfillment map during the analysis of the current state. In some cases, companies can learn what they needed to learn to make the desired changes to their strategy. This is why the analysis using the product fulfillment map is first performed. I include

Current State Grid

Buyer utility map (fulfilled items)	Current offerings and impacting factors
• Item 1 • Item 2	• Offering/factor 1 • Offering/factor 2 • Offering/factor 3 • Etc.
Buyer utility map (unfulfilled items)	
• Item 1 • Item 2	

Figure 9.3   Current state grid. (From Anthony Sgroi Jr.)

this step because it can (on its own) identify those missing links to an optimized future strategy for some companies.

The second form of strategy modification comes from the form of the internal industry perspective. The internal industry perspective is the creation of new ideas that will fill gaps according to those problems and solutions familiar within your current industry. Such ideas can be created from customer interviews, ethnographic research, focus groups, customer complaints, problem solution statements, job mapping, etc. These forms of ideas are typically improvements along the line of what the company in a particular industry already offers. In this stage, it may be essential that companies obtain data from the insight of the customer.

Customer insight is gained by studying customers' wants, needs, preferences, and methods of transacting with your company. You must determine how people use (or don't use) the products or services of your industry. Only then can you determine the pain points (lack of value or too much waste) of the offerings of your industry. During your study, you will want to find new opportunities to unlock customer value. Thus, begin by analyzing:

■ Major customer pain points of the offerings of your company and your industry
■ Offerings your company or your industry lacks
■ Offerings having no value that can be eliminated
■ The ways customers use your or your competitor's offerings
■ Offerings being overserved that can be reduced (waste reduction)
■ Offerings being underserved that can be increased (value enhancement)

- Other ways customers deal with problems associated in your industry
- Recommendations that customers provide

You should not stop at your customers; you should also call on non-customers, lost customers, and competitors' customers. If the customer represents the end user, the same as the user, you need to extend your observations to the users. You must watch these people in action (go and see), experiencing the products or services of your industry. You can utilize the product fulfillment map as you observe customers. You can also use the aspects of the product fulfillment map during discussions with customers. This can provide more insight into what your company or industry lacks.

Now that you have spent time with the various customers, keep track of the major feedback and list it in a customer feedback grid. A customer feedback grid is shown in Figure 9.4 and provides useful information for companies. This grid allows companies to understand what customers are trying to achieve, what is lacking and unnecessary, what is desired, and other important requirements. Ensure that you capture the feedback of several customers, lost customers, and competitors' customers. If necessary, a separate customer feedback grid can be used for each group to better analyze their buying preferences.

Customer Feedback Grid

Problems Customers are Solving	Customer Wants
Customer pain points	Unnecessary offerings
	Offerings levels to reduce
	Offering levels to increase
Lacking offerings	Other important requirements

Figure 9.4 Customer feedback grid. (From Anthony Sgroi Jr.)

Once you identify some of these areas that are lacking, you can then generate ideas to fill these gaps. Such methods include job mapping or the use of the problem solution statement. Refer to the earlier discussions contained in Chapter 4, or use your favorite method of idea generation. Some companies choose an outside facilitator to help generate ideas. These are acceptable, but ensure that key company personnel are involved in the entire process. As a note, there may be offerings that can be reduced in level or simply eliminated if they are not providing customer benefits. This can help reduce the cost of providing the much needed and desired benefits to customers that companies should be focusing on.

The third form of strategy modification comes from an external perspective. This perspective will unlock new offerings based on gathering new ideas from external frames of reference, such as a different industry, a different strategic group, buyer chain modification, the definition of a total solution, functional emotional shifts, and adaptation to a trend. These ideas can result in modifications to a product line or even the creation of a new business model. Managers should understand that the external perspective can be limitless in terms of the possible choices. Therefore, a good rule of thumb is to begin your selection by choosing an external perspective that targets a major lacking of your current industry. This can be the easiest way to begin this exercise. Before this exercise, it is best to review the external perspective portion of Chapter 4 in full detail.

At this stage, you should have a series of new ideas for consideration. Depending on your list of ideas, you may have some that are unrelated. Such unrelated ideas should be separated in categories defining separate themes. For example, consider the generation of 10 potential offering ideas. Five represent a modification to a current product targeting your current customer base. The other five represent a new product that seems to target a totally different customer base. You should separate these ideas for separate analysis. In Chapter 11, I will introduce the concept of using position statements to help you choose the appropriate theme that best aligns to your company's capabilities. Nevertheless, once a series of new ideas are generated, they need to be ranked and prioritized. Consider these categories for idea ranking:

- Value or benefits to the customer
- Market size
- Opportunity levels for the company
- Barriers to imitation

Idea Prefilter Grid

	Enter Levels (low, medium, high)				
	Customer Value (benefits)	Cost of Offering	Market Size	Opportunity Level	Barrier to Imitation
Offering 1	High	Low	High	High	Medium
Offering 2	High	High	Low	Medium	Medium
Offering 3	Medium	Low	High	Medium	Medium
Offering 4	Low	Medium	Medium	Low	Medium
Offering 5, etc.	Low	High	Low	Medium	Low

Figure 9.5 Idea prefilter grid. (From Anthony Sgroi Jr.)

■ Cost position
■ Pricing power

The items contained in the above list can serve as ranking criteria and can have any weight desired. They will also allow for the strategy icon to be created, as well as the market size gage for the new strategy.

To begin ranking, if you did not perform a quick pass through the product fulfillment map, go ahead and perform this task, as this may quickly filter out some ideas that may not be desirable. Next, you can begin to list the ideas that you have generated. During the generation of the list, you may identify those ideas that are obvious to eliminate. Finish your list by listing the remaining ideas in a grid, which I call the idea prefilter grid. This grid allows one to list the ideas and keep track of certain metrics associated with them. Since this is a prefiltering grid, you only need to know whether the potential offerings have high levels, medium levels, or low levels of specific attributes. The idea prefilter grid is illustrated in Figure 9.5.

By use of the idea prefiltering grid, managers can begin to discuss the various new potential offerings. This tool will allow for quick decisions in the retention or removal of new potential offerings. This tool will be the first filter that you will use to decipher through your list of new potential offerings before the requirement of a more detailed analysis. I find it useful to rank the new potential offerings by customer value (benefits) first, as the ultimate way to drive sales is to offer your target market high levels of benefits. I then look at the cost of the offering, market size, opportunity level, and finally, barriers to imitation. If you desire, you can add other metrics, such as pricing power. On the other hand, you can remove a metric or two if they are not applicable to your business. It should be noted that the idea prefiltering grid is a discussion tool used to help managers decide which offerings should be immediately removed. Immediate removal eliminates the waste of including nonessential offerings to detailed analysis when it is not necessary.

The final list will be subject to evaluation using the Kano evaluation table and by asking targeted customers to rate the relative importance and satisfaction for the potential ideas. The ideas that remain from this stage will finally be analyzed using the offering ranking matrix, if needed.

It should be noted here that this exercise requires extensive knowledge of the targeted customer. There is no process or series of tools that can transform a mediocre strategy to an optimum strategy without a good understanding of the targeted customer. Therefore, managers should strive to understand the target customer as well as the tools provided to you in this book. Once you understand both, you will have a better understanding of the use of the tools and how often they should be utilized. For example, you may choose to have targeted customers run through the Kano evaluation table several times as you fine-tune your strategy. If you do not have a good understanding of the targeted customer, this exercise will undoubtedly confuse you more. If you still require filtering after the Kano evaluation process, the offering ranking matrix can be the final method to finish off your idea selection process. Of course, these tools are discussion tools, as they are highly dependent on user input. So ensure that the strategy transformation process is a team-driven event and a team decision. Such teams should consist of members that fit the team of responsible experts criteria discussed in the beginning of this book.

Once the ideas are ranked, the ideas that represent good opportunities for the new strategy are then grouped together to form a theme. A focused theme is desired, as this allows the strategy to make sense and have a purpose. Therefore, if the offerings complement each other, this is most desirable, as it forms a focused strategy. A strategy would not make sense if one offering contradicted another. For example, a very small economical car having a heavy-duty towing package does not make sense for a company's offerings. One would never equip a lightweight car of low horsepower with a towing package. Therefore, ensure that the offerings of the strategy align with the common objective. By ensuring this alignment, it would be easy to describe the strategy in few words. This is another important characteristic of a strategy. If the strategy can be defined by a few words, it is very clear, transparent, and easy to communicate. Companies should strive for this.

Next is the creation of the new strategy icon with respect to the newly chosen offerings. You will also define a strategy icon for the competitor in view of the newly chosen offerings. Run through each offering and determine if a single strategy icon can be used for the new strategy. Next, analyze each icon parameter for your new set of offerings and complete the strategy icons.

Don't forget about the market size gage. Determine the total potential market and your expected first year's market share and the potential impact of your competitors' market shares, if desired.

Finally, the visual strategy map future state (VSMFS) can be drawn. Draw the visual strategy map future state by listing the offerings on the horizontal axis and map their corresponding levels on the vertical axis. If you have not yet defined price and offering levels, complete this step now. Do this for your newly proposed strategy and ensure that you capture the levels of these new offerings with respect to your competitors. Ensure that you include the newly created future state strategy icon in the appropriate areas and the latest market size gage. Finally, shuffle the offerings around until the curves are as smooth as possible.

Next, you should study the strategy. Are your curves different compared to your competitors'? They should be different, as a different curve represents a unique strategy. A unique strategy ensures that you are offering something different and should be more in tune to what customers want per your analysis. If the curves are the same, they represent a similar strategy, and this is not desirable, as you would not stand apart from your competition. Also, compare the levels of the offerings. You want to ensure that you are not providing excessively high levels (overserving customers with waste) of the offerings. You also want to ensure that you are not underserving your customers by not providing enough levels of valued offerings. Finally, study the strategy icon. Does your strategy provide better value at the same or better cost position? This should be the case. If your cost position is the same as your competitors, you had better provide more (and different) value. Next, your new strategy should represent a larger opportunity than your previous strategy and those of your competitors. A larger opportunity means that you have targeted an important customer characteristic that is not fully satisfied. Finally, do you have a good level to the barriers to imitation? You of course want to prevent imitation, or at least delay it as long as possible.

With respect to the market size gage, do you see a large market size that will enable long-term growth? This would be depicted by comparing the future market share portion to the market size portion. Finally, with all of this said, does your offering price position coincide with what you are offering? Make sure your price levels reflect the levels and benefits of your offerings. For example, if you are pricing higher than the competition, you should be offering better value than your competitors. Pricing must also reflect what the market can bear. You must align price with value offered and always know the affordability levels of your target customers and what they would be willing to pay. Understand the appropriate price first, and then verify if you can profit from the chosen offering price. If you attempt to adjust your offering price as dependent on your cost (normally called cost-plus profit), you may deter sales due to an excessive price.

If you have defined several ideas of different themes or categories, it may make sense to draw several visual strategy maps (future state). Once they are drawn and analyzed as described above, you may want to have team members and management personnel vote on the strategies. Hang all of your visual strategy maps (future states) on a wall illustrating the new strategies. Spend 10 minutes presenting each VSMFS to the audience, and give each member a chance to judge the new strategies. Have each judge explain why he or she chose particular strategies, and also why he or she did not pick particular strategies, as this will provide a final level of feedback. From the chosen strategies and the final levels of feedback, you can finalize your strategy. Create the final visual strategy map future state and ensure it has focus, is unique (different from the competition), and can be described in few words.

As stated above, this process may require some work and effort with many cycles dealing with both internal team members and targeted customers. It may also be an iterative process where a first set of ideas may add up to nothing after several weeks of research. This is why it is essential to understand the targeted customer base and the reasons that drive their purchase decisions. Form a cross-functional team of responsible experts comprising members from the specific disciplines from your company. For example, such a team can comprise marketing, product development, operations, service, customer service, sales, and legal. Depending on your company, you may have more or less members for your team.

You now have learned some of the considerations and tools to create your optimized strategy. However, the best way of learning is to use the process. Therefore, Chapter 10 will run through a detailed example.

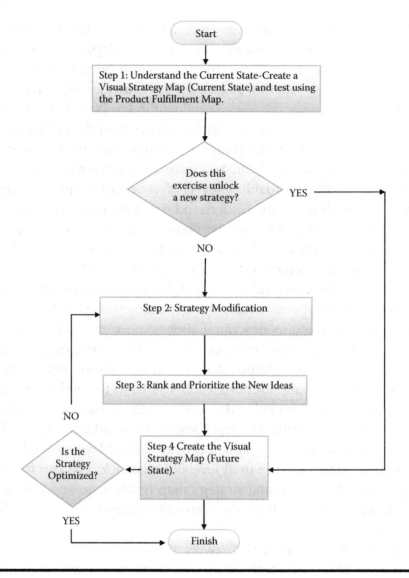

Figure 9.6 Strategy transformation process flowchart. (From Anthony Sgroi Jr.)

The example to be discussed will illustrate the tools and discussions up to this point. Study the example and the process of working through the example. I have also attached a general flowchart to help you visualize the strategy-transformation process shown in Figure 9.6. Figures 9.7 through 9.10 illustrate the details of Figure 9.6.

Step 1: Understand the Current State—Create a Visual Strategy Map (current state).

- List your Offerings, Competitor's Offerings, and industry factors (if applicable) in a Cost-to-Benefit Grid.

- Define the levels of all offerings, relative price, and draw the 2-D Map.

- Create Strategy Icon and Market Size Gage (The Product Fulfillment Map may assist the creation of the Strategy Icon).

- Draw your Visual Strategy Map (current state).

Test the Offerings of the current state.

- Thoroughly run all offerings through the Product Fulfillment Map to test for customer value (you can also include the competitor's offerings if you want to test their contribution to consumer value)

- If this unlocks a new strategy, proceed to Step 4.

- Keep track of the current offerings, fulfilled, and unfulfilled items in a Current State Grid.

Figure 9.7 Step 1 of the strategy transformation process. (From Anthony Sgroi Jr.)

Step 2: Strategy Modification (Talk to Customers)

- Perform Voice-of-Customer Analysis of your offerings and those common in your industry.

- Track the feedback by completing a Customer Feedback Grid.

- Generate new potential Offerings based on Customer Input (Utilize internal and/or external industry perspectives).

- If multiple ideas can form alternate themes, group the new ideas into distinct groups or clusters.

Figure 9.8 Step 2 of the strategy transformation process. (From Anthony Sgroi Jr.)

Step 3: Rank and Prioritize the New Ideas.

- Run all new ideas through the Product Fulfillment Map as a first pass (eliminate unwanted ideas).

- Begin to list and rank the selected ideas in a Idea Pre-Filter Grid to find the better ideas for analysis.

- Perform an analysis of the optimum ideas. Get customer feedback of new offerings by running through the Kano Evaluation Table and obtaining the relative importance for each potential idea. Also, obtain importance and satisfaction scores for the potential ideas. Process the data through the Opportunity Calculator and created a Ranked Opportunity Score for your list. This fulfills the BENEFIT and Opportunity portions of the Strategy Icon for the selected ideas.

- Use the Benefit and Opportunity results to filter your latest list of potential offerings.

- Finally, run the remaining Offerings through the Offering Ranking Matrix for final selection.

- Create a prioritized list of the final Offerings; maintain them in cluster form if they define different strategies.

Figure 9.9   Step 3 of the strategy transformation process. (From Anthony Sgroi Jr.)

Step 4: Create the Visual Strategy Map (Future State).

- Name the theme of the strategy: Your strategy should consist of a single theme if possible. If you have multiple themes, confirm that they collectively add up to a valid and aligned strategy.

- Create subcategories for the offerings based on your final list of ideas. The subcategories can possible define individual Strategy Icons.

- Complete the Strategy Icon(s).

- List the offerings of your new strategy and assign offering levels. Include the levels of the competitors as well.

- Create your Visual Strategy Map (Future State).

- Analyze the strategy and modify if necessary.

Figure 9.10   Step 4 of the strategy transformation process. (From Anthony Sgroi Jr.)

Chapter 10

Strategy Transformation Example

In the previous chapters, we have discussed the steps and tools necessary to transform a company's strategy into an optimum version using Lean principles. In this chapter, the reader will experience the entire strategy transformation process utilizing the tools previously discussed. This chapter will run through the process in detail, including an explanation for each step. After completion of this chapter, the reader should understand how to derive customer value with minimal waste for the delivery of profitable innovation.

This chapter will work through the entire process using an example[1] of a new natural cleaning product developed by a fictitious chemical cleaning company. In this example, the fictitious chemical cleaning company will be called Acme Cleaning Company. This example will reference some of the information contained in a case study, as well as other various additions for the purposes of explaining the strategy transformation process. This example will run through the entire process, using the creation of a new line of natural cleaners launched in early 2008. The name of the new product will be called Miracle Works, and in this chapter we will illustrate all of the tools for the creation of this business model. The actual case study is cited in the bibliography for those readers who are interested in studying it.

Acme Cleaning Company is a global leader in the areas of traditional chemical cleaners. It has enjoyed growing revenues and is certainly a product leader in its categories. It has been in business for several years and has a good brand name in the marketplace. Like many good companies, it also has competitors and would like to grow the business according to new customer needs and wants. The strategy transformation process is triggered by the understanding that new offerings are necessary to allow for Acme Cleaning Company to differentiate itself from the competition and create a unique and new strategy.

The strategy begins by understanding the current state. We will begin by utilizing the elements of step 1 with respect to the strategy process flowcharts. For simplicity, the elements of step 1 are listed below:

Step 1: Understand the current state—create a visual strategy map (current state).
  – List your offerings, competitor's offerings, and industry factors (if applicable) in a cost-to-benefit grid.
  – Define the levels of all offerings, relative price, and draw the 2-D map.
  – Create a strategy icon and market size gage (the product fulfillment map may assist in the creation of the strategy icon).
  – Draw your visual strategy map (current state).
Test the offerings of the current state:
  – Thoroughly run all offerings through the product fulfillment map to test for consumer value (you can also include the competitor's offerings if you want to test their contribution to consumer value).
  – If this unlocks a new strategy, proceed to step 4.
  – Keep track of the current offerings, fulfilled and unfulfilled items in a current state grid.

Thus, we begin by listing the offerings in a cost-to-benefit grid for Acme Cleaning Company and those of their main competitors. The basic offerings of the traditional chemical cleaning products sold by Acme Cleaning Company are shown in the cost-to-benefit grid in Figure 10.1. In addition, the offerings of their competitors are substantially the same and are depicted in Figure 10.2. I have shifted the levels slightly to allow for the insertion of distinct curves that will be drawn on the visual strategy map (current state). This will allow for the visual verification of all strategies when drawn on the visual strategy map.

The cost-to-benefit grids in this example depict the current state of just about all of the major players in the industry with respect to traditional cleaning chemicals. From the cost-to-benefit grids, we can see that the prices are affordable, as these products are mass-produced and are available in most retail outlets. Hence, this allows for a low-cost production model. The packaging is also inexpensive due to simplicity and economies of scale.

Acme Cleaning Company: Cost-to-Benefit Grid

Traditional Chemical Cleaners			
Customer Offerings and Impacting Factors	*Benefit Level of the Offerings (low, medium, high)*	*Company Cost of the Offering (low, medium, high)*	*Offering Level (user-defined scale, i.e., 1–4)*
Customer purchase price			1
Effective cleaning	High	Low	3.8
Availability	High	Medium	3.8
Strong chemical fragrance	High	Medium	3.2

Figure 10.1 Cost-to-benefit grid for Acme Cleaning Company. (From Anthony Sgroi Jr.)

Main Competitors: Cost-to-Benefit Grid

Traditional Chemical Cleaners			
Customer Offerings and Impacting Factors	*Benefit Level of the Offerings (low, medium, high)*	*Company Cost of the Offering (low, medium, high)*	*Offering Level (user-defined scale, i.e., 1–4)*
Customer purchase price			0.9
Effective cleaning	High	Low	3.7
Availability	High	Medium	3.7
Strong chemical fragrance	High	Medium	3.1

Figure 10.2 Cost-to-benefit grid for the main competitors. (From Anthony Sgroi Jr.)

Therefore, since the average targeted consumer can afford these products, the levels for price are designated a value of approximately 1.

With respect to the remaining attributes, we can state the following for each:

- Effective cleaning: All are effective in cleaning, as they are equipped with agents that break up dirt and kill bacteria (e.g., bleach). Any consumer that purchases an Acme Cleaning Company product would be very satisfied with the promise the company makes. Many competitors also provide this same effective cleaning, and thus the levels are close to 4.

■ Availability: Acme Cleaning Company products and competitive products are available everywhere, from grocery stores to pharmacies to retail outlets. No matter where you shop, it is very likely that you will find Acme Cleaning Company cleaning product you desire, and thus the levels are also close to 4.

■ Strong chemical fragrance: The traditional chemical cleaners all have some sort of differentiating scent. No matter the scent, they all tell the same story of clean. After using traditional chemical products, the user knows that the surface is clean and, in many cases, disinfected. The strong scent certainly triggers the notion of effective cleaning. Despite the scents being strong, they are not unbearable, and thus receive a level close to 3. However, in some cases, the scents are harsh and require ventilation during use, causing some safety concerns.

From the comparison of the two cost-to-benefit grids, it is clear that just about every major player selling traditional cleaning chemicals has the same general strategy. They are basically offering customers the same set of product characteristics. In addition, traditional chemical cleaners are basically all effective in the eyes of the users.

We next begin to define the strategy icons (current state). The strategy icon can be developed by use of the icon generation grid. As seen in Figure 10.3, the icon generation grid is configured to create a single icon for the entire strategy. As a note, if more than one offering feature stands apart, it may be necessary to create an individual strategy icon for a plurality of offering features. This would require a dedicated icon generation grid for each specific offering. The icon is defined by taking a pass through each icon parameter (benefits, opportunity, barriers to imitation, cost position of offerings) for the traditional chemical cleaning products for both Acme Cleaning Company and the competitors. This is shown in Figure 10.3.

Figure 10.3 depicts the results of the analysis of each parameter of the strategy icon for Acme Cleaning Company. If desired, a more detailed analysis can be conducted with respect to the parameters of the icon by reference to the product fulfillment map. However, for purposes of this example, simplicity is best for the description of the process. The analysis takes into account that Acme Cleaning Company is very successful with respect to its traditional chemical cleaning products. Thus, the new growth opportunities

Acme Cleaning Company: Icon Generation Grid

Icon Parameter	Parameter Level	Discussion
Benefits	High (green or black quadrant)	Current products clean very well and function as intended. Many kill bacteria.
Opportunity	Low (red or white quadrant)	Many cleaning products are basically commodities. New growth may be possible by targeting a new target customer group.
Barrier to imitation	Medium (yellow or gray quadrant)	There are some levels of protection, but some aspects are subject to imitation.
Cost position of offerings	High (green or black quadrant)	Currently, the cost is relatively low to deliver.

Figure 10.3   Icon generation grid for Acme Cleaning Company. (From Anthony Sgroi Jr.)

will reflect the understanding that Acme Cleaning Company would not prefer to lose market share of its traditional chemical cleaning products, but rather define a new target customer group for new growth opportunities.

By reference to Figure 10.3, a strategy icon can be drawn. The strategy icon drawn is displayed in Figure 10.4. The icon in Figure 10.4 is illustrated in a black-and-white format with the appropriate levels (black = high, gray = medium, white = low) defined and also includes the graphics. However, if you do not have access to software that has graphics capability, a simpler icon can be used without the graphics, as shown in Figure 10.5.

The strategy icon depicted in Figure 10.4 also suffices with respect to the competitors. This is the result of similar strategies from the chemical companies. Hence, we can deduce that Acme Cleaning Company and its main competitors will have substantially the same curve and strategy icon displayed on the visual strategy map (current state). The last component that we need to address is the market size gage (MSG), which captures the market size and the relative market share.

Current market size information may already be known by companies. If not, these data can be obtained by purchasing market research data. Such research is available from companies such as Nielsen, Kantar, Freedonia, and others. This research information can be costly. In some examples,

Figure 10.4 Strategy icon for Acme Cleaning Company. (From Anthony Sgroi Jr.)

Figure 10.5 Strategy icon for Acme Cleaning Company depicted without graphics. (From Anthony Sgroi Jr.)

Market Size $4.6 Billion
Current Market Share $1.44 Billion

Figure 10.6 Market size gage for Acme Cleaning Company. (From Anthony Sgroi Jr.)

categories of information can cost approximately $5,000 per report. Therefore, companies should ensure that they target the appropriate information to avoid excessive costs. This holds true when defining new markets. Marketers should ensure that they are defining the appropriate target market prior to purchasing such costly data. In this example, we are interested in pursuing new target customers, and thus are not so concerned about the exact market size of current traditional chemical cleaners. Therefore, we will choose to perform a quick analysis to gage the market size. From a quick overview of Freedonia, the U.S. household chemical cleaning market in 2007 was approximately 4.6 billion. Acme Cleaning Company net sales from its 2007 annual report is 4.8 billion. Now Acme Cleaning Company states that 31% of its sales is due to chemical cleaners. Thus, we can approximate 31% of 4.8 billion for 2007 to be about 1.44 billion. This will help us define the approximate market size of 2007. Thus, the market size gage can be shown as in Figure 10.6.

We now have the necessary information to create the visual strategy map (current state). From use of the above discussions and as seen in Figure 10.7, we can list the offerings along the horizontal axis and their corresponding levels on the vertical axis. Along the right portion of the visual strategy map (current state), I have included the icon key with a description of the icon parameters. In close proximity, I have included the market size gage that highlights the total market size and the current share of the market for Acme Cleaning Company. Above the market size gage is a curve key that depicts the line style to properly identify the curve of Acme Cleaning Company and the competitors. Finally, contained in the map is an strategy icon for each curve. In this example, I have utilized a single strategy icon for each strategy. As a note, the reader can verify, as discussed above, that the strategy icons are substantially the same. This is due to the fact that Acme Cleaning Company and its competitors have substantially the same strategies. Nevertheless, the visual strategy map (current state) depicts the entire strategy of Acme Cleaning Company with respect to its competitors for traditional cleaning chemicals. The advantage here is that with a single map, managers can visually verify and understand the entire strategy of their

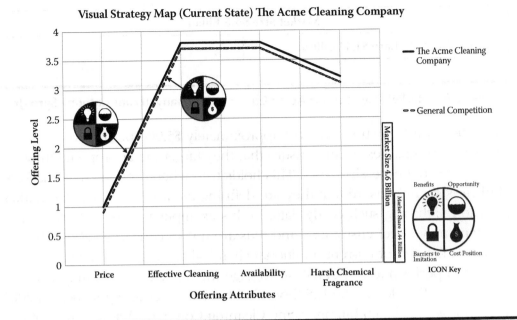

Figure 10.7 Visual strategy map (current state) of Acme Cleaning Company vs. general competition. (From Anthony Sgroi Jr.)

company in relation to their competitors. If desired, the combined competitor market shares can be included. This has been left out intentionally to keep this example as short as possible. Refer to earlier chapters for a more complete form of the market size gage.

Once the visual strategy map current state (VSMCS) is drawn, it is time to analyze the current strategy using the product fulfillment map. To begin using the product fulfillment map, we can work through each product fulfillment target individually, scanning through each corresponding product life cycle touch point. Recall that each cell is labeled using this label convention:

- F-number: *F* denotes fulfillment and *number* indicates the level of fulfillment, where 1 is very low fulfillment and 10 is completely fulfilled; for example, in F-5 the 5 indicates 50% fulfillment (based on a scale of 1 to 10).
- U: *U* indicates unfulfilled.
- If the cell does not apply, it can be left blank.
- An integer is placed in front of each label for purposes of cell identification (tracking), allowing for a written description (i.e., 1F-5, 2U, etc.).

Product Fulfillment Map

	Product Life Cycle Touch Points				
	Acquisition (purchase/ destination/ setup)	*Product Use*	*Barriers to Use (skills or supplements)*	*Product Reliability (service/ maintenance)*	*End of Life (trade-in/ residual value/ disposal)*
Product Fulfillment					
Utility (job completion)		1F-10			
Risk (safety, technical, etc.)		1U			2U
Simplicity or Convenience	2F-10				
Emotion or Social Well-Being		3U			
Supports Green Movement		4U			5U
Financial					

Figure 10.8   Current state product fulfillment analysis. (From Anthony Sgroi Jr.)

The product fulfillment map is illustrated in Figure 10.8 for the current state. An explanation of the current state is as follows. For the fulfilled items:

- 1F-10 indicates that current chemical cleaners boost customer productivity during the use stage; traditional cleaners provide very effective cleaning.
- 2F-10 indicates that current chemical cleaners are simple and convenient in the purchase stage; they are available everywhere, such as grocery stores, department stores, pharmacies, etc.

For the unfulfilled items:

■ 1U indicates that current chemical products have some risk associated with them due to the harsh chemicals. Gloves are sometimes required, in some cases harsh vapors exist, and storage can be an issue with children in the home.
■ 2U indicates risk in the disposal stage. It is not proper to pour chemicals in the sink, outside, etc.
■ 3U indicates a block to the emotional side. Storing chemicals for use in the house near children is always a concern (risk/safety).
■ 4U and 5U indicate blocks to environmental friendliness during the use and disposal stage. Many harsh chemicals are not good for the environment.

Based on the analysis, it is clear that traditional chemical cleaners provide productive cleaning and are available in many convenient locations. In addition, we have identified five unfulfilled items. As explained previously, we can choose to attack some of these unfulfilled items and immediately modify our strategy to create a potential new future state. However, based on the list of unfulfilled items, there is no quick modification that comes to mind that can transform the strategy. Therefore, it would seem proper to run through a more detailed idea generation exercise. This could result in the definition of a new target market and should unlock new and higher levels of value for the new target market. At this time, we will capture the current state by filling out a current state grid. This will allow for the capture of fulfilled items, unfulfilled items, current offerings, and impacting factors. The entire current state is captured in list form in the current state grid and is illustrated in Figure 10.9.

Figure 10.9 concludes step 1 of understanding the current state. The next series of events involve the acquisition of new potential ideas based on working with customers and generating ideas from either the internal or external industry perspective or a combination of both. These events define step 2 of the strategy transformation process. As with step 1, I have included the events of step 2 from the process flowchart.

Step 2: Strategy modification (talk to customers).
  – Perform voice of customer analysis of your offerings and those common in your industry.
  – Track the feedback by completing a customer feedback grid.

Current State Grid (Acme Cleaning Company)

Buyer utility map (fulfilled items)	Current offerings and impacting factors
• Productive in the product use stage • Convenient in the acquisition stage	• Effective cleaning • Availability • Harsh chemical fragrance
Buyer utility map (unfulfilled items) • Harsh chemicals can be a risk in the use stage (safety). • Risk in the disposal stage • Concern when storing chemicals when children are in the home	

Figure 10.9 Current state grid (Acme Cleaning Company). (From Anthony Sgroi Jr.)

- Generate new potential offerings based on customer input (utilize internal or external industry perspectives).
- If multiple ideas can form alternate themes, group the new ideas into distinct groups or clusters.

Acme Cleaning Company then decided to gain the voice of the customer. It began to study the ways customers experience their current chemical cleaning products. It wanted to gain insight on how people used and stored the various products. During this study, Acme Cleaning Company performed some various internal industry perspective studies, beginning with interviews, focus groups, and finally, home cleaning studies (go and see), watching people clean their homes. They determined that women were the individuals making 85% of the purchase decisions for chemical cleaning products. Acme Cleaning Company then focused its research on all forms of chemical cleaning products in hopes that new opportunities could be discovered. After the study, Acme Cleaning Company identified a large group sharing a large commonality. The group was not defined by age, income, or geography, but had a shared belief that chemicals might be dangerous to a family's health and well-being. The shared belief did not motivate a concern for the environment or to act in a socially responsible manner. Rather, the shared belief defined a target customer group motivated to keep their families safe as one of their main roles in life. Thus, this group was dubbed the chemical-avoiding naturalist and represented a large potential market.

To gain a better understanding of the chemical-avoiding naturalist, Acme Cleaning Company performed in-depth customer interviews and followed up with in-home visual studies to observe people cleaning with chemicals. The mannerisms by those using chemical cleaners highlighted the fact that many women had concerns using and storing chemicals in the home. In this exploration stage, many customers talked about "kitchen lab" chemistry, using vinegar and water to clean instead of harsh "gagging" chemicals. When asked why these people did not use natural cleaners, the responses indicated that these people (among others) were extremely skeptical of "green" products currently available on the market. All those who tried these green products became dissatisfied, as they could not effectively clean, and thus repeat purchases or word-of-mouth recommendations did not result. The use of kitchen lab chemistry did boost emotional well-being for some; however, those using these alternatives did not like the vinegar smell, and instead strongly preferred a pleasant fragrance. By the end of the exploration stage, Acme Cleaning Company confirmed the discovery of a new market segment consisting of the chemical-avoiding naturalist. It determined that the customers of this new market segment would switch to natural products if their skepticism could be eliminated. In addition to keeping the home safe, Acme Cleaning Company discovered these explicit customer requirements:

■ Support their deep emotional commitment to protect their family by dramatically reducing the use of harsh chemicals
■ Not compromise functional performance
■ Not compromise convenience or ease of use
■ Be priced right
■ Be readily available
■ Offer assurance that the cleaner comes from a credible and trustworthy source (eliminating skepticism)

The major feedback from spending time with customers is a result of the internal perspective approach. This feedback from customers and competitor's customers can be captured in a customer feedback grid. This feedback will serve as a guide when generating new ideas from the external perspective approach since there is now a better understanding of what is important to customers. The results from the customer feedback grid are shown in Figure 10.10.

I will run this example through all components of the external perspective approach to illustrate how the tools can unlock or confirm certain offerings. The readers of this book may choose to run through all components or less, if desired. However, I recommend utilizing all of the components of the

Customer Feedback Grid

Problems customers are solving	Customer wants
• Cleaning around the home • Effective and convenient cleaning • Home safety using and storing chemical cleaners	• Safe and effective cleaners that are safe to keep in the house • Better understanding of green cleaners due to skepticism
Customer pain points	Unnecessary offerings
• Current green products are safer but do not provide effective cleaning • Most are skeptical that green products are not effective	• Harsh chemical fragrance • Gagging from harsh chemicals
Lacking offerings	Other important requirements
• Effectiveness of safe cleaners • Safer products are not readily available everywhere	• Priced right • Available everywhere • Produced by a credible source • Pleasant fragrance • Ease of use

Figure 10.10   Results of customer feedback. (From Anthony Sgroi Jr.)

external perspective approach, as this increases the chance of triggering a new idea, resulting in an improved strategy.

As previously explained, instead of looking within the confines of a company's business, companies can look beyond them to create a totally new business model. First, we will begin this process by looking to alternate industries. In addition to alternate industries, we will also look to alternate strategic groups, across the different buyer groups, and across complementary product and service offerings; add or remove functional or emotional orientations of an industry; and finally, identify new trends across time. This process will be performed by running through the tools illustrated in the idea generation chapter, followed by a brief discussion of each. We begin looking to alternate industries by working with the substitute-alternative chart (Figure 10.11) and the benefit–disadvantage chart (Figure 10.12).

Looking to alternate industries has certainly generated many ideas. However, the alternatives do not seem that they would fit the target customer. In many cases, some of the ideas generated would create various

Substitute–Alternative Chart

Industry	Basic Objective	Substitute Offering Different form, same function	Alternative Offerings Different form, different function, same objective
Liquid chemical cleaners	Cleaning Disinfecting Breaking up dirt Etc.	Solvents Alcohol Acetone Paint thinners	Mechanical cleaning: Sand paper Razor scraping Automotive buffing compounds High-pressure washing
Notes	Effective	Still are chemical based	Potentially damaging

Figure 10.11 Analysis using the substitute–alternative chart. (From Anthony Sgroi Jr.)

Benefit–Disadvantage Chart: Chemical Cleaning

	Alternative	Main Disadvantage	Main Benefit
Your industry	Chemical cleaners	Safety	Effectiveness
Industry 2	Solvents	Damage to surfaces, safety	Quick-drying evaporation of the liquid
Industry 3	Automotive compounds	Damage to surfaces, safety	Abrasiveness
Industry 4	Razor scraping	Damage to surfaces, surfaces must be flat, safety	Effectiveness
Industry 5	Sandpaper	Damage to surfaces	Very effective
	Good ideas, but require preliminary ranking with respect to fitting the need of the target customer group		

Figure 10.12 Analysis using the benefit–disadvantage chart. (From Anthony Sgroi Jr.)

Strategic Group Blending Chart

Strategic Group	Disadvantages	Benefits
Liquid chemical cleaners	Safety	Effectiveness
Green liquid cleaners	Effectiveness	Safety
Comparison	It is clear that green cleaners are safer than traditional chemical cleaners. If an effective and safe formula can be created at an affordable price, this could have a large potential.	

Figure 10.13 Analysis using the strategic group blending chart. (From Anthony Sgroi Jr.)

safety concerns and can also damage surfaces to be cleaned. We will verify these concerns during the ranking process.

Next, we will move on to looking at alternative strategic groups. By utilizing the strategic group blending chart (Figure 10.13), we can list one or more ideas that eliminate or mitigate the main disadvantage of our current offerings, focusing on the aspect of an alternate strategic group within the same industry. If you recall, alternate strategic groups focus on the same types of customer needs, but along different dimensions. For example, some may include more elaborate and expensive solutions, whereas others can include simple, lower-cost solutions. Regarding chemical cleaning, the alternate strategic groups comparable to traditional (existing) liquid chemicals that come to mind are green liquid cleaners, homemade solutions (i.e., baking soda, vinegar cocktails, bleach-water mixtures), and natural or green cleaners. Judging from this list, the optimum strategic group that has commercial potential would be the natural or green cleaners.

This exercise is almost obvious from our study of the target customer. It would seem that if a very effective natural green cleaner can be developed that is available everywhere, trusted, affordable, and safe for children and pets, consumers would purchase this offering.

Next, we look across the different buyer groups to verify if the company is marketing to those who make the purchase decision. This is accomplished by the exercise using the buyer chain grid. The results are shown in Figure 10.14. From these results, we can verify that our marketing efforts properly focus on the target customer, which is comprised of women. Therefore, no new activity is necessary with respect to this area, except we may consider modifying our packaging to have more of a feminine appeal.

Buyer Chain Grid

	Purchasers	Users	Influencers
Which group are your offerings focused on?		Women	
Who makes the purchase decision?		Women	

↓

Focus already achieved, as these 2 columns are aligned vertically

Figure 10.14 Analysis using the buyer chain grid. (From Anthony Sgroi Jr.)

Next, we look across complementary product and service offerings with respect to the category of natural cleaning. To find the total solution, we can run through the complementary offering grid and analyze the pain points before, during, and after the use of current green cleaners. The results of the complementary offering grid are illustrated in Figure 10.15.

Complementary Offering Grid

	Before	During	After
Pain point	Hard to find natural cleaners (not available in most retailers) Ineffective terminology on products	Not effective during cleaning No appropriate fragrance to indicate clean	Fear that surfaces are not properly cleaned
Pain point elimination method	As a reputable supplier of liquid chemical cleaning products, we will use our technology and our vendor relationships to create an effective natural cleaner that will have a fragrance that will indicate the effectiveness of our new product. We will make it available in all of our channels, so it will be available to everyone. We will also properly communicate the value the product can bring.		

Figure 10.15 Analysis using the complementary offering grid. (From Anthony Sgroi Jr.)

From the results shown in Figure 10.15, we confirm the already known fact that natural cleaners are not preferred and can be difficult to find. We also know that natural cleaners (purchased and homemade) are not very effective and do not have a strong fragrance to indicate the surfaces have been cleaned properly. Also, current green cleaners do not communicate their ability to clean, as the current terminology is ineffective. Thus, this exercise confirms the key offering features that can target the chemical-avoiding naturalist.

The next area to look to is the functional emotional components of the offerings. Are the offerings adding too much function and not enough emotion? Or is the reverse the case? Using this tool, we can verify if the use of natural green cleaners complements our existing business model. The process of using the functional emotional grid is shown in Figure 10.16.

This exercise confirms that natural cleaners will address the emotional concerns of the target customers. Safety is always a large emotional component for people that use products having safety concerns. Thus, by ensuring effective and safe cleaning as well as safe storage, the emotional component can be satisfied and unlock new growth.

Functional Emotional Grid

	Functional Appeal	*Emotional Appeal*
Your company: Acme Cleaning Company	Current liquid chemical cleaners are effective but do not add to the emotional feeling of safety.	
Competitor: Green Cleaners (for this potential category)		Natural green liquid cleaners are safe, and this allows people to feel better about using and storing cleaners
There is an opportunity to add an emotional appeal to liquid cleaners by ensuring family safety as green cleaners claim. There is also an opportunity to add function to current green liquid cleaners with an effective formula. This will stimulate growth for our business if the customer concerns are addressed properly from both the functional and emotional perspectives.		

Figure 10.16 Analysis using the functional emotional grid. (From Anthony Sgroi Jr.)

Time Trend Matrix

Trends Applicable to Your Business	Predictability Can you visualize the future activities based on this trend?	Staying Power Will this trend last?	Influence Factor Will many people be influenced by this trend?
Enter trend for analysis or discussion: Safe and effective natural cleaners	More and more users are searching for *safer* liquid cleaners to be used and stored within the home. The need is clearly defined.	Many companies are developing green cleaning products. When they become effective, they will have enormous staying power. Users continue to request the availability.	Most houses include a family with children or visiting grandchildren. If effective safer alternatives are available and are affordable, more people will switch to these types of products.
Business Assessment	We will create an effective natural cleaning product that will have high levels of effectiveness compared to current chemical cleaners. We will leverage our *brand name* and educate the public on the effectiveness of this new product. We will seek endorsements from well-known and respected organizations to further communicate our cleaning effectiveness and family safety. We are confident that this trend will continue if offered at an affordable price.		

Figure 10.17 Analysis using the time trend matrix. (From Anthony Sgroi Jr.)

Finally, we verify if new trends can be identified or created across time by running the concept of natural cleaners through the time trend matrix. The results of this exercise are shown in Figure 10.17.

From the time trend matrix, it is clear that this trend should be sustainable for an acceptable duration. People will always desire safety for their children and pets, as families will always be created and pets will always be a key part of many families. Thus, the cost to develop an effective and safe natural cleaner can be justified in the creation of a new brand of natural liquid cleaners.

This completes the ideation from the external perspective. The results are summarized in Figure 10.18. In addition, it is clear that natural cleaners seem the most promising. We can also verify that this exercise did not produce

External Perspective Summary

External Perspective Component	Action Items
Alternate industries	Ideas from chosen alternate industries cause damage to surfaces or have home safety concerns
Alternate strategic group	Strategic group of green cleaning provides insight to a highly desirable product if effectiveness can be achieved
Buyer chain (purchase decision)	Already achieved: We are targeting the customers making the purchase decisions; 85% of women are the actual users and purchase liquid cleaners
Complementary offerings	Creating a highly effective natural cleaner from a credible source will address all pain points before, during, and after the purchase
Functional/emotional	Product safety will allow women to feel good about their purchase decision (keep family safe)
Time trend	Natural cleaning has a clear trajectory and staying power if it can be made effective for cleaning

Figure 10.18 Summary of ideas generated from the external perspective analysis. (From Anthony Sgroi Jr.)

ideas having multiple themes. Thus, there is no need to group the new ideas into distinct groups or clusters.

The summary, as shown in Figure 10.18, concludes the events of step 2. At this point, we have captured a series of new potential ideas and are ready for the events of step 3, where the new ideas are ranked and prioritized. The events for step 3 are shown below.

Step 3: Rank and prioritize the new ideas.
  – Run all new ideas through the product fulfillment map as a first pass (eliminate unwanted ideas).
  – Begin to list and rank the selected ideas in an idea prefilter grid to find the better ideas for analysis.
  – Perform an analysis of the optimum ideas. Get customer feedback of new offerings by running through the Kano evaluation table and obtaining the relative importance for each potential idea. Also,

obtain importance and satisfaction scores for the potential ideas. Process the data through the opportunity calculator and create a ranked opportunity score for your list. This fulfills the benefit and opportunity portions of the strategy icon for the selected ideas.
- Use the benefit and opportunity results to filter your latest list of potential offerings.
- Finally, run the remaining offerings through the offering ranking matrix for final selection.
- Create a prioritized list of the final offerings. Maintain them in cluster form if they define different strategies.

In order to begin prefiltering our new ideas, we should first list all of the potential items for consideration. We begin by listing the key learnings from the customer feedback grid, followed by the newly generated ideas. Based on our study, it seems we will be pursuing the natural cleaner strategy, and thus our ideas will support the theme of natural cleaners. All of the general ideas and factors are:

- Safe to keep in the house
- Clean effectively
- Eliminate skepticism and have a better understanding of natural or green cleaners (effective terminology and trust)
- Eliminate harsh chemicals (gagging)
- Affordably priced
- Available everywhere
- Boost emotional well-being
- Produced by a credible source
- Have pleasant fragrance
- Are easy to use
- Solvents
- Alcohol
- Acetones and paint thinners
- Sandpaper
- Razor scraping
- Automotive buffing compound
- High-pressure washing

We can take these ideas and begin to filter them. The first intention is to eliminate those ideas that are not aligned with customer or company values. We

Ideas Supporting Natural Cleaners

Idea	Status	Notes
Home safety	Keep	Prioritize later (i.e., Kano)
Effective cleaning	Keep	Prioritize later (i.e., Kano)
Effective terminology (reduce skeptism)	Keep	Prioritize later (i.e., Kano)
Harsh chemical fragrance	Eliminate	Safety during use and disposal
Affordable	Keep	Analyze levels later
Availability	Keep	Prioritize later (i.e., Kano)
Credible source (reduce skeptism)	Keep	Prioritize later (i.e., Kano)
Solvents	Keep	Prioritize later (i.e., Kano)
Alcohol	Eliminate	Safety during use and disposal, potential damage to property
Acetones—paint thinners	Eliminate	Safety during use and disposal, potential damage to property
Sandpaper pads	Keep	Prioritize later (i.e., Kano)
Razor scraping	Eliminate	Safety during use and disposal, potential damage to property
Automotive buffing compounds	Keep	May provide potential cleaning solutions
Pressure washing	Eliminate	Safety, cost, and damage concern
Emotional well-being	Keep	Analyze levels later
Produced by a credible source	Keep	Prioritize later (i.e., Kano)
Pleasant fragrance	Keep	Prioritize later (i.e., Kano)
Ease of use	Keep	Prioritize later (i.e., Kano)

Figure 10.19 Listing of potential ideas. (From Anthony Sgroi Jr.)

can tabulate the new potential ideas and provide notes as per the status (eliminate or keep). Those to keep will be subject to a detailed analysis and ranked. The ideas, with their corresponding notes, are illustrated in Figure 10.19, and those ideas eliminated reference an analysis using the product fulfillment map.

Idea Prefilter Grid (Natural Cleaners) Quick Analysis

	Enter Levels (low, medium, high)				
	Customer Value (benefits)	Cost of Offering	Market Size	Opportunity Level	Barrier to Imitation
Home safety	High	Medium	High	High	High
Effective cleaning	High	Medium	High	High	High
Availability	Medium	Medium	High	High	Medium
Pleasant fragrance	High	Low	High	Medium	Medium
Emotional well-being	Medium-high	Medium	High	High	Low
Availability	High	Medium	High	High	Medium
Ease of use	High	Medium	High	High	High
Automotive buffing compounds	Low-medium	High	Low	Low	Low
Credible source	High	Low	High	High	High
Effective terminology and trust	High	Low	High	High	Low
Solvents	Medium	Medium	Medium	Medium	Medium
Sandpaper pads	Medium	Medium	Medium	Medium	Low

Figure 10.20   Using the idea prefiltering grid. (From Anthony Sgroi Jr.)

The ideas that are to be kept from Figure 10.19 can now be inserted into the idea prefilter grid. This allows for another round of idea elimination, and additional prioritization. As we can verify from Figure 10.20, we performed an adequate job of idea selection and filtering, as those that are left in the idea prefilter grid show medium-high levels of potential. The only exceptions are solvents, sandpaper pads, and automotive buffing compounds. We can see right away that automotive buffing compounds would define an undesirable strategy icon. The customer benefits are not high enough to justify a high cost. The market size would also be low, as this could damage surfaces, except for items like stove tops and other hard, nonscratchable items. Thus, it would seem that the opportunity is low, as this market seems to already be satisfied. Since we are not specialized in this technology, we may have to license with a manufacturer, and thus we would not have any forms of patent protection. Hence, this idea can be eliminated from use of the idea prefilter grid.

We can now subject the rest of the ideas to a Kano evaluation. To begin, we define a series of questions in the Kano format. We are interested in determining the offering requirement type (must-have, one-dimensional, and attractive) and the importance and satisfaction ratings to compute the ranked opportunity scores. Thus, for each potential offering (idea) we will arrange a set of questions that asks participants (30 participants) to answer the functional and dysfunction forms of the feature question. This will determine the requirement type. We then include the importance and satisfaction questions so we can compute the opportunity scores. This is illustrated in Figure 10.21 for the offering idea of pleasant fragrance. If desired, one can include asking targeted customers to rate the level of satisfaction of certain competitors' offerings. The remaining ideas are repeated, similar to Figure 10.21, and included in the questionnaire.

After all 30 participants have been administered the questionnaire, the answers are evaluated by running them through the Kano evaluation table, calculating the opportunity scores, and finally, selecting using majority rules or other statistical means. The results are illustrated in Figure 10.22 based on majority selection. Refer to the earlier chapters to refresh your memory.

Now we can rank the ideas based on the opportunity scores. This is shown in Figure 10.23. As a note, when equal opportunity scores are found, they should be subranked according to those having the larger importance rating, as is done in Figure 10.23.

From Figure 10.23, we can verify that we have satisfied a series of must-have requirements as well as two attractive requirements. The one-dimensional requirements will also have adequate levels to ensure customer satisfaction. The data also illustrate a good distribution of important offerings. In some areas, the data seem to be conflicting, such as the lower than expected opportunity score of 5 for pleasant fragrance. Many times customers do not answer questions in a way that complements what they say during ethnographic research. This is why decision makers must go and see for themselves. Thus, although the opportunity is only a 5, decision makers

Potential Feature: Pleasant Fragrance for a Natural and Effective Cleaner

If your natural and effective cleaner had a pleasant fragrance, how would you feel?	1. I like it that way. 2. It must be that way. 3. I am neutral. 4. I can live with it that way. 5. I dislike it that way.
If your natural and effective cleaner did not have a pleasant fragrance, how would you feel?	1. I like it that way. 2. It must be that way. 3. I am neutral. 4. I can live with it that way. 5. I dislike it that way.
How important is it to have a pleasant fragrance for a natural and effective cleaner? (1 = not important, 10 = very important)	1 2 3 4 5 6 7 8 9 10 Circle the most appropriate score.
How satisfied are you with the fragrances of natural cleaners currently available on the market? (1 = not important, 10 = very important)	1 2 3 4 5 6 7 8 9 10 Circle the most appropriate score.

Figure 10.21 Sample questions for a specific product feature taken from a questionnaire. (From Anthony Sgroi Jr.)

should not ignore these offerings, as these must complement the more important features, namely, effective cleaning. In addition, lower opportunity scores may be subject to higher levels of the offerings to ensure customer satisfaction. Therefore, our strategy should have high levels of pleasant fragrance, among the others to enhance customer satisfaction. This also makes sense, as pleasant fragrance is a one-dimensional requirement, and the more that is given, the more satisfied customers will be. The goal is to create a strategy in which the offerings complement one another and collectively add up to high levels of valuable benefits. We cannot lose sight that questionnaires ask questions on an individual basis, but the strategy must be envisioned on a collective basis. Depending on the way questions are asked or interpreted, the answers obtained may potentially be misleading.

The last ideas (solvents and sandpaper pads) do not seem promising and may not be applicable for a few reasons. One reason is that solvents and

Potential Offering (Idea)	Offering Type	Importance	Satisfaction	Opportunity
Home safety	M	10	4	6
Effective cleaning	M	10	2	8
Availability	A	8	2	6
Pleasant fragrance	O	8	3	5
Solvents	O	5	4	1
Sandpaper pads	O	4	8	–4
Emotional well-being	O	8	4	4
Ease of use	O	8	2	6
Credible source	M	8	2	6
Effective terminology and trust	A	9	1	8

Figure 10.22   Calculation of opportunity scores. (From Anthony Sgroi Jr.)

sandpaper pads do not complement the strategy of natural cleaning. In addition, the importance scores are rather low, and the current satisfaction scores are rather high. Therefore, the opportunities are low. However, before we eliminate these ideas, let us subject them to final ranking.

We can run the offerings through the offering ranking matrix for final selection. With respect to weights, I have doubled the level of barrier to imitation to 20, as I feel that the entire success on this project is the ability to prevent others from imitation. The key to success will be in the formula, and I would like to see high levels of barrier to imitation. Therefore, the results are tabulated in Figure 10.24, and the final ranked results are shown in Figure 10.25. As a note, the importance scores trigger the benefit scores as indicated by customers. The opportunity scores are taken from our early analysis, as shown in Figures 10.22 and 10.23. The barriers to imitation and the cost positions are analyzed individually for each potential offering.

As suspected, the ideas of utilizing solvents and sandpaper pads are not feasible, as they receive very low percentage scores of 0.42 and 0.24, respectively. Therefore, we can remove them from the final list.

We have now completed step 3 of the strategy transformation process. The next and final step will comprise the activities to draw our visual strategy map (future state). However, there are a few tasks necessary to perform

Potential Offering (Idea)	Offering Type	Importance	Satisfaction	Opportunity
Effective cleaning	M	10	2	8
Effective terminology and trust	A	9	1	8
Home safety	M	10	4	6
Availability	A	8	2	6
Ease of use	O	8	2	6
Credible source	M	8	2	6
Pleasant fragrance	O	8	3	5
Emotional well-being	O	8	4	4
Solvents	O	5	4	1
Sandpaper pads	O	4	8	−4

Figure 10.23 Ranked opportunity scores. (From Anthony Sgroi Jr.)

Offering Dimensions	Value (Benefits)	Opportunity	Barrier to Imitation	Cost Position of Offering		
Symbol					Total Score	% of Perfect Score
Perfect Possible Score	10	10	20	10	50	N/A
Offering Attributes						
Effective Cleaning	10	8	18	5	41	0.82
Effective Terminology and Trust	9	8	10	2	29	0.58
Home Safety	10	6	18	5	39	0.78
Availability	8	6	15	6	35	0.70
Ease of Use	8	6	18	5	37	0.74
Credible Source	8	6	15	6	35	0.70
Pleasant Fragrance	8	5	18	5	36	0.72
Emotional Wellbeing	8	4	18	5	35	0.70
Solvents	5	1	10	5	21	0.42
Sandpaper Pads	4	0	3	5	12	0.24

Figure 10.24 Using the offering ranking matrix. (From Anthony Sgroi Jr.)

Offering Dimensions	Value (Benefits)	Opportunity	Barrier to Imitation	Cost Position of Offering		
Symbol					Total Score	% of Perfect Score
Perfect Possible Score	10	10	20	10	50	N/A
Offering Attributes						
Effective Cleaning	10	8	18	5	41	0.82
Home Safety	10	6	18	5	39	0.78
Ease of Use	8	6	18	5	37	0.74
Pleasant Fragrance	8	5	18	5	36	0.72
Availability	8	6	15	6	35	0.70
Credible Source	8	6	15	6	35	0.70
Emotional Wellbeing	8	4	18	5	35	0.70
Effective Terminology and Trust	9	8	10	2	29	0.58
Solvents	5	1	10	5	21	0.42
Sandpaper Pads	4	0	3	5	12	0.21

Figure 10.25 The offering ranking matrix ranked. (From Anthony Sgroi Jr.)

before we can draw the visual strategy map (future state). They are the items of step 4:

Step 4: Create the visual strategy map (future state).
  – Name the theme of the strategy: Your strategy should consist of a single theme, if possible. If you have multiple themes, confirm that they collectively add up to a valid and aligned strategy.
  – Create subcategories for the offerings based on your final list of ideas. The subcategories can possibly define individual strategy icons.
  – Complete the strategy icon(s).
  – List the offerings of your new strategy and assign offering levels. Include the levels of the competitors as well.
  – Create your visual strategy map (future state).
  – Analyze the strategy and modify if necessary.

In this case, there is one theme. The theme will be natural liquid cleaners, and the offerings from our final ranking are:

■ Effective cleaning
■ Home safety
■ Ease of use

- Pleasant fragrance
- Availability
- Credible source
- Emotional well-being
- Effective terminology and trust

In this example, we can create a dominant subcategory. The offerings effective cleaning, home safety, ease of use, and pleasant fragrance are all dependent on the chemical formula. Therefore, the dominant subcategory can be titled "chemical formula." We can also base the strategy icon on this subcategory for our entire strategy. The offerings of availability, credible source, and effective terminology and trust are a result of our business model practices and do not require a strategy icon. Finally, emotional well-being is a result of the combination of the offerings, and thus is denoted as an industry factor.

Two of the four quadrants with respect to the strategy icon (benefits and opportunity) have already been analyzed. Benefits are directly related to the importance ratings, where opportunity is a calculation of importance minus satisfaction. This makes sense, as high importance dictates high benefits to be targeted. Since the offerings of the strategy complement each other, they collectively add up to high consumer benefits and high levels of opportunity. The remaining two items of the strategy icon can be completed via a discussion.

With respect to barriers to imitation, chemical companies have always understood that copying formulas or the process of making chemical products has always been a challenge for competitors to imitate. Therefore, our newly developed formula will be protected by trade secrets. In addition, our channel partners have significant trust in our company. We will illustrate how our natural cleaners will result in highly satisfied customers, unlike current green products in the marketplace. This trust will most likely prevent our channel partners from switching to one or more products that may be developed by our competitors in the future. Thus, we can safely surmise that we have achieved high levels of barriers to imitation.

With respect to cost position, we understand that new sales will absorb considerable research and development costs to arrive at the best and most effective formula that adheres to all of the customer requirements. In addition, we also understand that this potential market size may be smaller than the lower-cost traditional chemical cleaner market. Therefore, we will most likely experience lower sales volume. Hence, we should consider that we

Figure 10.26 Proposed future strategy icon of the new offering. (From Anthony Sgroi Jr.)

will have a medium-level cost position to deliver this product to our target market. However, we also know that we can price higher than our traditional chemical cleaning products, and yet still price lower than current ineffective green products. Therefore, we feel that we have an optimum cost position for our new natural cleaner.

With these discussions in mind and our previous analysis, we have identified an optimum strategy icon, which is illustrated in Figure 10.26.

We now define the strategy icon for our main competitors. In this case, our main competitors are current green cleaners as well as some traditional chemicals, as some customers may refuse to purchase natural cleaners. For current green cleaners, we have already discussed the ineffectiveness of their cleaning ability. Also, they are not available in many outlets, and thus are subjected to low opportunity levels. Even though the chemistry is ineffective, there still exists some sort of barrier to imitation, as any chemical formula has some level of difficulty for imitation. Finally, the cost position is medium, as reflected by the higher offering prices and low volumes. Therefore, the strategy icon for current green cleaners is illustrated in Figure 10.27.

Finally, we can generate a strategy icon for traditional chemical cleaners. Although we are targeting the chemical-avoiding naturalist, it doesn't hurt us to include a strategy icon for traditional chemicals. We discussed the

Figure 10.27   Future strategy icon for current green chemicals based on the attributes of the new offering. (From Anthony Sgroi Jr.)

effectiveness of traditional chemicals; however, there is a safety risk in the use and storage stage. Thus, the risk portion in relation to the cleaning benefits, as compared to effective natural cleaners, causes the benefit level to be medium on a comparative basis. Since traditional chemicals are commoditized, the opportunity levels are low. With respect to barriers to imitation, all chemical companies have some levels of protection from imitation, and thus have medium levels along this parameter. The argument for medium instead of high is that some formulas have been copied in the marketplace (e.g., bleach, ammonia). Finally, the cost position is optimum, as these companies have enjoyed large volumes of sales and have perfected the formulas. Therefore, the strategy icon for traditional chemical companies is depicted in Figure 10.28.

We can finally list all of the offerings for our new strategy and assign the offering levels for them. We will at the same time include the offering levels of the current competitors. This may take a few iterations until accuracy occurs. Be patient in this step so accuracy is maintained. This list is illustrated in Figure 10.29.

The last item to generate is the market size gage. In this example, I am going to formulate a quick estimation of the market size. Of course, more elaborate means are possible with better data. However, for purposes of this illustration, this method will suffice. Let us look to www.census.gov for

Figure 10.28   Future strategy icon for current traditional chemicals based on the attributes of the new offering. (From Anthony Sgroi Jr.)

Assigned Offering Levels (Our Company and Competitors)

Offering Name	Our Company Levels	Current Green Levels	Traditional Chemical Levels
Offering price	2	3.8	1
Effective cleaning	3.9	1.4	3.8
Home safety	3.9	3.0	0.5
Ease of use	3.4	1.5	3.8
Pleasant fragrance	3.5	1.5	0.8
Availability	3.5	1.5	3.8
Credible source	3.8	0.5	3.8
Emotional well-being	3.2	3	0.5
Effective terminology and trust	3.8	0.8	3.5

Figure 10.29   The new offering attributes and their respected levels. (From Anthony Sgroi Jr.)

Total Market Size	Households Having Children Younger Than 9 Years of Age	17,302,500
Awareness	Percent of potential customers we could make aware of the product (i.e., advertising, effective packaging)	50%
Trial	Percent of aware customers who are willing to try product (have actual interest)	60%
Availability	Percent of distributors we can convince to carry product (grocery, mass, etc.)	80%
Repeat	Percent of those who are willing to try the product to actually purchase the product	50%
Forecasted families to be interested	The total possible target group is multiplied by the corresponding percentages to obtain the forecast	2,076,300
Annual purchases in dollars	This represents the annual spending for the new natural cleaner in the first year for each new customer	$20
First-year annual revenue	This represents gross sales or top-line revenue	$41,526,000

Figure 10.30 Potential market size for Acme Cleaning Company using ATAR. (From Anthony Sgroi Jr.)

the number of households with children under the age of 18. For 2010, this number is 34,605,000. We can cut this number in half to gage the number of households having children under 9. This is about 17,302,500 families. Therefore, if we can reach all of these families, and their annual purchase for chemical cleaners is about $20 annually, the total market size would be about $346 million in revenue (top line). Now we can use an awareness-trial-availability-repeat (ATAR) analysis to approximate the first year's potential revenue. From a somewhat conservative perspective, this calculates to approximately $42 million in revenue (top line). The first year's potential revenue is depicted in Figure 10.30.

We are now ready to create our visual strategy map future state (VSMFS). We take the offerings and map the names on the horizontal axis and locate their respective offering levels for our company and our competitors along the vertical axis. We then connect these points to form distinct curves. In some cases,

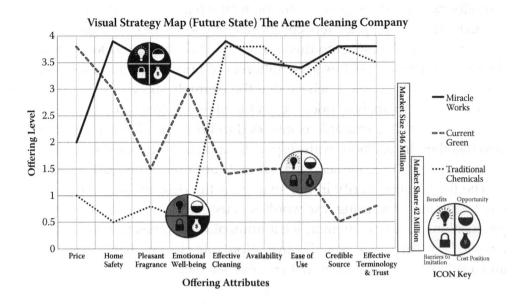

Figure 10.31 Future state visual strategy map for Miracle Works Offered by Acme Cleaning Company. (From Anthony Sgroi Jr.)

we may be forced to move certain offerings around to achieve the smoothest curves possible. We insert the strategy icons and the market size gage. The VSMFS is illustrated in Figure 10.31 for the newly transformed strategy.

Next, we study the strategy. First, we want to ensure that our curve is different than that of our competitors. We can easily verify this upon inspection. The different curve defines a unique strategy. A unique strategy ensures us that we are offering something different. In addition, our process should define a strategy more in tune to what customers want. If our curves matched those of our competitors', we would not be offering anything different. Next, we compare the levels of the offerings. From our analysis of the customer, we feel that the levels are where they need to be. Finally, we can compare the strategy icons. Our strategy provides better value at the same or better cost position. This is even the case compared to traditional cleaning products. We can also verify from the strategy icons that our new strategy does represent a larger opportunity than that of our competitors. This means that we have targeted important characteristics that are not fully satisfied. Finally, we can verify that we have high levels of barriers to imitation.

With respect to the market size gage, we can see that after the first year's sales, we still have tremendous opportunities to gain additional market share. This will enable long-term growth. Finally, our offering price is lower than our green competitors'. With the levels of benefits we are offering, we feel that our offering price does in fact coincide with what we are offering. We also feel that our offering price reflects affordability levels of our target customers.

As a note, with respect to this example, I chose not to include running through the profit model exercise in terms of price elasticity in relation to the fixed and variable costs. I believe that the example shown in Chapter 5 fully illustrates how to analyze price vs. profitability. I therefore decided to leave this step out, as this example is intended to bring the elements of the process together. In addition, with respect to applying the elements of this book to your strategy, I recommend that all tools are used or at least considered.

The final item to verify in our strategy is the description. Can the strategy be summarized using few words so customers can understand the value proposition? As a first attempt, what immediately comes to mind is the following: "A natural, safe, yet effective affordable cleaner that is easy to use and available everywhere from a credible source."

Conclusion

This concludes the strategy transformation process. The length of this chapter was necessary to illustrate the steps of the strategy transformation process and their associated sequence. After a few cycles of running through this process, you will have the ability to visually imagine current and proposed offerings on a visual strategy map. The VSM, with all of its parts, will also allow you to have quick talking points anytime the word *strategy* is stated. A company's strategy is all about getting sales and winning against the competition. This is possible by offering customers a set of offerings that entices them to buy from you. You then want the optimum set of offerings and the appropriate levels, compared to the competition. The VSM will not only show this, but also the key considerations, as depicted in the strategy icon. Pricing for what is being offered is also depicted on the VSM, so you can see what you are offering for the prices, compared to the competition. The market size gage communicates the total possible market size and your relative market share and those of your competitors, if you choose to include them. Finally, once the VSM can be imagined in your head, you will also have all of the necessary talking points with respect to company planning or the term *strategy*.

Chapter 11

Alignment and Position Statements

In the previous chapters we utilized the principles of Lean to create a visual process of creating innovation for customers. This focused on activities that maximized value and minimized waste for customers and companies. We created a process and included the steps so that any company can transform its current strategy to an optimum strategy. In that process, we generated a series of ideas and filtered them to define a theme. Finally, after final ranking and filtering, we displayed a new and unique strategy on a future state visual strategy map. In our example, it was very easy to define the theme of the new strategy, as many of the offering ideas were consistent with a single theme. The question that remains to be answered is, how can the optimum theme be chosen for the new strategy when several possible themes arise from the idea generation phase? How can managers ensure that ideas align to the capabilities of the company? Finally, how can decision makers determine what the goals of the company are so that optimum themes are created and ultimately chosen?

Well-run companies typically have a vision that is intended to provide long-term guidance for the company. The vision is usually stated in a short and concise vision statement. The vision statement is an inspiring unifying focal point for the entire organization. A good vision statement will always attempt to leap far beyond what is capable. This is synonymous to a stretched target. The statement is bold and can strive beyond what is possible and even beyond present reality. A vision statement can capitalize on core competencies, company history, customer base, strengths, unique

227

capabilities, resources, and assets. Its intention is to be inspiring, to provide a vivid image in people's minds as to which direction the company is heading long term. This provides employees with a sense of purpose. It must also be motivating so that employees are driven by the vision. Finally, it should provide a picture of what the business could look like in the future.

Consider IKEA's vision statement:[1] "To create a better everyday life for many people."

This simple and short vision statement describes IKEA's vision. IKEA's main purpose is providing affordable products so that many people can live a better life. IKEA's products are priced far cheaper than their competitors' with respect to their offerings, so that it can reach as many people as possible. This pricing is only possible by the consistent and aligned activities that IKEA lives by.

From the above vision statement, the reader can verify that the statement provides very high levels of guidance. That is the typical format of a vision statement. Thus, for more and focused guidance, i.e., for daily activities, companies create a mission statement to provide more immediate guidance for their present activities. The mission statement is a statement of the present that supports and directly aligns to the vision statement.

The elements of the mission statement must reflect the company's purpose. The mission statement must fit the current market environment and must be focused on satisfying customers that represent the target market. The mission statement must be based on the company's core competencies, in other words, what the company does best. It must be realistic, clear, specific, and as short as possible. The mission statement should be written to be sharply focused and memorable. This will provide immediate guidance to inspire and motivate employees. In the event that employees feel that their managers are not providing proper guidance, a properly written mission statement should direct them to what needs to be done. In support of the vision statement for IKEA, those that read its mission statement can agree that it does in fact support the long-term vision of IKEA and also provides immediate guidance.

IKEA's mission:[2] "Our business idea supports this vision by offering a wide range of well-designed, functional home furnishing products at prices so low that as many people as possible will be able to afford them."

This mission statement is very clear. Simply stated, IKEA will be the low-cost provider of all types of home furnishings so that most people will have the opportunity to buy them. This means that if the people working for IKEA are striving to provide lower-cost home furnishings that maintain expected functional requirements, they would be supporting the mission and vision of IKEA. However, if one or more employees strive to create a product that is overdesigned and expensive to manufacture or ship, they would not be supporting the mission and vision of IKEA. Thus, IKEA has identified a large customer group and has aligned its vision and mission to fulfill them. The mission statement, which provides more guidance, is aligned to the vision statement. The mission statement is designed to inspire employees to be aligned to that mission, where of course the mission is aligned to the target customer.

The final topic that deserves some attention is company values. Values are the beliefs, traits, and behavior norms that company personnel are expected to display in conducting the company's business and pursuing its strategy according to the strategic vision of the company. They provide guidance down to the individual to aid in decision making. Typically, if one makes a decision that reflects the core values of the company, he or she has not made the wrong decision. Over time, the values can define the culture of a company. The culture of a company is the *unwritten* beliefs and traits that exist within an organization that drive the general way the organization operates.

Below are the values for IKEA,[3] with a description associated with each. Note how some of the values support the mission and the vision.

■ Humbleness and willpower:
  – We respect each other, our customers, and our suppliers. Using our willpower means we get things done.
■ Leadership by example:
  – Our managers try to set a good example, and expect the same of IKEA coworkers.
■ Daring to be different:
  – We question old solutions, and if we have a better idea, we are willing to change.
■ Togetherness and enthusiasm:
  – Together, we have the power to solve seemingly unsolvable problems. We do it all the time.
■ Cost-consciousness:
  – Low prices are impossible without low costs, so we proudly achieve good results with small resources.

■ Constant desire for renewal:
  – Change is good. We know that adapting to customer demands with innovative solutions saves money and contributes to a better everyday life at home.
■ Accept and delegate responsibility.
■ We promote coworkers with potential and stimulate them to surpass their expectations. Sure, people make mistakes. But they learn from them!

The above values provide each employee of IKEA with the necessary guidance to aid in decision making. For example, IKEA respects its suppliers as well as its customers. That statement clearly implies that IKEA would most likely frown upon any individual wrongfully passing blame on a supplier.

The vision statement, mission statement, and values of IKEA are written so well that any new employee can understand the behavior expected upon entering IKEA. They are also highly aligned and complement each other, and thus it is clear that IKEA offers home furnishings at the absolute lowest possible cost. This means that innovation and problem solving are critical to the success of IKEA. For example, how can a particular product be designed to ship in the absolute smallest packaging to save on shipping costs? This takes incredible thought and teamwork. And once this is achieved, now reduce the volume of the package again by another 10%. More innovation and thought will be required by the team.

IKEA is successful by proper alignment. The entire company is aligned to the target customers, in this case, those seeking quality home furnishings at low cost. In order to deliver low-cost home furnishings to customers, IKEA must find the absolute lowest-cost operating model. Thus, the designs must be low cost and functional. This requires the use of low-cost materials using innovative designs to maintain expected levels of functionality. To keep shipping and inventory costs at a minimum, the products are shipped flat and in the smallest possible package to create large storage densities. This allows IKEA to ship and store a vast number of products at the lowest possible cost. Just think, if it cost $3,000 to ship a container via water, it would be more cost-effective if one could fit 400 units on the container compared to 50. IKEA also looks into the lowest-cost shipping routes. Thus, the entire business model is aligned in the offering of functional home furnishings at the lowest possible cost.

Any well-managed company should have a clear vision and mission statement with an associated set of values. If this is the case, it is very easy to write a position statement for the company. A position statement is a statement that instantly identifies a company's (or individual's) unique characteristics. A well-written position statement allows for the quick determination of what the company stands for. The same holds true with respect to an individual.

When the characteristics of a company are easy to identify in the market, or when an individual is easily labeled in terms of his or her unique characteristics, we say that the company or individual is well positioned. One could also make the argument that the company or individual is well branded. If the answer to the following question is apparent, the company or individual is well positioned. Just answer this question:

> What instantly comes to mind when you think of [company's name or individual's name]?
> Answer: The first thing that comes to mind when one thinks of [company's name or individual's name] is _____.

Based on discussions with colleagues, we can look at an example with respect to Walmart. By applying the question above, we can ask: What instantly comes to mind when you think of Walmart? A possible answer could be:

The first thing that comes to mind when one thinks of Walmart is good products at low prices as a result of its powerful supply chain management. Therefore, a possible position statement could be:

> We at Walmart offer good products at low prices as a result of our powerful supply chain management.

Walmart is positioned well in the market as having a good selection of products, and they are priced lower than those of the competition. This is an example of clear and focused company position.

Now consider another example regarding the positioning of an individual. What comes to mind when you think of Jack Welch? Based on discussions from an MBA course, the answer could be:

> The first thing that comes to mind when one thinks of Jack Welch is great, high-energy, and passionate leadership, with highly effective execution skills.

Jack Welch knew GE required changes at the beginning of his tenure, despite that the company seemed to be performing well. He formulated his three-circle strategy and stated that each strategic business unit (SBU) was going to be number 1 or number 2 in the markets it served. If it was not, it would be fixed, sold, or closed. Thus, a position statement for Jack Welch could be:

> Jack Welch is known for his great, high-energy, and passionate leadership style and is not afraid of executing the tough decisions to lead GE in creating high levels of shareholder value.

If a company is following a well-written vision statement, mission statement, and living aligned values, the position statement will be synonymous with what is already written. However, if a company does not have these statements in place, it may be worth first identifying the current position of the company by writing a position statement. This is done by first answering this question:

> What instantly comes to mind when you think of [company's name]?

If this question is easy to answer, then the company seems to have a general understandable position in the marketplace. This will allow for an easy task in the generation of a position statement. If this holds true, then the theme for the new strategy can align to the position statement.

Now let us assume that this question is difficult to answer. Let us also assume that there is no vision or mission statement present. In this case, one choice of action is to understand the company's core competence and draw a position statement from the core competence. A company's core competence is that set of activities that a company is good at and passionate about. It also represents those activities in which that company has a chance to be the best in the world. Once this is considered, a position statement can be written and communicated inside and outside the organization to build awareness and brand power. Therefore, in this case one can derive a position statement based on the answer to the following question: "What comes to mind when you think of [company's core competence]?" When the question is asked in this fashion, it may be easy to answer and ultimately write a position statement.

Consider the pharmaceutical company Abbott.[4] In 1964, the majority of Abbott's revenues were mostly due to its antibiotic product lines. It was around this time that Abbott realized it had lost the opportunity to be the best pharmaceutical company in the world. Companies like Merck had developed huge research facilities and were truly positioned to the best in the world at developing new pharmaceuticals through advanced research. The leaders of Abbott then decided to explore what it could truly be the best in the word at. Despite pharmaceuticals being its main source of revenue, Abbott shifted its focus and targeted a new opportunity. It designed products to help patients quickly regain their strength after surgery. In addition, it focused on diagnostic devices that properly diagnosed patients. This substantially reduced the cost of healthcare. Soon Abbott realized that it could be the best in the world with respect to postoperative recovery and accurate diagnostics. These two areas allowed Abbott to reposition itself as a company that could lower the cost of healthcare. During the period of transition, Abbott could have written a position statement to reflect its new area of focus. Thus, we can proceed by answering this question:

> What instantly comes to mind when you think of Abbott's newly discovered core competence?
> Answer: The first thing that comes to mind when one thinks of Abbott's new core competence is that Abbott could become the best in the world in lowering the cost of healthcare.

Thus, Abbott's position statement could read:

> We at Abbott are positioned to create a portfolio of products that lower the cost of healthcare.

Despite that 99% of Abbott's revenues consisted of pharmaceuticals, Abbott realized that it could not be the best in the world in developing next-generation pharmaceuticals. Therefore, Abbott confronted reality and shifted its focus to creating a portfolio of products that contributed to lowering the cost of healthcare. It first focused on hospital nutritionals, diagnostics, and hospital supplies.

With the new position statement in mind, Abbott could now easily recognize the themes to focus on during idea generation. In addition, the themes also serve as a filter for the elimination of ideas that would not fit its position statement. For example, if during idea generation the idea of a new pharmaceutical product emerged that required extensive research to develop, Abbott could quickly eliminate it based on the fact that this idea would not fit the new position statement that properly describes Abbott's core competence.

Company position is also highly related to the value discipline[5] of the company. Therefore, if a particular company is having a difficult time developing a position statement based on its core competence, consider another approach with respect to the value discipline of a company. As you recall, we discussed in detail the concept of value, particularly value in the form of benefits in view of the customer. We also used the term *value proposition*. Value proposition is a promise a company makes to customers to deliver a particular combination of value, being price, quality, performance, simplicity, selection, convenience, etc. These are the benefits of the company's offerings. There are three types of customer value that can be delivered as defined by the term *value discipline*. Value disciplines are the three desirable ways in which companies can combine their operating models and value propositions to be the best in their markets along a chosen discipline. Each discipline produces a different kind of customer value. The first is product leadership, where companies strive to deliver the best product or service, second to nobody within their industry. For example, consider the products of Apple. Apple is the innovator and strives to deliver the next-best product. The second value discipline is operational excellence. Operational excellence strives to deliver the value proposition in the most efficient and cost-effective manner. Those that have operational excellence have the lowest cost of delivery within their industry in the delivery of their value proposition. Just consider Walmart's supply chain management. The final value discipline is customer intimacy. This focuses on personalized service. Consider IBM's business model of delivering its value proposition in a personalized manner to its customers.

Companies should focus on one dominant value discipline, but maintain a threshold of standards with respect to the other two. They should strive in improving their value discipline each year and always ensure that their primary value discipline delivers unmatched value. Below are the basic highlights of the three value disciplines:

Operational excellence:
- Reliable products and services
- Sufficient and consistent selection of product and services
- Lowest possible cost of ownership and usage
- Main focus is price and speed of delivery
- Minimal acquisition cost and effort for customer

- No mistakes or good recovery from mistakes
- Product and services meet or exceed customer expectations
- Good predictability on supply chain due to consistent selection of product and services

Product leadership:
- Innovative
  - Renewing
  - Creative
  - Leading edge
  - Great upgrades or extensions to products
  - Creation of new applications ahead of market
  - Helping customers innovate
  - Creation of new markets
- Predictability on supply chain is not as certain, especially with promotions

Customer intimacy:
- Vast amount of time spent on fewer customers
- Personalized service coupled with customized products specific to customer requirements
- Highly responsive to customer needs
- Highly attentive to the details of a single customer
- Flexibility
- Helping customers succeed in their business on a personal level
- Products or services adapt to customer's changing needs

Thus, if companies are having a difficult time in writing a position statement, it may be worth the effort to understand your value discipline and formulate a position statement around that value discipline. Remember, the entire purpose of formulating a position statement is to aid in idea generation and selection that is consistent with your company. It is essential that your company first aligns with your target customer. By understanding your chosen target market (hopefully a large-sized market), you can then begin to align your company to the needs and wants of these targeted customers. This forms the beginning in defining the new strategy. In order for the company to be aligned to a target market, each department within the company must also be properly aligned to each other. In most companies, marketing is aligned to the customer, product development is aligned to marketing, operations and manufacturing are aligned to the needs of product development and marketing, and quality is aligned to every stakeholder, especially the customer. Companies that run in perfect alignment ensure that all departments communicate well cross-functionally and are also aligned to the customer.

An important characteristic of alignment is consistency. Maintaining consistency in defining key unmet needs and wants of the customer is critical in defining the optimum offering attributes. These offering attributes define the value proposition and must be consistent across the company. For example, if a strategy is defined by a key unmet need for a high-performance automotive tire, the project management activities must be consistent with that strategy. The marketing team must understand the customer perceptions of what is acceptable for a high-performance automotive tire. This prevents the company from overdelivering or underdelivering with respect to the performance of the tire. Overdelivery would result in a more expensive tire the customer may not be willing to invest in. Underdelivery may result in a lower than expected quality tire, causing customer dissatisfaction and thereby preventing repeat purchases and the desired market buzz. Marketing must also have a good understanding of the market size and sales forecast. This is essential for demand planning. For a high-performance tire, the material science team must strive to deliver an ultra-high-end rubber that performs as specified. If the material science team proposed a lower-cost and lower-quality rubber, they would *not* be aligned to the strategy. Operations must choose the optimum method of manufacture to ensure high levels of product quality. The sales literature and training of the sales force must properly communicate the high-end benefits offered by the new tire compared to the tires made available by the competitors. Notice how each portion of the company maintains consistency. This is essential, as a lack of consistency ultimately confuses customers.

Alignment internal to the company is also important. For example, if operations was given a sales forecast of 10,000 units per year, it would plan the requirements for the quantity of tools and inspection equipment required to deliver 10,000 units. Now let us assume that marketing was not aligned with customer demand and the company later learned during the first year that customer demand was in the range of 50,000 units. That would result in a 40,000-unit shortfall. This could trigger certain shortcuts affecting product quality to meet demand. In the end, a majority of customers could receive inferior tires, inconsistent with everything the company was striving for. This would clearly place the company in an unfavorable quality position with respect to the customer. This is why alignment is critical, beginning from the customer and funneling through to each and every task necessary to properly deliver the value proposition.

Consistency in your products or services and in the methods by which these offerings are manufactured, delivered, and communicated to customers is the recipe for success. For example, consider a strategy where your company wishes to deliver a series of products having acceptable user benefits with the utilization of an ultra-low-cost operating model. This strategy would define quality products for a lower price than that of your competitors. With this strategy, you would most likely choose lower-cost materials for your products, employ a lower-cost supply chain for your products, advertise quality products at the lowest prices, and be consistent with your message. For example, if you want to sell low-cost disposable pens, you must ensure that the product design is robust despite having minimal components, you are using low-cost materials, producing in low-cost regions, using low-cost transportation, utilizing low-cost selling methods, advertising the benefits in low-cost packaging materials, and ultimately providing a lower price than your competitors. In this example, each business part must understand the common strategy and must support this strategy by aligning the efforts of these individual parts (i.e., product design, marketing, operations, sales force) to service the whole, or the strategy will fail. If, for example, the product design team designed the pen in the above example using several difficult-to-assemble components in highly exotic materials such as polished stainless steel, the company would be forced to price the pen higher than originally intended to maintain the predetermined profit target. This would create an inconsistent chain of events from product creation to customer delivery, and these inconsistencies create an unaligned strategy and confuse customers.

Conclusion

In conclusion, use the tools in this chapter to aid in defining themes for your strategy. By writing a position statement, you can better align idea generation and selection techniques to these defined themes. This can reduce time in the strategy transformation process. Finally, ensure that your entire company is aligned to the target customer and made aware of the customer requirements. This will maintain consistency across the departments, so that each department can support each other rather than conflict with the requirements of the target customer.

Chapter 12

Epilogue

There is a very famous quote used in business that states, "The only constant is change." There is yet another quote used frequently that states, "If it ain't broke, don't fix it." We will not worry or argue about the origins of these quotes. They both have meaning and are certainly used often. However, there is a contradiction to both of them. The first states that change is inevitable. The second states that if all seems good, there is no need to worry about change. The real question is the conflict of when change should occur.

This conflict is overcome by strong visionary leadership that understands no matter how great things look in the present, the future is unknown and threats are imminent. Good visionary leaders know that they must be ready for change before a new unseen threat takes over.

Leaders need to worry about the plans their competitors have for taking their market share. In addition, if their competitors better understand customers, this poses more of a threat. So the question is, how do leaders know when to pursue change?

The answer to the question is twofold. Leaders should engage themselves in both present and future thinking. Present thinking is simply delighting current customers with current offerings and responding to their immediate needs as evident in the marketplace. This, of course, requires companies to be close to their customers by understanding their current needs. Leaders can also optimize their present situation by driving waste out of their processes in the delivery of their products and services to customers.

Future thinking is the ability to foresee what customers would want, need, and desire in the future. This can be linked, by example, to new trends, new technologies, or future forces such as new laws. This is where visionary leaders make the difference. Only through successful vision and of course luck can the proper choices be made to pursue successful change. Leaders can make attempts to anticipate future customer problems or find new ways of helping customers produce their desired outcomes.

Is there a simple way to get started with all this? The answer to this question can be answered by another question: What does your strategy icon look like? By ensuring that the present icon is accurate, we can begin to understand the current threats. As we track the strategy icon over time, we can determine if we need to make more immediate changes to preserve the present.

For the future, we can formulate a series of future state strategy icons and verify if they seem to fit future trends. These icons can be derived by proposing new future offerings. By studying the marketplace, alternate industries, alternate technologies, foreign laws, etc., leaders can attempt to gage whether the trends fit their new strategy icons. Leaders may realize that their efforts are not successful. This is the norm and is acceptable, providing learning is achieved and retained. If leaders do nothing, they will never anticipate change. If they make several attempts, they stand a better chance of winning over the competition.

Some last pieces of advice to give:

Understand value in the eyes of the customer. This can be in the forms of utility, emotion, or a combination of both. Refer to earlier discussions for these details.

Understand waste, on both an internal and an external perspective. External waste is overdelivery of features to customers, resulting in higher cost, product confusion/difficulty, and unnecessary features. Internal waste is the waste associated with getting the job done from all aspects of the company, such as useless meetings, useless processes, useless reports, and other forms of useless activities. All activities should be linked to (1) understanding customers and (2) the efficient delivery of value to customers. Anything else is pure waste and should be eliminated or at least reduced. If there must be waste, this is called necessary waste and should be kept to a minimum.

Strive for simplicity. Anything difficult will lead to confusion. Make sure products are simple for customers. In addition, ensure that all company processes such as product development and management systems are also simple.

Understand your core competence. Companies must understand what they do best or what they can be the best at doing. This should be aligned across the organization and also to a profitable target market.

Strive for transparency! Although some think that perception is reality, most often it is not. If your company has evolved to a bureaucracy where many have climbed the ladder of success at the company's expense, it will eventually suffer. Ensure that all activities are transparent to everyone so that waste and politics can be driven out of the organization.

Appoint technical managers at the senior level. This cannot be overemphasized. Too often, members of senior management consist of few individuals from a technical background. It is very easy to teach business skills to technical individuals in comparison to teaching technical skills to business people.

Implement change in small manageable batches. This book has been written to allow the reader to utilize the entire process or portions of the process. Change occurs by at least trying something. If company culture does not allow a process overhaul, begin by selecting and using one tool, such as the product fulfillment map. After success, new tools can be incorporated one at a time.

Good luck in your endeavor in understanding your customers and delivering innovative offerings to them. May you profit from your activities!

Bibliography

"What Is Strategy?"
  Michael E. Porter
  Harvard Business Review, November–December 1996, reprint 96608

Lean Product and Process Development
  Allen C. Ward
  The Lean Enterprise Institute, September 2009

The PIMS Principles Linking Strategy to Performance
  Robert D. Buzzell, Bradley T. Gale
  Free Press, 1987

What Customers Want: Using Outcome-Driven Innovation to Create
  Breakthrough Products and Services
  Anthony Ulwick
  McGraw-Hill, 2005

Invention Analysis and Claiming: A Patent Lawyer's Guide
  Ronald D. Slusky
  ABA Publishing, 2007

Mastering Lean Product Development: A Practical, Event-Driven Process
  for Maximizing Speed, Profits, and Quality
  Ronald Mascitelli
  Technology Perspectives, 2011

Strategic Planning for Dummies
  Erica Olsen
  Wiley Publishing, 2007

Managerial Economics and Organizational Architecture, 3rd edition
James A. Brickley, Clifford W. Smith, Jerold L. Zimmerman
McGraw Hill, 2004

Blue Ocean Strategy
W. Chan Kim and Renee Mauborgne
Harvard Business School Press, 2005

The Discipline of Market Leaders
Michael Treacy, Fred Wiersema
Basic Books, 1995

Crafting and Executing Strategy: Text and Readings, 14th edition
Arthur Thompson Jr., A.J. Strickland III, John Gamble
McGraw-Hill, Irving Publishing, 2005

Patent It Yourself, 12th edition
David Pressman
Nolo, 2006

Good to Great
Jim Collins
HarperCollins Publishers, 2001

The Next Economy
Elliott Ettenberg
McGraw-Hill, 2002

www.edmunds.com

Executive MBA program
University of New Haven, West Haven, Connecticut, 2007

Choosing the Best Method for Listening to the Customer
Pam Hunter
www.isixsigma.com

www.authenticwatches.com (Rolex watches)

"Plane Crew Is Credited for Nimble Reaction"
   Matthew L. Wald
   New York Times, January 15, 2009

Master Lock Case Study
   http://www.dcontinuum.com/seoul/portfolio/11/228/07. Master Lock-
      Padlock Innovation Strategy

LifeSync case study
   http://www.dcontinuum.com/seoul/portfolio/11/231/02. GMP-LifeSync
      Wireless medical device uses Bluetooth technology
   Other information taken from http://www.lifesynccorp.com/index.html

"The Kano Model: How to Delight Your Customers"
   Elmar Sauerwein, Franz Bailom, Kurt Matzler, Hans H. Hinterhuber
   Department of Management, University of Innsbruck
   Preprints Volume I of the IX International Working Seminar on
      Production Economics, February 1996

www.cdc.gov (Centers for Disease Control and Prevention)

www.census.gov (U.S. Census Bureau)

Jack Welch visit and interview with Harvard Business School
   Viewed in the Executive MBA Program
   University of New Haven, West Haven, Connecticut, 2007

Manual of Patent Examining Procedure (MPEP)
   Revision, July 2010

Overview and use of the tools in the IP toolbox
   Ned McMahon, October 2011

www.uspto.gov

www.heinz.com

www.CPSC.gov

"The Story of Clorox Green Works™"
   Sumi. N. Cate, David Pilosof, Richard Tait, Robin Karol
PDMA Visions Magazine, March 2009

http://www.samples-help.org.uk/mission-statements/ikea-vision-statement.
   htm

www.ikea.com

Idea Stormers
   Bryan W. Mattimore, Jossey-Bass
   Wiley, 2012

http://www.businessdictionary.com

http://www.balancedscorecard.org/BSCResources/
   AbouttheBalancedScorecard/tabid/55/Default.aspx

The Innovator's Solution
   Clayton M. Christensen, Michael E. Raynor
   Harvard Business School Press, 2003

Managing Customer Value: Creating Quality and Service That Customers
   Can See
   Bradley T. Gale
   Free Press, 1994

Appendix 1

On January 16, 2009, minutes after departing La Guardia Airport, US Airways Flight 1549 flew into a large flock of birds,[1] causing both engines to shut down. US Airways Flight 1549 was ascending and lost power only 3,200 feet above the ground. Capt. C.B. "Sully" Sullenberger, the US Airways pilot, immediately took control from the first officer and began making quick decisions. The first decision was the order for the attempted and failed restart of the engines. The second was the decision to land the aircraft in the Hudson River despite the instructions from air traffic control. Air traffic control instructed US Airways Flight 1549, a twin-engine airbus A320, to land at Teterboro Airport in New Jersey. However, final authority resides with the pilot in command, and Captain Sullenberger knew that the plane could not glide that far. Therefore, Captain Sullenberger decided immediately that the best choice would be to land the plane on the water near a boat that could potentially help to evacuate passengers. After clearing the George Washington Bridge by about 900 feet, Captain Sullenberger was able to control the gliding decent of the aircraft above the water. He maintained ground effect (the float) of the aircraft just above the water in a slight nose-up position. Captain Sullenberger had to ensure that the wings landed parallel to the water with the aircraft in a nose-up position in order to prevent potentially massive damage to the aircraft and loss of life. Thinking logically, the aircraft was traveling more than 100 mph, and if the aircraft did not contact the water at just the precise angle, one or more portions of the aircraft would be forced to decelerate suddenly, possibly causing the structure to be torn apart. Captain Sullenberger ensured that the wings simultaneously contacted the water with the nose slightly elevated so the aircraft could "drag" to a full stop. A nose-down entry into the water could have caused the aircraft to become jammed into the water, causing the aircraft to possibly flip forward. Captain Sullenberger made the landing of Airbus A320 look like a normal water landing, as if the aircraft had pontoons. Major injuries were avoided and the entire plane was evacuated. Captain Sullenberger announced his retirement several months following his heroic event.

This major event was all over the news. Videos were floating all over the web, and so were the countless interviews with Captain Sullenberger and several of the passengers. In my opinion, I believe that any airline could have capitalized on this event. A smart airline could have pushed for the recruitment of Sullenberger to represent a particular airline. Imagine all of the free press and publicity that this major event could have provided. Any airline that successfully recruited Sullenberger, no matter the cost, could have launched a new internal training program led by Captain Sullenberger. This internal training program could have been highly publicized during this media frenzy. This smart airline could have promoted that all of their pilots will strive to be the safest in the world by embarking on a new safety training program headed by Captain Sully. They could have allowed Captain Sullenberger to work with top flight safety experts and made this reality. In addition, all of this could have been advertised for free by the media. The airline could have created a new tagline boasting this program and the new levels of safety resulting from the new training program. Perhaps premium pricing would have been possible. Let us see what this could look like when used in the time trend matrix introduced in Chapter 4. This is shown in Figure A1.1.

Time Trend Matrix: Making the Safest Airline Possible

Trends Applicable to Your Business	Predictability Can you visualize the future activities based on this trend?	Staying Power Will this trend last?	Influence Factor Will many people be influenced by this trend?
New branding as the airline having the safest pilots in the world trained by Captain "Sully"	Safety is always a concern when traveling, especially flying. This event will help us drive the initiative as we have already created a positive experience with the public.	We will truly train our pilots and perform additional inspections on our aircraft, thus reinforcing safety. We will alert the media every quarter as to new initiatives to keep the message strong.	Most people that fly would choose a safe airline. Our new branding will be reinforced by all of our marketing support to achieve maximum influence.
Business Assessment	We will launch a new program that would allow Captain Sullenberger to work with top flight safety experts and make this reality for our airline. With the heroic actions of Captain Sullenberger, we can alert the media and get free publicity. We will create a new tagline boasting this program and the new levels of training in safety.		

Figure A1.1 Making the safest airline using the time trend matrix. (From Anthony Sgroi Jr.)

Appendix 2

While I was preparing the manuscript for this book, I came across a very ingenious method of evaluating offering attributes. In his book *Managing Customer Value*,[1] Bradley Gale teaches a method that utilizes a questionnaire directed to customers. This questionnaire allows customers (current, lost, competitor) to enter numeric values for various aspects of the attributes. By utilizing an innovative method of transforming the data, a numerical value can be calculated that provides a total comparative score of the total offering. This method evaluates the total offering based on the perceived benefits and the perceived cost of the attributes. In some cases, the offering attributes may already be known and can be simply evaluated by customers. In other cases, the offering attributes are proposed and require customer evaluation. In still other cases, the offering attributes can be generated by customers for evaluation.

The method has several components and is summarized:

- The method allows for the comparison of a company to one or more competitors.
- The offering attributes, in terms of perceived benefits, are individually rated on a predefined numeric scale. This allows customers to enter a numerical value within that scale, for example, in the range of 0–10. Each offering attribute is compared to the competitor's on a relative basis.
- The offering attributes, in terms of perceived price, are rated independently from the perceived benefits. As with the perceived benefits, the perceived price is also rated on a predefined numeric scale. Each price attribute is also compared to the competitor's on a relative basis.
- The offering attributes (both perceived benefits and perceived price) are evaluated on a weighted scale. This allows for the more important attributes to be identified. This also allows companies to better choose the attributes to focus on for the delivery of higher levels of fulfillment.

This method provides executives with the relative weights of various offering attributes.

■ In addition to perceived benefits and perceived price, the questionnaire also has customers rate, on an independent basis, the percent importance of the benefits in relation to percent importance of price. This is typically based on 100%.

The questionnaire can be arranged in several formats. For purposes of discussion, I chose to begin with relative weights.

Relative Weights

We can ask customers to provide the relative weights (importance) of a series of offering attributes. The questionnaire will ask a targeted customer to rate each offering attribute from a list of offerings in terms of percentages. Each attribute is to be given a percentage, and the total list is to add up to 100%. If desirable, the weights can be entered in decimal format where the sum would add up to 1. This can be summarized by an example, as shown in Figure A2.1.

In Figure A2.1, we can verify that attribute 4 is the most important to the customer, whereas attribute 1 is the least important. We can also state that attribute 4 is four times as important as attribute 1.

Offering Attributes	Weight (enter % importance) Sum = 100%
Attribute 1	10%
Attribute 2	20%
Attribute 3	15%
Attribute 4	40%
Attribute 5	15%
Total weight	100%

Figure A2.1   Relative weights of offering attributes. (Adapted from Bradley T. Gale, *Managing Customer Value: Creating Quality and Service That Customers Can See,* Free Press, 1994.)

Customer Perceived Benefits

Next we can have the target customer evaluate the offering attributes as to the levels of fulfillment on a *comparative* basis using a predefined scale. Such a scale can be any chosen range, such as 0–10. If the company conducting the analysis is marketing the product, then we can include it to gage how it is doing compared to its competitors. However, if the company is not currently marketing the product, then the analysis can indicate if there is an opportunity. This is illustrated in Figure A2.2. In this example, we are comparing our company to our top competitor.

From Figure A2.2, we can begin to gage the level of fulfillment of the various attributes. From a quick inspection, we can see that the competitor achieves higher fulfillment with respect to attributes 5, 4, 3, and 2. Our company only achieves higher fulfillment with respect to attribute 1. Figure A2.2 does not tell the entire story, as it does not factor in the relative weights. The use of relative weights better analyzes the combined attributes as a whole. This is also necessary because the more important attributes should have relatively higher levels of fulfillment, whereas the less important attributes may not need high levels of fulfillment. Also, by utilizing relative weights, we can get a better understanding as to which attributes can be adjusted to provide better value (benefits).

To better analyze value, we can define a ratio that compares the attribute ratings of our company to that of our competitor. Thus in this example, let us define a ratio where the rating for our company is divided by the rating of the competitor for each attribute. This would create a convention where

	Enter Level of Fulfillment in the Range of 0–10	
Attribute No.	Our Company	Competitor
Attribute 1	6	3
Attribute 2	4	5
Attribute 3	3	5
Attribute 4	3	6
Attribute 5	4	8

Figure A2.2   Comparing the levels of fulfillment for offering attributes. (Adapted from Bradley T. Gale, *Managing Customer Value: Creating Quality and Service That Customers Can See*, Free Press, 1994.)

Attribute No.	Weights	Enter Level of Fulfillment in the Range of 0–10		Ratio Our/Theirs	Weight × Ratio
		Our Company	Competitor		
Attribute 1	10%	6	3	2.00	0.20
Attribute 2	20%	4	5	0.80	0.16
Attribute 3	15%	3	5	0.60	0.09
Attribute 4	40%	3	6	0.50	0.20
Attribute 5	15%	4	8	0.50	0.08
Total	100%	(Perceived benefit ratio) sum of weight × ratio $\rightarrow$			0.73

Figure A2.3 Perceived benefit ratio analysis. (Adapted from Bradley T. Gale, *Managing Customer Value: Creating Quality and Service That Customers Can See,* Free Press, 1994.)

a number that is greater than 1 is desirable. On the reverse, if the number is less than 1, this would indicate that the competitor is superior in the fulfillment of the attribute.

Next, we can introduce another convention where the ratio is multiplied by the weights obtained for each attribute. This final product of each attribute is summed to produce a final score that communicates the level of fulfillment for the total perceived benefit portion. This is shown in Figure A2.3.

From Figure A2.3, we form the conclusion that the sum of weight × ratio is 0.73 and is less than 1. This is denoted as the perceived benefit ratio. This states that our company is 73% as effective as our competitor in terms of perceived benefits. We can also state that our competitor is 27% better than our company.

To test the validity of the calculations and this model, let us assume that our company and our competitor fulfill the perceived benefits exactly the same. This should yield a dividend of 1 that carries through the table, providing a perceived benefit ratio of 1.00. A perceived benefit ratio of 1.00 would indicate that both companies are equal. This is confirmed in Figure A2.4.

Next, let us use the analysis for the purpose of decision making. What simple change can our company make to provide better value than our competitor? By a quick inspection of Figure A2.3, we first verify that attribute 4

Attribute No.	Weights	Enter Level of Fulfillment in the Range of 0–10		Ratio Our/Theirs	Weight × Ratio
		Our Company	Competitor		
Attribute 1	10%	6	6	1.00	0.10
Attribute 2	20%	4	4	1.00	0.20
Attribute 3	15%	3	3	1.00	0.15
Attribute 4	40%	3	3	1.00	0.40
Attribute 5	15%	4	4	1.00	0.15
Total	100%	(Perceived benefit ratio) sum of weight × ratio →			1.00

Figure A2.4 Perceived benefit ratio analysis of equal levels of fulfillment. (Adapted from Bradley T. Gale, *Managing Customer Value: Creating Quality and Service That Customers Can See*, Free Press, 1994.)

has the highest relative importance (40% out of 100%). We can also see that our competitor fulfills this attribute with a value of 6, and our level of fulfillment is only a 3. Therefore, a proper question to ask is could our company achieve better total perceived benefits if we were to increase this attribute? Based on a hypothetical analysis, we determine that we can provide this attribute at a level of 9 comparatively. Thus, by one simple modification to our offering, we can provide more value and obtain a higher perceived benefit ratio. This is depicted in Figure A2.5. By one simple adjustment, our company is now 13% better in perceived benefits compared to our competitor. This confirms the advantage of using relative weights.

Customer Perceived Price

The perceived price requires equal emphasis. Based on the discussion above, we can also apply the same logic with respect to perceived price.

We can ask customers to provide the relative weights (importance) of a series of price attributes. As with perceived benefits, the questionnaire will ask a targeted customer to rate each price attribute from a list of price offer-

Attribute No.	Weights	Enter Level of Fulfillment in the Range of 0–10		Ratio Our/Theirs	Weight × Ratio
		Our Company	Competitor		
Attribute 1	10%	6	3	2.00	0.20
Attribute 2	20%	4	5	0.80	0.16
Attribute 3	15%	3	5	0.60	0.09
Attribute 4	40%	9	6	1.50	0.60
Attribute 5	15%	4	8	0.50	0.08
Total	100%	(Perceived benefit ratio) sum of weight × ratio $\longrightarrow$			1.13

Figure A2.5 **Perceived benefit ratio analysis of modified offering attribute. (Adapted from Bradley T. Gale,** *Managing Customer Value: Creating Quality and Service That Customers Can See,* **Free Press, 1994.)**

ings in terms of percentages. Each attribute of the total list will add up to 100%. This is summarized in Figure A2.6.

Thus, in the example in Figure A2.6, we can verify that attribute 2 is the most important to the customer in terms of price, whereas attribute 1 is the least important.

Next, we can have the target customer evaluate the perceived levels of the various price attributes on a *comparative* basis using a predefined numeric scale. The scale is defined on a range from 0 to 10, where a lower

Offering Attributes	Weight (enter % importance) Sum = 100%
Price 1 (i.e., acquisition)	10%
Price 2 (i.e., maintenance)	60%
Price 3 (i.e., residual trade-in)	30%
Total weight	100%

Figure A2.6 **Visualizing the levels of perceived prices. (Adapted from Bradley T. Gale,** *Managing Customer Value: Creating Quality and Service That Customers Can See,* **Free Press, 1994.)**

Price Attribute No.	Enter Level of Fulfillment in the Range of 0–10	
	Our Company	*Competitor*
Price 1	4	8
Price 2	6	7
Price 3	8	2

Figure A2.7 Comparing the levels of perceived prices. (Adapted from Bradley T. Gale, *Managing Customer Value: Creating Quality and Service That Customers Can See*, Free Press, 1994.)

value indicates a least desirable cost position in view of the customer. This is done independent of the benefits. For example, the acquisition cost of our company's offerings is directly compared to the acquisition cost of the competitor's without considering the level of the benefits provided. This is illustrated in Figure A2.7.

From Figure A2.7, we can begin to gage the level of fulfillment of the various price attributes. We can instantly verify that our competitor has superior pricing attributes with respect to prices 1 and 2. We are superior with respect to price 3.

Similar to perceived benefits, to better analyze perceptive pricing, we can define a ratio that better compares the total price attribute. We can define a similar convention as illustrated above. This is shown in Figure A2.8.

From Figure A2.8, we form the conclusion that the sum of weight × ratio is 1.76 and is greater than 1. This is denoted as the perceived price ratio. This states that our company is 76% superior to our competitor in terms of perceived price. We can also state that our competitor is 24% inferior to our company in terms of perceived offering prices.

In summary, we now have some quantitative numbers describing perceived benefits and perceived prices. However, does this information suffice to properly compare the offerings of one or more companies? The answer to that question can be obtained by understanding the trade-offs of price vs. benefits as a whole. For example, how much are customers willing to pay for a certain level of benefits? How much more can we charge for an associated jump in benefits? Can a cluster of customers willing to pay more be identified?

The answers to the questions above are dealt with by again going to the customer. By allowing customers to provide the relative importance or weighted importance of benefits vs. price, we can begin to see various

Price Attribute No.	Weights	Enter Level of Fulfillment in the Range of 0–10		Ratio Our/Theirs	Weight × Ratio
		Our Company	Competitor		
Price 1	10%	4	8	0.5	0.05
Price 2	60%	6	7	0.86	0.51
Price 3	30%	8	2	4.00	1.20
Total	100%	(Perceived price ratio) sum of weight × ratio			1.76

Figure A2.8 Perceived price ratio analysis. (Adapted from Bradley T. Gale, *Managing Customer Value: Creating Quality and Service That Customers Can See*, Free Press, 1994.)

buying preferences of customer groups. Similar to our previous discussion, the two weights are to add up to 100%. This is reflected in Figure A2.9.

If this question is asked to a group of customers, you may receive differing percentages. This can define the preferences of certain groups of customers and form a basis for segmentation. For example, let us assume that we map salary range in terms of benefits sought in relation to price for a certain product offering. These results are displayed for 400 people surveyed and are shown in Figure A2.10.

From the data in the table, we can begin to group market sizes in terms of salary ranges. In this example, the majority of the people fell in the 25K–49K salary range and comprises approximately 64% of the market. Thus, if desired, we can target this market and use its values obtained for

Parameter	Enter Weights for Benefits vs. Price
Benefits	Enter benefits % (% importance of benefits)
Price	Enter price % (% importance of price)
Sum	100%

Figure A2.9 Input weights of benefits vs. price. (Adapted from Bradley T. Gale, *Managing Customer Value: Creating Quality and Service That Customers Can See*, Free Press, 1994.)

Benefit vs. Price Preference of 400 People Surveyed

Parameter	Salary Range 15K–24K	Salary Range 25K–49K	Salary Range 50K–100K
Benefits	10%	30%	60%
Price	90%	70%	40%
Totals	78 people	257 people	65 people

Figure A2.10   Survey of benefits vs. price preferences. (Adapted from Bradley T. Gale, *Managing Customer Value: Creating Quality and Service That Customers Can See,* **Free Press, 1994.)**

the importance of benefits vs. price. This target market rates the importance of price to be 70% out of 100%, compared to only 30% for benefits. Thus, the people in this market make their purchase decision primarily on price.

This entire discussion and analysis allows for the creation of a final numerical calculation that compares our company to our competitor's for a chosen target market. This combines the perceived benefit ratio, perceived price ratio, and weighted importance of price vs. benefits.

This done by a simple calculation and is denoted as the customer value ratio (CVR). This equation is shown in Figure A2.11.

Based on the customer value ratio, we can obtain an overall number that communicates the total perceived score of how our company compares to our competitor. We can also use a spreadsheet tool to automate the calculations for purposes of comparison. For example, what are the customer value ratios for differing perceived benefit ratios (Figures A2.3 and A2.5) in relation to an 85% weighted benefit preference and a 15% weighted price preference? We can run these values and obtain overall customer value ratios for these conditions. The results are illustrated in Figure A2.12.

The final calculations of 0.88 and 1.22 define two distinct customer value ratios with respect to alternate parameters. In the first case, the CVR of 0.88

Customer Value Ratio =

(Weighted Benefit % × Perceived Benefit Ratio)
+ (Weighted Price % × Perceived Price Ratio)

Figure A2.11   Calculation of the customer value ratio. (Adapted from Bradley T. Gale, *Managing Customer Value: Creating Quality and Service That Customers Can See,* **Free Press, 1994.)**

Customer Value Ratio Based on Alternate Parameters (CVR)

CVR Calculation	0.88	1.22
Benefit weight	85%	85%
Price weight	15%	15%
Perceived benefit ratio (Figures A2.3 and A2.5)	0.73	1.13
Perceived price ratio	1.76	1.76

Figure A2.12   Customer value ratio comparison. (Adapted from Bradley T. Gale, *Managing Customer Value: Creating Quality and Service That Customers Can See,* **Free Press, 1994.)**

communicates a less desirable condition than that of our competitor. In this case, our competitor is 12% superior in its total offering to our company. On the other hand, the second case tells us that our company is 22% better than our competitor. This, of course, reflects that customers place more importance on benefits instead of cost.

Conclusion

In this discussion, numerous examples were provided that required an individual to input values in a questionnaire. In reality, questionnaires would be provided to multiple people, and the data would then be converted into a form to be entered into the analysis discussed. The conversion is possible by various methods. For example, one method can be by taking the averages of the scores. Another method can be by identifying a series of ranges that correspond to various data points to be entered into the analysis. This analysis can also be adapted to compare several competitors. This would require various alterations to the analysis discussed.

Appendix 3

The details in Appendix 2 have inspired a new way of working with perceptual maps. In Appendix 2, the general comparison of companies utilized ratios. The ratios allowed for the comparison of one or more companies to a baseline, such as a reference company. In those examples, we compared two companies by dividing the ratings of the companies, specifically our company divided by the comparison or competitive company. In this discussion, we illustrate an analysis that uses an absolute scoring convention (i.e., no ratios). The final results will be mapped onto what is referred to as the 2-D weighted perceptual map.

As detailed in Appendix 2, the analysis used a questionnaire directed to various customers. For this discussion, we will also seek the input of customers. Customers will enter numeric values for various offering attributes. This analysis will also use weights to gage the relative importance of the offerings. Instead of using ratios, the scores of each attribute will be multiplied by the respective weights and then summed for a variety of companies. This will allow for an overall numeric score for each company. Similar to the analysis in Appendix 2, the first analysis will be directed to customer perceived benefits. Since we are dealing with absolutes, this quantity will be termed absolute customer perceived benefits.

To simplify this discussion, we will illustrate the absolute customer perceived benefits using an example. For this example, we will look at the attribute ratings of several fictitious cellular phone providers. This example will analyze six offering attributes, summarized:

- Number of service towers (i.e., national coverage)
- Download speed (i.e., 4G, 3G)
- Sound quality of the phones
- Phone choices (variety of appealing phones)

■ Available apps
■ Dropped calls (minimized occurrences)

The analysis of the above attributes is illustrated in Figure A3.1. As seen in the figure, the analysis begins with the identification of each offering attribute along the left portion of the table. The gray shaded cells allow for user input. First, the attributes are entered. Next, the weights are identified for the offering attributes where the sum adds to 100%. Each attribute is then rated for each company on a scale from 1 to 10. A rating of 0 indicates that the attribute is not fulfilled in view of the customers. A rating of 10 indicates full fulfillment. These entries are all based on the questionnaire provided to customers. The rest of the table generates the final values by multiplying each attribute by the respective weight, and then summing for each respective company. The sum produces a final value representing the absolute perceived benefit score for each company. These values represent a set of horizontal data points on the 2-D weighted perceptual map.

Similar to the absolute perceived benefit scores, the same logic is applied for the absolute perceived price scores. As seen in Figure A3.2, there are three pricing attributes that contribute to the purchase decision with respect to cellular providers. They are outlined:

■ Acquisition cost (actual cost of purchasing the phone and entering into the contract)
■ Monthly cost (includes cost of voice, data, texting, etc.)
■ Contract lock (this is primarily the cost of early cancellation of service)

For cost attributes, various customers enter the ratings on a scale from 0 to 10. A rating of 0 would indicate low pricing preference according to the customer's point of view. On the contrary, a rating of 10 would indicate the best price in view of the customer. Thus, by example, a value of 10 for a certain price attribute would indicate total customer satisfaction with respect to that price. Similar to the analysis depicted in Figure A3.1, the values and analysis for each company's absolute perceived price score are illustrated in Figure A3.2.

The table depicted in Figure A3.2 is identical to that shown in Figure A3.1, with the exception of the bottom row containing the inverse of the sums. These values represent the vertical data points used on the 2-D weighted perceptual map. This is necessary, as the chosen convention with respect to price attributes would not represent actual pricing on a graph. For

Benefits (what customer gets)	Weights	Our Company Rating (0–10)	Weight × Rating	Cellular Provider 2 Rating (0–10)	Weight × Rating	Cellular Provider 3 Rating (0–10)	Weight × Rating	Cellular Provider 4 Rating (0–10)	Weight × Rating	Cellular Provider 5 Rating (0–10)	Weight × Rating
No. of service towers	25%	3.00	0.75	8.00	2.00	2.00	0.50	10.00	2.50	2.00	0.50
Download speed	20%	4.00	0.80	9.00	1.80	5.00	1.00	9.00	1.80	3.00	0.60
Sound quality	15%	6.00	0.90	7.00	1.05	4.00	0.60	8.00	1.20	5.00	0.75
Phone choices	10%	5.00	0.50	6.00	0.60	7.00	0.70	8.00	0.80	2.00	0.20
Available apps	15%	1.00	0.15	8.00	1.20	2.00	0.30	9.00	1.35	4.00	0.60
Dropped calls	15%	5.00	0.75	7.00	1.05	4.00	0.60	6.00	0.90	1.00	0.15
Sum	100%	Sum	3.85	Sum	7.70	Sum	3.70	Sum	8.55	Sum	2.80

Figure A3.1 Absolute perceived benefit scores. (From Anthony Sgroi Jr.)

| Cost (what customer pays) | Weights | Our Company | Rating (0–10) | Cellular Provider 2 | Rating (0–10) | Cellular Provider 3 | Rating (0–10) | Cellular Provider 4 | Rating (0–10) | Cellular Provider 5 | Rating (0–10) |
		Rating (0–10)	Weight × Rating	Rating (0–10)	Weight × Rating	Rating (0–10)	Weight × Rating	Rating (0–10)	Weight × Rating	Rating (0–10)	Weight × Rating
Acquisition cost	50%	1.00	0.50	2.00	1.00	5.00	2.50	0.25	0.13	10.00	5.00
Monthly cost	40%	2.00	0.80	5.00	2.00	6.00	2.40	0.25	0.10	9.00	3.60
Contract-lock	10%	2.00	0.20	4.00	0.40	4.00	0.40	1.00	0.10	9.00	0.90
Sum	100%	Sum	1.50	Sum	3.40	Sum	5.30	Sum	0.33	Sum	9.50
		Inverse	8.50	Inverse	6.60	Inverse	4.70	Inverse	9.68	Inverse	0.50

Figure A3.2 Absolute perceived price scores. (From Anthony Sgroi Jr.)

example, a rating of 10 indicates the most optimum cost position, which is the lowest relative cost needed to be depicted on the 2-D weighted perceptual map.

In this example, we chose a scale for benefits and price to be in the range of 0–10. This convention would allow for a maximum possible absolute benefit and price score of 10 and a minimum of 0. Therefore, the *average* offering price and benefit attribute would each have a rating of 5. This is half of the chosen range of our scale and represents the middle average zone (absolute perceived benefit = 5 and absolute perceived price = 5). Similarly, we can define a zone called the low-end zone, which can be in the benefit range of about 1 to about 4 for both absolute perceived benefits and price. This can represent a target market seeking low value and low prices. Finally, we can define a high-end zone in the benefit range of about 6 to about 9. This can represent a target market seeking high value at high prices. This can also indicate benefits subjected to cost reductions. In this case, companies may choose to maintain the same level of benefits or reduce the level and also reduce costs. A final zone that represents low benefits at relatively high prices can be called the improvement zone. This zone would require a transformation to shift the offering attributes to a more desired zone better aligned to target customers.

With the above analysis and discussions, we can create the 2-D weighted perceptual map. This is depicted in Figure A3.3. From Figure A3.3, we can instantly make the following statements:

■ Our company is in the improvement zone. We offer low perceived benefits at a high-cost position. We clearly need to modify our offerings.
■ Cellular provider 2 is a high-end provider. It offers high benefits at a relatively high cost to the customer. However, it is still at a better cost position than our company for the better benefits.
■ Cellular provider 3 should consider lowering its cost or improving its benefits to customers.
■ Cellular provider 4 is also in the improvement zone. It offers higher benefits at a slightly higher cost than us.
■ Cellular provider 5 offers low benefits for a low price.

The above discussion serves as a basis to either improve our offerings or optimize the understanding of our offerings. For example, it is quite possible that we do have better than scored benefits, as customers may not understand the true value we offer. Nevertheless, there is work to do.

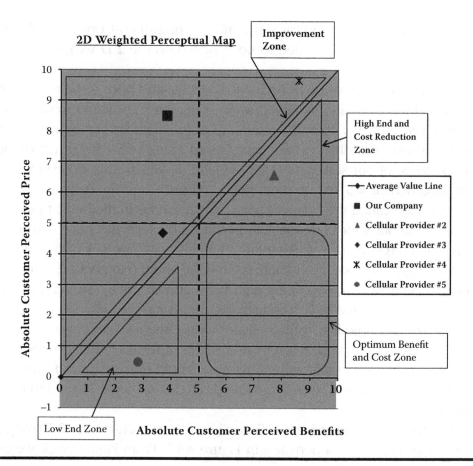

Figure A3.3   Two-dimensional weighted perceptual map. (From Anthony Sgroi Jr.)

Our fictitious example continues with the following modifications to our strategy. First, we did not properly communicate the fact that we have built and acquired a series of new towers. Therefore, upon a quick analysis, our rating (on a comparative basis) for number of service towers should be 8 instead of 3. This should directly affect the download speed and the number of dropped calls. Upon analysis, we are able to determine that the download speed will increase to a rating of 7 from 4. Also, the added towers will boost our rating to minimizing the dropped calls to 9 from 5. We have also improved the sound quality and can rate this attribute as a 9 from a 6 rating. In terms of cost, we have successfully cost reduced our way of doing business. Therefore, we are now competitive on all three cost attributes.

We can run the new ratings through an updated analysis and map the results. Figure A3.4 illustrates the absolute perceived benefit scores for each company based on the new ratings for our company. For the updated price attribute ratings, Figure A3.5 illustrates the resultant absolute perceived price

Benefits (what customer gets)	Weights	Our Company Rating (0–10)	Weight × Rating	Cellular Provider 2 Rating (0–10)	Weight × Rating	Cellular Provider 3 Rating (0–10)	Weight × Rating	Cellular Provider 4 Rating (0–10)	Weight × Rating	Cellular Provider 5 Rating (0–10)	Weight × Rating
No. of service towers	25%	8.00	2.00	8.00	2.00	2.00	0.50	10.00	2.50	2.00	0.50
Download speed	20%	7.00	1.40	9.00	1.80	5.00	1.00	9.00	1.80	3.00	0.60
Sound quality	15%	9.00	1.35	7.00	1.05	4.00	0.60	8.00	1.20	5.00	0.75
Phone choices	10%	5.00	0.50	6.00	0.60	7.00	0.70	8.00	0.80	2.00	0.20
Available apps	15%	1.00	0.15	8.00	1.20	2.00	0.30	9.00	1.35	4.00	0.60
Dropped calls	15%	9.00	1.35	7.00	1.05	4.00	0.60	6.00	0.90	1.00	0.15
Sum	100%	Sum	6.75	Sum	7.70	Sum	3.70	Sum	8.55	Sum	2.80

Figure A3.4 Revised absolute perceived benefit scores. (From Anthony Sgroi Jr.)

Cost (what customer pays)	Weights	Our Company Rating (0–10)	Weight × Rating	Cellular Provider 2 Rating (0–10)	Weight × Rating	Cellular Provider 3 Rating (0–10)	Weight × Rating	Cellular Provider 4 Rating (0–10)	Weight × Rating	Cellular Provider 5 Rating (0–10)	Weight × Rating
Acquisition cost	50%	5.00	2.50	2.00	1.00	5.00	2.50	0.25	0.13	10.00	5.00
Monthly cost	40%	7.00	2.80	5.00	2.00	6.00	2.40	0.25	0.10	9.00	3.60
Contract-lock	10%	4.00	0.40	4.00	0.40	4.00	0.40	1.00	0.10	9.00	0.90
Sum	100%	Sum	5.70	Sum	3.40	Sum	5.30	Sum	0.33	Sum	9.50
		Inverse	4.30	Inverse	6.60	Inverse	4.70	Inverse	9.68	Inverse	0.50

Figure A3.5   Revised absolute perceived price scores. (From Anthony Sgroi Jr.)

scores based on our updated ratings. Finally, Figure A3.6 illustrates the updated 2-D weighted perceptual map.

Based on the analysis, we can immediately verify that our company is now in the optimum benefit and cost zone. We can also verify that we are in a unique position in the marketplace. Our nearest competitors are cellular providers 3 and 2. In terms of cellular provider 3, it is in the improvement zone and currently is not a threat. Cellular provider 2 has an incremental improvement of benefits, but at a higher cost. Therefore, the lower prices we are offering to customers should drive sales.

Conclusion

This discussion used an absolute scoring convention to gage offering attributes. More specifically, this analysis allowed for the determination of benefits and cost considerations in view of the customer. This can help to directly gage the benefit parameter of the strategy icon. It can also indirectly help to understand the cost position of the strategy icon by working with profit calculations based on the desired prices customers are willing to pay. The map can depict a unique position in the marketplace, as verified in Figure A3.6. This can lead to a better understanding of market opportunities, coupled with opportunity scores obtained from importance and satisfaction data. Finally, the price preferences obtained from this analysis can help companies place the appropriate pricing levels on the visual strategy map for comparisons.

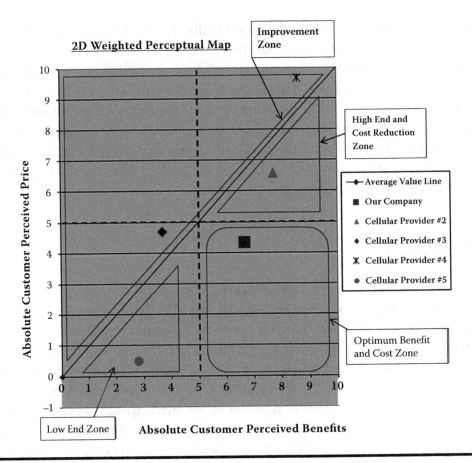

Figure A3.6   Revised 2-D weighted perceptual map. (From Anthony Sgroi Jr.)

Notes

Introduction

1. Allen C. Ward, *Lean Product and Process Development*, Lean Enterprise Institute, September 2009.
2. For a detailed discussion of the many parts of Lean briefly described, see Allen C. Ward, *Lean Product and Process Development*, Lean Enterprise Institute, September 2009.

Chapter 2

1. For more information about 2-D maps, see discussions about the strategy canvas by W. Chan Kim and Renee Mauborgne, *Blue Ocean Strategy*, Harvard Business School Press, 2005.

Chapter 3

1. For a detailed discussion of customer satisfaction in relation to offering requirements, see the paper by Elmar Sauerwein, Franz Bailom, Kurt Matzler, and Hans H. Hinterhuber, "The Kano Model: How to Delight Your Customers," Preprints Volume I of the IX International Working Seminar on Production Economics, Department of Management, University of Innsbruck, February 1996.
2. The product fulfillment map is adapted from the buyer utility map in W. Chan Kim and Renee Mauborgne, *Blue Ocean Strategy*, Harvard Business School Press, 2005.
3. For more discussions on desired outcomes, jobs, and constraints, see Anthony Ulwick, *What Customers Want: Using Outcome-Driven Innovation to Create Breakthrough Products and Services*, McGraw-Hill, 2005.

4. The opportunity scores in this book are numerical calculations of market gaps, and the format is adapted from the opportunity algorithm. The opportunity algorithm allows for various market conditions to be mapped. For more on this topic, see Anthony Ulwick, *What Customers Want: Using Outcome-Driven Innovation to Create Breakthrough Products and Services*, McGraw-Hill, 2005.

Chapter 4

1. See Pam Hunter, *Choosing the Best Method for Listening to the Customer*, www.isixsigma.com.
2. See Ronald D. Slusky, *Invention Analysis and Claiming: A Patent Lawyer's Guide*, ABA Publishing, 2007.
3. See Anthony Ulwick, *What Customers Want: Using Outcome-Driven Innovation to Create Breakthrough Products and Services*, McGraw-Hill, 2005.
4. See Bryan W. Mattimore, *Idea Stormers*, Jossey-Bass, 2012.
5. The concepts of the external perspective approach to idea generation are adapted from the six paths framework in W. Chan Kim and Renee Mauborgne, *Blue Ocean Strategy*, Harvard Business School Press, 2005.
6. Example adapted from a case study searched on the Internet and from the company website during the time of the writing. See LifeSync case study, http://www.dcontinuum.com/seoul/portfolio/11/231/02.GMP-LifeSync Wireless medical device uses Bluetooth technology. See also http://www.life-synccorp.com/about/corporate-overview.html.
7. Example taken from a case study searched on the Internet during the time of the writing. See Master Lock case study, http://www.dcontinuum.com/seoul/portfolio/11/228/07.Master Lock-Padlock Innovation Strategy.
8. See www.authenticwatches.com (Rolex watches).

Chapter 5

1. http://www.businessdictionary.com.
2. See Elliott Ettenberg, *The Next Economy*, McGraw-Hill, 2002.
3. For more on this topic, see James A. Brickley, Clifford W. Smith, Jerold L. Zimmerman, *Managerial Economics and Organizational Architecture*, 3rd edition, McGraw Hill, 2004.
4. This Q × P profit model concept and the associated graphs (Figures 5.3 through Figure 5.6) were authored by Tom Giordiano and taught to this author in a marketing management class in an executive MBA program at the University of New Haven, West Haven, Connecticut, in 2007. This is presented by permission.

5. This ATAR analysis model was taught to this author in a marketing management class in an executive MBA program at the University of New Haven, West Haven Connecticut, in 2007. It is presented by permission.
6. See Anthony Ulwick, *What Customers Want: Using Outcome-Driven Innovation to Create Breakthrough Products and Services*, McGraw-Hill, 2005.

Chapter 6

1. Author's recollection and experience with the brand. Also see www.heinz.com.

Chapter 7

1. Adapted from Erica Olsen, *Strategic Planning for Dummies*, Wiley Publishing, 2007.
2. Adapted from http://www.balancedscorecard.org/BSCResources/AbouttheBalancedScorecard/tabid/55/Default.aspx. See also Robert S. Kaplan and David P. Norton, "Using the Balanced Scorecard as a Strategic Management System," *Harvard Business Review*, January–February 1996, 76.
3. See Clayton M. Christensen and Michael E. Raynor, *The Innovator's Solution*, Harvard Business School Press, 2003.

Chapter 8

1. Figure 8.1 is adapted from Elmar Sauerwein, Franz Bailom, Kurt Matzler, and Hans H. Hinterhuber, "The Kano Model: How to Delight Your Customers," Preprints Volume I of the IX International Working Seminar on Production Economics, Department of Management, University of Innsbruck, February 1996.
2. Figure 8.2 is adapted from Elmar Sauerwein, Franz Bailom, Kurt Matzler, and Hans H. Hinterhuber, "The Kano Model: How to Delight Your Customers," Preprints Volume I of the IX International Working Seminar on Production Economics, Department of Management, University of Innsbruck, February 1996.
3. Figure 8.3 is adapted from Elmar Sauerwein, Franz Bailom, Kurt Matzler, and Hans H. Hinterhuber, "The Kano Model: How to Delight Your Customers," Preprints Volume I of the IX International Working Seminar on Production Economics, Department of Management, University of Innsbruck, February 1996.
4. The ski example up to Figure 8.6 is adapted from Elmar Sauerwein, Franz Bailom, Kurt Matzler, and Hans H. Hinterhuber, "The Kano Model: How to Delight Your Customers," Preprints Volume I of the IX International Working Seminar on Production Economics, Department of Management, University of Innsbruck, February 1996.

5. Adapted from Elmar Sauerwein, Franz Bailom, Kurt Matzler, and Hans H. Hinterhuber, "The Kano Model: How to Delight Your Customers," Preprints Volume I of the IX International Working Seminar on Production Economics, Department of Management, University of Innsbruck, February 1996.

Chapter 10

1. Case study adapted from Sumi N. Cate, David Pilosof, Richard Tait, and Robin Karol, "The Story of Clorox Green Works™," *PDMA Visions Magazine*, March 2009.

Chapter 11

1. See www.ikea.com.
2. Taken from Ikea's business idea; see www.ikea.com. See also http://www.samples-help.org.uk/mission-statements/ikea-vision-statement.htm.
3. See www.ikea.com.
4. Adapted from Jim Collins, *Good to Great*, HarperCollins Publishers, 2001.
5. See Michael Treacy and Fred Wiersema, *The Discipline of Market Leaders*, Basic Books, 1995.

Appendix 1

1. Matthew L. Wald, "Plane Crew Is Credited for Nimble Reaction, *New York Times*, January 15, 2009.

Appendix 2

1. Bradley T. Gale, *Managing Customer Value: Creating Quality and Service That Customers Can See*, Free Press, 1994. See also www.cval.com.

Index

About the Author

Anthony Sgroi Jr. is a broadly experienced innovative thinker with a rare combination and proven track record in the disciplines related to customer fulfillment. Mr. Sgroi is highly experienced in the fields of engineering, manufacturing, and law, with a strong understanding of marketing and business strategy. He has considerable experience in defining value-added customer offerings utilizing the principles of Lean product development.

Mr. Sgroi has worked for many well-known companies in the areas of product development. Mr. Sgroi has developed a multitude of products that are currently on the market today. Mr. Sgroi began his career in the areas of product design and procurement. After successfully launching several products, Mr. Sgroi decided to broaden his skill set by studying business, where he acquired a strong interest in marketing and strategy. This understanding allowed him to better contribute across the various disciplines of business. Understanding the level of importance and to further differentiate himself, Mr. Sgroi successfully passed the patent bar, where he is admitted to practice before the U.S. Patent and Trademark Office regarding patent matters. Mr. Sgroi is the holder of 40 patents with an additional 30 pending in the areas of compressed butane lighters, hydrogen generating devices for fuel cells, and various inventions related to cleaning tools.

Mr. Sgroi has several forms of hands-on experience and multiple degrees. His degrees are in physics, and mechanical engineering, where he graduated magna cum laude. He also has a master's in business administration.

Mr. Sgroi resides in Wallingford, Connecticut, with his wife of 21 years and their two children.

Mr. Sgroi can be contacted at HYPERLINK "mailto:innovative.lean.enterprise@gmail.com" \t "_blank" innovative.lean.enterprise@gmail.com.